# Impure Migration

# JEWISH CULTURES OF THE WORLD

Edited by Jeffrey Shandler, Rutgers University and Marcy Brink-Danan, Hebrew University of Jerusalem

Published in association with the Allen and Joan Bildner Center for the Study of Jewish Life, Rutgers University

## Advisory Board

# Impure Migration

~

*Jews and Sex Work in*
*Golden Age Argentina*

M IR  Y ARFITZ

RUTGERS UNIVERSITY PRESS
NEW BRUNSWICK, CAMDEN, AND NEWARK,
NEW JERSEY, AND LONDON

Library of Congress Cataloging-in-Publication Data

Names: Yarfitz, Mir, author.
Title: Impure migration : Jews and sex work in golden age Argentina / Mir Yarfitz.
Description: New Brunswick : Rutgers University Press, [2019] | Series: Jewish cultures of the world | Includes bibliographical references and index.
Identifiers: LCCN 2018027679 | ISBN 9780813598154 (cloth)
Subjects: LCSH: Jews—Argentina—Buenos Aires—History—19th century. | Jews—Argentina—Buenos Aires—History—20th century. | Prostitution—Argentina—Buenos Aires—History. | Human trafficking—History. | Jews—Migrations—History. | Jews, European—Argentina—Buenos Aires—History. | Buenos Aires (Argentina)—Emigration and immigration—Social aspects—History. | Europe, Eastern—Emigration and immigration—Social aspects—History. | Social reformers—Argentina—Buenos Aires—History. | Buenos Aires (Argentina)—Social conditions.
Classification: LCC F3001.9.J5 Y37 2019 | DDC 982/.11004924—dc23
LC record available at https://lccn.loc.gov/2018027679

A British Cataloging-in-Publication record for this book is available from the British Library.

♾ The paper used in this publication meets the requirements of the American National Standard for Information Sciences—Permanence of Paper for Printed Library Materials, ANSI Z39.48-1992.

www.rutgersuniversitypress.org

Manufactured in the United States of America

*With gratitude to all my beloved communities*

# Contents

# Note on Translation and Transliteration

I have wrestled with spelling and naming consistency in this work, as the sources contain tremendous variety. The Society at the center of the book was sometimes called the Varsovia and sometimes the Zwi Migdal—I generally refer to it as the Society, and use Varsovia or the Society as the name unless discussing a source that uses Zwi Migdal.

Yiddish orthography is often nonstandard, and transliteration varies substantially between Spanish and English. I have tried to consistently use the YIVO transliteration system, including spelling out Hebrew words as these Yiddish speakers would have done. If terms and titles were already transliterated not in accordance with the YIVO system, I leave them as is and note the distinction. Unless otherwise noted, translations from Spanish and French are by me, and from Yiddish by Will Runyan and me. I take full responsibility for any errors.

# Acronyms and Abbreviations

EN      Ezres Noshim
GdF     "Juzgados de instrucción: Número 3—asociación ilícita," *Gaceta del Foro* 15, no. 4729 (November 1, 1930)
IBSTW   International Bureau for the Suppression of the Traffic in Women
IWO     Yidisher Visnshaftlekher Institut, or Instituto Judío de Investigación, Buenos Aires
JAPGW   Jewish Association for the Protection of Girls and Women
JCA     Jewish Colonization Association
NVA     National Vigilance Association

# Impure Migration

# Introduction

## WHITE SLAVE WIVES ON THE ROAD
## TO BUENOS AIRES

On June 2, 1928, Raquel Liberman walked into Buenos Aires police commissioner Julio Alsogaray's office to denounce her husband for deceiving her and entrapping her into prostitution. Liberman had come from Eastern Europe to Argentina along with many other Jewish migrants who joined the massive transatlantic population flow of the late nineteenth and early twentieth centuries. Although she'd worked as a prostitute before, at the time of her marriage she was running her own antique store, in the heart of the new Jewish section of downtown Buenos Aires. As she narrated to the commissioner and in court two years later, as soon as she married she discovered that her new husband was in fact a brothel owner and that he had seduced her as part of a deliberate scheme to bring her back into prostitution and profit from her labor. To do so, he deployed not only his power as a husband, but his leverage as a member of the Varsovia Israelite Mutual Aid and Burial Society, an organization of several hundred Jewish brothel owners, pimps, madams, and traffickers in women.

The Varsovia Society, legally incorporated in a Buenos Aires suburb in 1906, provided burial and other social services to Eastern European Jews who, because of their association with sex work, were excluded from communal burial rites.[1] The organization grew over the next several decades, until it was dismantled by the 1930 court case triggered by Liberman's denunciation. By that time it was infamous among local Jews and international opponents of prostitution. At its peak of power and visibility in the 1920s, the Society had over four hundred members on its rolls. Members circulated loans to develop properties into brothels throughout the Argentine capital and in other provinces and outfitted a lavish mansion as headquarters to host meetings, parties, and religious services. The mansion included a synagogue, since the larger Jewish community refused to allow Society members into its spaces of worship.

Terrified that all Jews would be stigmatized and their immigration and assimilation thereby restricted, other local Jews struggled for decades to keep those
involved in sex work out of mainstream Jewish institutions. The term *tmeim*, a
biblical Hebrew word meaning "impure" or "ritually unclean," became an in-
group code that "respectable" Jews used to refer to Varsovia Society members
and those with whom they worked.[2] Leaders of this "boycott" were thrilled to
join Liberman and local authorities in building a case against the tmeim, and
the Yiddish press celebrated the series of dramatic raids in May 1930 on brothels and individual residences in the Argentine capital and provinces associated
with the Varsovia Society. Although the sweeps captured only around a hundred
of the Society's members and all were freed within eight months, the related media
frenzy as well as the increased power of Jewish reform institutions and a simulta-
neous military coup closed the forty-year chapter in which the Jewish "white slaver" was feared, scapegoated, and contested locally and around the world.[3]

Liberman's testimony to Judge Manuel Rodriguez Ocampo, reiterated in the
Spanish, Yiddish, and English press, meshed with other stories of young women's
entrapment in prostitution, familiar from the era's international anti–white slave
trafficking campaigns. In response to massive migrations of men and women
across the Atlantic in the late nineteenth and early twentieth centuries and their
attendant social dislocations, a perceived crisis of "white slavery" or "traffic in
women" stirred the popular press and social activists in Europe and the Americas.[4] Narratives of white slaves, young European victims of swarthy male exploiters who fooled or forced them into brothels across international borders,
inspired sensational news stories and transnational feminist organizing for the
half century straddling 1900. The traffic in women was the biggest transnational
women's rights issue after suffrage. International reform organizations from late
nineteenth-century women's rights groups to the League of Nations debated the
causes of what appeared to be a major rise in the cross-border movement of
women for sexual purposes during this period of mass migration. Self-styled new
abolitionists opposed the public health regulatory regimes that legalized prostitution in many countries and proposed restrictions on international mobility,
particularly for suspicious and vulnerable groups. Argentina became a flash
point for these controversies, with its half century of government-regulated
brothels and largely male migrant labor force. The group most often blamed as
a collectivity for the entrapment of innocent women, bound in secret multinational conspiracies, ever unscrupulous in search of lucre, was Europe's wandering
ur-Others, the Jews.

The popular connection between the Jewish Pale of Settlement and prostitution was so pervasive that *polaca*, referring to immigrant women from Eastern
Europe, implicitly Jewish, became a common term for "prostitute" in Argentina
and Brazil. Long-standing antisemitic tropes of the Jew as an unscrupulous
exploiter in financial matters corresponded to the moment's unique flourishing

of highly visible Jewish management of international sex trafficking. Displacement of blame for trafficking onto the Jews stretched from the British panic of the 1880s to the Nazi claim that Jews were responsible for 98 percent of the international sex trade.[5] Indeed, Argentine Jews' continuing fear of antisemitic reprisal for publicizing this connection has not been pure paranoia. In the early 1980s, during a brutal and antisemitic military dictatorship, urban street corner newspaper kiosks sold a propaganda piece that reproduced police photographs from the 1890s to lay exclusive blame on the Jews for the existence of prostitution in Argentina.[6]

The history of local Jewish pimps and prostitutes continues to be well known and still a source of shame among Argentine Jews but is often framed as "unknown," a "silenced story," and is frequently exoticized by scholars and journalists with an audience beyond Latin America.[7] Many scholars who have acknowledged Jewish participation in international prostitution between the 1890s and 1930s have tried to absolve Jews as a whole for responsibility by juxtaposing Jewish pimps and prostitutes with the energetic fight of Jews around the world against these rogue elements. Historians of Argentine Jewry, like the "respectable" Jewish Argentines of the past, have often tried to minimize the topic in favor of others casting the community in a more favorable light. They have done so by mentioning the Society and the mainstream Jewish community's opposition as a colorful footnote in a larger narrative of rural settlement and urban institutional formation.[8] New work on Argentine Jewish women aims to redress the overidentification of the group with prostitution.[9]

Although antisemites and nativists exaggerated Jewish masterminding of white slavery, a transnational network of Eastern European Jews did in fact play an important role in this era in transporting women for sexual purposes across national borders, with exceptional visibility in the South American terminus. Jews were not the only immigrants in Buenos Aires managing places of assignation, but they were the most tightly organized and identifiable. From the 1890s, when Eastern European Jews first began to arrive in substantial numbers in Argentina, prostitutes and their managers made up a large and highly visible percentage of this community's population. Self-protective fears prompted mainstream Argentine Jewish leaders to organize against Jewish sex work and make common cause with local and international reformers and authorities. Although Jews worked both separately and together with other opponents of white slavery around the world, Argentine Jews were particularly aggressive and organized, using the local Yiddish press, the legal system, and other forms of collective pressure to defend their community's reputation. This struggle engaged central questions of Jewish identity and legitimacy, defining acceptable limits of work and leisure, family structure, and religious expression.

This book analyzes the causes and implications of the central position Argentina and Eastern European Jews held in this era's international discussion of sex trafficking and compares the behavior of sex workers with that of their coreligionists and other immigrants. New archival sources help detail the networks, strategies, and values of Jewish sex workers and their managers in the context of transnational migration. Such an approach provides a way to analyze the tropes and functions of international narratives of Jewish sex trafficking between the 1890s and 1930s. Large numbers of Jews were involved both in commercial sex and in opposition to it, but this is rarely interpreted as central to Jewish mobility or class ascension. Opponents gained social status in working transnationally with non-Jews on the problem of the traffic in women.

Between the late nineteenth century and the interwar period, Jewish migrants to Argentina from Eastern Europe, the Middle East, and North Africa created the largest Jewish population concentration in all of Latin America and the Caribbean. Although often erased in discussions of Argentine Jewry, usually reflexively characterized as Ashkenazi, from Eastern Europe and originally Yiddish-speaking, a significant percentage identified as Sephardi, of North African and Middle Eastern background and speaking Arabic or Ladino.[10] Although divided by language, ethnic identity, class, and politics, Jews would also be characterized as one collectivity, sometimes strategically from the inside, and sometimes from the outside, particularly as an antisemitic strand of nativism gained traction in the 1930s.[11]

Ashkenazi Jews had been mostly excluded from the dominant form of labor in Eastern Europe, farming, and thus lacked the skills and experience to participate in the predominant sectors of the Argentine economy, agriculture and livestock raising, which drew most other European migrants.[12] Jews were also excluded from many professions and sometimes access to education. Ashkenazi job skills thus concentrated in urban artisanal fields such as tailoring, then in insufficient demand in most New World cities to accommodate the level of migrant supply, with the notable exception of New York City's garment industry. Traditional avenues into the Latin American elite, including the Roman Catholic Church, the military, and landownership, would have been closed to Jews, and budding professions were not particularly friendly. While Jews increasingly found their way into a range of occupations, the organization and management of what was then largely legal sex work drew men and women with few other attractive options. As more educational, professional, and industrial options became available, they would move on, but in this time of mass migration, gray zones of employment drew Jews along with other marginalized groups.

As the Argentine capital's downtown Jewish district first developed in the late nineteenth century, its residents' involvement in prostitution was highly evident, and its flashy beneficiaries were among the immigrant group's wealthiest members. According to one local Jewish observer, when new migrants arrived at the Buenos Aires docks in 1891, madams in furs and men in flashy suits called to young women to join them in the lucrative underworld.[13] Buenos Aires exemplified a common gender imbalance in "frontier" communities: the belle epoque capital was dominated by single male immigrants (mostly from Spain and Italy) who flocked to homosocial spaces from the brothel to the café.[14] Among the foreign-born, men outnumbered women by nearly two to one. The numbers of men per 100 women were 251 in 1869, 173 in 1895, 171 in 1914, and 138 in 1947.[15] Due to resultant demand and the legal status of regulated prostitution, the city gained a reputation as a magnet for sex workers, and drew women already working in prostitution in less lucrative places, where male emigration fed a decrease in brothel prostitution.[16]

The visibility of Jews in sex work provoked a defensive reaction from other Jews. "Respectable" Jews tried to exclude the tmeim from Jewish institutions such as cemeteries and burial societies, synagogues, community organizations, and the Yiddish theater. This battle played a key role in the foundational and long-term development of the new immigrant community's identity and institutional life. Ironically, the exclusionary tactics of mainstream Jews in fact fed the intensification of the tmeim's power and visibility: underworld members defiantly declared their Jewishness through synagogue events and holiday celebrations, a cemetery gate decorated with a giant menorah, extensive property ownership in the central Jewish neighborhood, and dominance of the Yiddish theater.[17]

At the center of this story, the Buenos Aires–based Varsovia Society was the most tightly organized and powerful hub of generally informal international sex work networks. After the Society's legal dissolution in 1930 in the dramatic court case launched by Liberman and Alsogaray, Jews did not return to their influential position in the Argentine underworld.[18] The legal system of prostitution was soon dismantled. The government seized six million pesos worth of property and other assets belonging to the Society and its members, and the provincial educational body took over its lavish Cordoba Avenue headquarters. The Society ceased to exist; most Jews had moved with the rest of the Argentine population into the middle class. As the more pressing concerns of the 1930s preoccupied Jewish institutions, Jewish visibility in Argentine sex work fell to lower priority levels for social reformers and antisemites alike.

## BUENOS AIRES RESPONDS TO PROSTITUTION AND CRIME

During the massive migrations out of Europe in the late nineteenth and early twentieth centuries, Argentina became a land of new immigrants even more so than the United States. The capital city boomed with hungry arrivals, mostly male laborers, and export-led economic development during its "golden age," roughly 1890 to 1913.[19] New technology increased the wheat production of the pampas and international investment promoted primary export growth. Class stratification encouraged radical labor and social movements, particularly anarchism and socialism. Continuing the demographic growth pattern, the 1914 census recorded the population of Argentina as 30 percent foreign-born, twice as high as the corresponding percentage in the United States at that time, and Buenos Aires was 60 percent foreign-born.[20] Immigrant-driven growth continued in the interwar period, with the capital's population rising from 1.5 to 2.5 million in the 1920s and 1930s.[21] Buenos Aires developed a large middle class built through immigrant upward mobility. However, Lila Caimari argues that this upward mobility was recent enough that *porteños*—port dwellers, used to refer to denizens of Buenos Aires—could not take it for granted, which exacerbated certain social tensions. While the 1930 economic crash damaged Argentina less than other countries, it did undermine the hope of social mobility and shaped a fear-based social conservatism across the population in the 1930s.[22] Specifically, as some of its members improved their economic positions but felt these gains were tenuous, the Buenos Aires Jewish community developed certain conservative social attitudes.

The year 1930 has been viewed as a watershed in Argentine history by most scholars in several generations of historians, due to the world economic crisis and the September 6 presidential coup that ushered in a half century of politics dominated by the military.[23] In response to the economic crash, rural laborers fled struggling regions of the grain-producing interior for the capital city, and the thousands of newly unemployed exacerbated concern with public order.[24] My analysis of press and other sources suggests that the 1930 breakup of the Society shared causal factors with the end of electoral democracy and the institution of military dictatorship in the same year. The widely publicized coordination of police sweeps may have been a last-ditch effort to redeem the legitimacy of the prior regime, and the public fixation on the management of Jewish sex work, to the exclusion of other nationalities, was a part of the moment's larger nationalist consolidation.

The political quest for social order in this rapidly modernizing society inspired a series of regulations intended to corral the visibility and impact of the *mala vida*, literally the bad or dissolute life, a term that was used to refer to the port city's underworld and its denizens.[25] In 1875, Argentine municipal authorities, following the public health model then current in France, instituted the legal regulation of prostitutes, creating a state-sponsored brothel system that controlled the spread of venereal disease through regular examination and quarantine of prostitutes.[26] Prostitutes who remained healthy and plied their trade within certain parameters were given legal licenses, for which they were taxed and medically examined twice per week.[27] They were required to carry identification cards that noted their disease-free status, and their public mobility was limited, spatially and temporally.[28] No formal red-light district existed, but dense downtown zones mixed spaces of sex work with other leisure activities as well as housing and employment. Symbolic markers such as pink or white translucent front door curtains, unlike the traditional lace, wordlessly directed clients.[29]

Urban outskirts and expanding suburbs provided new sites for both the flour-ishing and suppression of illicit activity.[30] Legal regulation claimed to liberate sex workers from the control of pimps, promised the general population a clear distinction between prostitutes and other women, and tried to keep "dangerous women" away from recreational sites and public thoroughfares.[31]

Regulation was of limited success in meeting implicit and explicit goals and was continually challenged by anti–white slavery organizations and other invested constituents. Although regulations granted sex workers freedom from prosecution, the majority preferred to work "clandestine," outside of these inva-sive restrictions, risking fines if caught but generally not further punishment.[32] Until 1919, taxation of brothels provided an important source of income for the Buenos Aires municipality; officials targeted enforcement efforts at women work-ing out of unlicensed businesses, which could afford to pay fines, rather than clandestine streetwalkers.[33] Clients were not monitored, as women were seen as the critical disease vectors, and there was no effective treatment beyond quar-antine until the mass production of penicillin in the 1940s.[34]

Argentine laws were revised multiple times to address concerns ranging from public visibility to curbing the power of pimps over women. An 1894 ordinance responded to concerns with violations of women's civil rights by reducing limi-tations on public behavior and punishment of clandestine prostitutes, but the goal of increasing the registration rate was not met, and deaths attributed to syphilis rose.[35] The 1904 revision once again increased control of registered pros-titutes, increasing the age of majority from eighteen to twenty-two and reducing the number of women allowed in brothels, in which sanitation and behavior standards were tightened, reflecting concerns of public health practitioners and antitrafficking groups.[36] These constituents were unsatisfied with the results, and managers of brothels pushed back against these restrictions. A 1908 city revision reduced restrictions on brothel locations, pleasing owners but raising public ire and prompting public demonstrations by antitrafficking organizations.[37]

Visiting European reformers presumed that this system reflected a continu-ally favorable situation for pimps to exploit European-born women, feeding international narratives that blamed legal prostitution for the flourishing of white slavery.[38] In 1913, Congress passed the Palacios Law, named after its sponsoring Socialist Party deputy and responding explicitly to Argentina's infamy in Europe as a center for white slavery by providing legal recourse for any woman forced into prostitution.[39] Cases of white slavery failed to appear in court, however, and instead more women were arrested for scandalous behavior.[40] At the close of 1919, the Buenos Aires City Council tried to reduce the power of pimps by banning all licensed houses with more than one woman working as a prosti-tute, again altering the urban landscape of sex work. This had the opposite of the intended effect, increasing the expenses of sex workers who could no longer share high rents, expanding the power of property owners, and exacerbating police corruption.[41] In this context, the Varsovia Society, which helped members to remodel properties in accordance with changing regulations, achieved its greatest power. After the Society was disbanded and the country brought under military rule, the system of legal prostitution ended in 1934 in Buenos Aires and nationally two years later.

This is thus not only a transnational Jewish story, but a uniquely Argentine story, shaped by the particularities of Argentine immigration, rural and urban settlement, changing public health regulations, criminology and penal reform, and popular attitudes toward prostitution. The contours of Argentine economic and demographic growth, urbanization, and public health in the late nineteenth and early twentieth centuries shaped the porteño Jewish street.[42] The historiography on this metropolis is too large to be adequately addressed here, particularly in the rich realm generated by scholars working within Argentina. Relevant directions of Argentine work tied to international debates include multinational police cooperation and the social history of policing, urban history, and social control.[43] Until recently, scholars have given less consideration to racial categories in Argentine history than in the histories of many other Latin American countries. Argentines have tended to deny their country's racialized identity, often asserting minimal influence of indigenous and African populations and the predominance of European migration, drawing the nation closer to Europe and other European settler societies—the United States, Canada, and Australia—than to its South American neighbors.[44] New scholarship, however, highlights racial elements of the Argentine past and the complex ways racial categories have evolved and shaped Argentine identity.[45] Sandra McGee Deutsch's recent contribution to the history of Jewish racialization and Argentine national identity lays a foundation for assessing the particularities of Jewish whiteness in the Argentine context, on which this book builds more connections to sexuality and the transnational context.[46] Jewish arrivals both contributed to and challenged the evolution of Argentine national identity as white.

Historians of crime in Argentina and across Latin America have long emphasized the power dynamics inherent in state definitions of crime and the criminal, as efforts to structure public order also defined the boundaries of acceptable citizenship.[47] A recent flourishing of work on policing also highlights the social and cultural aspects of surveillance institutions and policing.[48] Argentina pioneered a late nineteenth-century fingerprinting system that was taken up by police forces across South America, and police tried to cooperate across international borders in response to mobile criminals.[49] Centering of Latin Americans' contributions to intellectual and practical systems of social control, from eugenics to policing, pushes against the implicit bias in much cultural history— that ideas generated in Europe and the United States were passively received in "peripheral" regions.[50] As the Argentine population exploded, particularly in the capital city, modern nation-building efforts tried to physically and symbolically separate order and disorder.[51] Ricardo Salvatore has argued that responses to crime "set moral limits to the expansion of market forces. The gambler, the delinquent, and the prostitute were emblematic of perverse market paths, of entrepreneurial energy allocated to immoral purposes."[52] Local prostitution debates were about economic growth as well as morality, imagining the modern nation's economic and social future. State regulation of prostitution and shifting restrictions on physical spaces where sex work could be legally performed aligned with broader social engineering efforts, as did the internal segregation of the "impure" attempted by many Jewish community leaders.

## JEWISH GAUCHOS IN THE CITY AND OTHER UNDESIRABLES

Beginning with the Argentine political and intellectual leaders of the Generation of 1880, the importation of desirable European bodies became a key part of the national improvement project. Late nineteenth-century Argentine governments incentivized immigration, particularly promoting rural settlement as part of the "pacification" of the interior's indigenous population and "colonization of the desert."[53] While the absolute majority of these immigrants came from Italy and Spain in search of manual labor, Eastern European Jewish centers also provided an important source of new Argentines.[54] Jews fleeing poverty and persecution in Eastern Europe in the 1880s and 1890s were invited to assist in this rural colonization, though treated with more caution than other Europeans. Jewish migrants were often sponsored not by the Argentine state, but by the London-based Jewish Colonization Association, which established Jewish agricultural projects in the provinces as part of the international effort to help persecuted Jews and counteract antisemitic stereotypes of parasitic mercantile Jews with the image of Jews as hardy physical laborers.[55] Few of these agricultural settlements flourished, but the image of the "Jewish gaucho," promoted in the first local Spanish-language Jewish work of literature, persisted in the mythmaking of a uniquely Argentine Jewish identity.[56]

Despite this effort to settle Jews in the countryside, the vast majority of Jews, like other immigrants, settled in the capital city. In Buenos Aires, Eastern European Jews generally congregated with others from the same background, more so than new arrivals from Italy and Spain, who were linguistically and culturally closer to native-born Argentines and generally migrated at younger ages. However, porteño residential segregation was less prevalent than in the urban United States; Jews in Buenos Aires never made up the majority in any particular neighborhood and learned language and customs from their neighbors.[57] Ashkenazi and Sephardi Jews generally created separate institutions, with further internal distinctions drawn between specific places of origin and, over time, ideologies such as Zionism and political or class differences.[58] Such internal divisions were not generally visible to those outside.

The linguistic and cultural association of pimping and prostitution with foreignness within Argentina echoed and reinforced negative popular perceptions and assisted in official efforts to divert moral criticisms from the Argentine state itself, by, for example, directing particular scrutiny at Jews among the masses of newly arriving European immigrants. Migration records kept by the Argentine government in this period single out these Jewish settlers for special attention, questioning the success of their acculturation as their numbers grew.[59] The national immigration department referred to these Jewish settlers as "so distinct from the rest, so separate from the Argentines, by race, tongue, religion and customs, that it is necessary to proceed vigorously with their education, taking into account that they are settled together, far from the national centers . . . so that . . . they do not become a social problem."[60] The government's effort to keep this population from flocking to the capital ultimately failed, and the rural Jewish agricultural settlements barely survived. New Jewish arrivals from Eastern Europe were criticized by immigration officials in the mid-1890s as generally upholding much lower hygiene standards than other new arrivals, mixing together dirty clothes with cooking utensils and lacking underwear entirely.[61] Multiple cited examples of families and individuals with insufficient underwear, while framed as hygienic criticism, also implied low sexual morality. At the same time as annual immigration reports gave particular attention to whether this particular population could assimilate and contribute to agricultural expansion, Jewish men in Buenos Aires were arrested for pimping in numbers far above their population percentage. While Jewish migrants were allowed as part of the national expansion and Europeanizing project, they were treated with particular moral suspicion.

Argentina maintained an open door to immigrants until the 1920s, and the urban Jewish population exploded along with the numbers of immigrants from other parts of Europe. National immigration policy tightened in 1923, reflecting trends originating in the United States and spreading across the hemisphere.[62] The annual government immigration publication that had scrutinized Eastern European Jewish arrivals in the 1890s had decided by 1927 that Central European Jewish migrants were not recommendable.[63] As in other arenas, 1930 was a turning point for the nation's openness to the outside world, with a more dramatic closing of the gates following the September coup. Throughout this period, the chief fear of the Jewish collectivity was that all Jews would be blamed for the traffic in women and therefore face antisemitic and anti-immigrant backlash. Late nineteenth-century concern with underpopulation, to be solved by attracting more desirable immigrants, had shifted by the 1930s to new overpopulation worries, as the bulk of the groups attempting to enter were seen as undesirable.[64] Epitomized by the brutal street violence of the 1919 "Tragic Week," an anti-leftist riot that targeted Jews, Jews were frequently blamed for leftist radicalism. Increasingly restrictive immigration policy followed at least one sector of this popular feeling.[65]

Prevention of such exclusionary policies inspired self-defensive social work. The international Jewish Association for the Protection of Girls and Women (JAPGW) was founded in Britain in the 1880s primarily to fight against Jewish involvement in cross-border prostitution. Trafficking to Argentina dominated the JAPGW's early discussions. In 1896 the Gentlemen's Committee found that "the traffic to, and the houses of ill-fame at Buenos Aires [were largely] in the hands of Jews."[66] The first JAPGW branch outside of Europe was established in Buenos Aires in 1901 and referred to locally as Ezres Noshim, or Women's Section, as in the segregated area for women in the traditional synagogue. This name referred to Ezres Noshim's focus on such women's issues as prostitution and trafficking, spousal abandonment and bigamy, divorce and alimony, and the custody of minor girls. Trafficking, not clearly distinguished from legal or voluntary prostitution, was the group's primary target. Men and women worked together as members.

Ezres Noshim quickly became by far the international JAPGW's most active local office, due to the high international profile of Jewish involvement in Argentina both as traffickers and prostitutes. Although its work was not universally supported by Argentine Jews, Ezres Noshim featured prominently in Yiddish press discussions of these issues, was a principal player in the boycott against the tmeim, sent dock inspectors to meet ships at the port looking for suspicious or endangered new arrivals, and marshalled evidence against the Varsovia Society in court.[67] However, minimal rescue of trafficked women resulted from this work. Although reformers' annual reports tried to spin the numbers more positively, daily dock inspections and other intensive efforts met with very low levels of success in rescue and rehabilitation.[68] Their paternalist approach undermined any trust sex workers might have held in their would-be rescuers. Stories of hapless victims circulated in multiple registers, serving several purposes for well-meaning parties, but also silencing more complex stories.

Through the 1930s, although Jews no longer had a significant presence in transnational prostitution or the Argentine mala vida, the moral argument about community identity continued via Jewish community institutions' efforts to regulate the boundaries of marriage and motherhood. Ezres Noshim capitalized on its role in the court case that dissolved the Varsovia Society and heralded the finale of organized Jewish-led prostitution. The office's routine work had long included literal gatekeeping at the docks, in which they assessed the moral fitness of potential new members of the local Jewish community. Its cooperation with Argentine authorities seems to have been rewarded with an ongoing sentinel role as immigration restrictions tightened during the military dictatorship. Even after prostitution ceased to be a central concern in the 1930s, the organization continued to monitor the Jewish community's family formation through the regulation of immigrant marriages via morality certificates, which required potential brides and grooms to prove through multiple references that they had never been involved with the tmeim. Such internal moral policing and the suppression of unsavory community aspects, while of course not unique to any particular collectivity, may have been more extreme among Argentine Jews than other groups due to ongoing antisemitism and incomplete social integration.[69] New arrivals fleeing social exclusion and persecution would have been particularly attuned to the reputational as well as economic ascension possibilities of *"Hacer la América"*—making it in America—often understood as anywhere across the Americas.[70]

Antitrafficking projects dovetailed with broader efforts to control migrant flows and the geographic and behavioral boundaries of the modern nation. While the JAPGW and Ezres Noshim focused on primarily Eastern European Jewish female migration, international antitrafficking bodies from the British International Bureau for the Suppression of the Traffic in Women to the League of Nations' Traffic in Women and Children Committee scrutinized broader cross-border population flows. Authorities inspected all single migrant women as potential prostitutes and suspicious men as traffickers. Port and border targets of antitrafficking scrutiny tended to be sites of broader racial and national demographic anxieties. The rhetoric of white slavery was inherently racialized, and its victim narrative and the institutions that both spread the story and were inspired by it engaged in racializing and nation-building work. Within the United States, the 1910 White Slave Traffic Act or Mann Act was used to police in particular interracial sexual and romantic relationships.[71]

Because the white slave's exploiter was rhetorically presumed to be nonwhite, the positioning of Jewish women and men in white slave narratives frequently served to whiten Jewish women, while darkening Jewish men. Although in the Jewish press all involved were understood to be Jewish, outside of the Jewish press the Jewishness of traffickers tended to be emphasized, while that of their victims was elided, making the narrative conform more closely to the standard white slave story of a white victim of a nonwhite man. On the ground, Jewish brokers and managers of sex workers almost exclusively dealt with Jewish women, but the innocent white women in narratives circulating outside the Jewish community were rarely coded as ethnically linked to their exploiters. Publicity around Jewish men as traffickers thus racialized all Jewish men. Jewish-led antitrafficking projects, in defending the reputation of Jews as a collectivity, also defended the whiteness of Jews and their suitability as modern national citizens.

Jewish community shame, the editorial decisions of Argentine police and military leaders over numerous repressive decades, and antisemitic destruction of Jewish community records have minimized the paper trail left by the infamous group and its opponents. In a fictional parallel to this erasure, in the opening scene of Nathan Englander's novel about the brutal military dictatorship that ruled Argentina from 1976 to 1983, descendants of the tmeim hire thugs to gouge the names of their less-than-illustrious forebears out of their tombstones.[72] Antisemitism has been more than a canard in this saga: only four of Ezres Noshim's archival boxes survived the 1994 bombing of the AMIA Jewish Community Center, in which eighty-five people were killed and hundreds injured as well as countless records destroyed, and access to these materials has since been restricted out of concern for the community's reputation.

## WHITE SLAVES AS VICTIMS AND HEROINES

As the 1930 court case against the Varsovia Society captured local and some international headlines, Raquel Liberman's story and those like it were already sufficiently familiar that newspapers and court records did not need to detail how she had entered sex work. The vagaries of her past were easily imagined to be in line with the countless narratives of poor women across Europe dislocated by industrial development and war, particularly the sensational stories of women kidnapped or otherwise tricked into white slavery. Jewish women, whose families were often weakened by pogroms and poverty, were known to be quick to accept the marriage offers of prodigal migrants whose wealth and cosmopolitan charm overcame families' fears of sending their daughters to a faraway continent rumored to doom foreign girls to brothels. Once on the steamship or foreign dock, the narrative went, the bridegroom would reveal his true profession as a trafficker in women. Her marital obligations, linguistic limitations, and lack of options would guarantee the young bride's imprisonment in a brothel, where she would be doomed to sexual subjugation to dark-skinned men, followed by a none-too-quick syphilitic death. Yiddish literature, theater, and press regularly dramatized these white slave stories, as did popular narratives in other languages across Europe and the Americas.

While the story of Liberman's particular fall remained vague, the details she gave to the court resonated with the familiar white slave narrative. But specific aspects of her story also reveal examples of women's decision making that challenge the boundaries of the victim narrative. Liberman arrived in Argentina as a married woman with children, and after her first husband's death decided to sell sex to support her family. She saved enough money to leave prostitution and open an antique store, where she met her second husband. According to the story she told in court, only after their marriage did she find out that her new husband was in fact a member of the Varsovia Society, and he enlisted the organization's power to push her back into sex work. Her attempt to free herself with official aid by denouncing these activities to the police commissioner only escalated the pressures against her: she was bribed with cash and jewels and threatened with facial disfigurement and death. Members warned her that she could not be allowed to successfully denounce the organization because she might inspire the other women forced into prostitution against their will to "rise up" against their oppressors.[73] This version of her story, which she told in court, inspired enthusiastic support from supporters of women's rights both at the time and over a half century later.

Although Raquel Liberman's name has been better known in Argentina than in the Global North, her story as a heroine who turned the tables on her oppressors has captured the imagination of authors, activists, dramatists, and filmmakers. Cultural products in Argentina inspired by her rebellion include an eight-hour television miniseries produced in 1993, several plays and novels (one a South American best seller), a poem series, and a recent documentary film.[74] In 2010, a biannual prize was established in her honor by the city of Buenos Aires's Subsecretariat of Human Rights and Cultural Pluralism to support the work of individuals or nongovernmental organizations "who promote and protect the rights of survivors of situations of violence against women."[75] Canadian journalist Isabel Vincent connects Liberman to Jewish prostitutes in Brazil, who started their own mutual aid society and cemetery.[76] All of these works highlight Liberman's bravery in standing up to her exploiters, as in these lines from Carlos Luis Serrano's eponymous play: "Raquel. . . . Her fate was that of a bird / that sings only in Spring. . . . You were the bird that took to flight . . . sings: I AM FREE! I AM FREE!"[77]

Liberman's heroism is framed as a ray of hope in the historical context of trafficked women's victimization and as a possible model for today's victims of sex trafficking. Her key role in "exposing the stinking swamp" of the Society and related underworld goings-on makes her an attractive symbol of women's agency.[78] Even previous scholarship that intends to avow women's agency generally suggests that the only way for prostitutes to manifest agency is to leave the underworld behind. Liberman is thus held up as an exemplar of prostitutes' agency, an ideal heroine who successfully denounced the Society of exploitative men. But before Liberman could become a heroine, she first became a victim among other victims. In Argentina, the Spanish and Yiddish press as well as reformers and court records consistently used only the term "exploiters" to discuss the Society members who propelled Liberman's re-entry into prostitution.[79] In contemporary and later tellings of her story, Liberman stood out from the silent mass of other exploited women for her willingness to risk violent reprisals. Her status as escaped victim underscores the unredeemed victimhood of other women.

After developing an analytical framework and further historical context, later sections of this book revisit Liberman's story and offer other possible readings and narrative structures that build on historical research and theoretical debates that suggest that most of what has been called transatlantic sex trafficking in the half century preceding World War II did not match the white slave as victim narrative. Both some contemporary observers and later scholars have argued that the problem's scale was exaggerated and that most women entered prostitution due to economic necessity and lack of other options, not because they were deceived or kidnapped. Sex workers' own voices, when audible, proclaim agency. Certainly violence permeated the underworld, but it also reached into the supposedly protected domestic sphere and other arenas of women's labor. From among limited options, most prostitutes made at least some of the decisions that led into sex work. If prostitution is framed as a form of labor, then this period's trafficking problem can also be viewed as the female side of the massive migration out of industrializing and war-torn Europe. Migrating women and men faced different sets of choices and were differently affected by international relocation.[80] The moral and physical risks for migrant women were greater and their opportunities fewer. Labor demands and restrictions meant that particularly at the beginning of the era selling sex was one of few available options for female migrants to make money in their new homes.

Just as Raquel Liberman gave up prostitution to open her own antique store, selling sex was often one of multiple economic strategies deployed at one time or over the course of a lifetime, despite the implication of permanent "fall" in most narratives. While the white slave narrative implied women's total victimization, most sex workers made certain choices along their migratory paths and continued to make choices after their "fall." To almost everyone, the white slave story was more palatable than the version articulated by the tmeim themselves: prostitution and its management provided the most lucrative occupational field for ambitious individuals with still-limited options on both sides of the migratory journey. Although brothel rent consumed generally half of their earnings and they had to share their earnings with property owners, doorkeepers or madams, brokers, and commodity suppliers, sex work offered women unrivaled financial opportunities. This could sometimes be parlayed into property ownership and a degree of future security that the Society in some ways supported. In Buenos Aires in the 1920s, a standard sexual act cost an average workman's daily salary.[81] Sex workers typically had up to fifteen to twenty clients a day, with oral sex as the main offering, which allowed them to service more clients than other acts. However, this pace could not be maintained forever, and their value to clients decreased with age.

Varsovia Society members responded to changing municipal regulations in the 1920s by pooling resources to build and renovate brothels to accommodate new restrictions, which stipulated that only one prostitute could work in a house and a woman over forty could serve as her doorkeeper. This latter position provided a needed job opportunity for women who had aged out of prostitution. Doorkeepers could rotate between properties and keep an eye on new tenants and frequently were married to male owners of these properties, maintaining overlapping business and familial ties among group members.

Remaining in the field of sex work in different positions, moving up from prostitute to madam or doorkeeper and from pimp to brothel owner, seemed to be a popular option for both men and women stigmatized as tmeim and was facilitated by their network. In the 1930 court case against the Varsovia Society, while a few other prostitutes' stories of abduction were brought into the trial as evidence in addition to that of Liberman and newspapers promoted the judge's request for further denunciations, the arrests and self-imposed exile of hundreds of Society members did not inspire an influx of victims seeking sanctuary. Without further denunciations, the judge struggled to make any charges stick to the group's members, and none remained in jail longer than a year. While many fled the country, other women and men presumably managed to eventually leave their stigma behind and become ordinary Argentines.

### MAPPING THE ROAD TO BUENOS AIRES

This book evaluates the institutions, methods, and narratives with which migrant Jewish sex workers and managers structured their life experiences in this period. Poor immigrant women could sometimes achieve new decision-making powers in sex work, in comparison to the limitations they faced in their old and new homelands. Collaborations with men, such as strategic marriage, migratory networks, and mutual aid, could increase women's choices, even as reformers viewed such relationships as necessarily coercive. The boycott of the tmeim failed to hold bright lines between "respectable" and "unclean" migrants, as sex work occurred on a continuum and broad networks shaded into other arenas. Sex workers' strategies evolved in response to the forces that tried to constrain them. Just as international media and organizations made political uses of the white slave narrative, people involved in sex work used victim rhetoric to their own ends. Their lived experience also challenged the stories told about them and stymied the efforts of international abolitionists, local advocates for the regulation of prostitution, and "respectable" Jews to erase them.

Not just a footnote to the development of communal institutions and identity, Jewish trafficking and the battle against it fundamentally shaped the Argentine Jewish community. Despite the potential risks involved with airing dirty laundry, this approach also contributes to the larger paradigm shift in European and international Jewish history away from the poles of victimization and triumphalism toward the moral ambiguity of everyday life.[82] As communities reshaped by migration and modernity reconstituted themselves, subgroups vied to define the parameters of Jewish identity. While mainstream Jews tried to persuade authorities and antisemites that they should be embraced as respectable modern citizens, the tmeim claimed their own form of respectability in similar terms. The structures they built for mobility, labor, and mutual support were generally portrayed as forcible, but may often have been experienced as better than other constrained choices. They also mirrored similar institutions and values of other migrants and engaged the central concerns of their opponents: Jewish reputation, community solidarity, and the future of the Jewish family. The stakes of this battle for reputation were substantial: constraints on migration, barriers to community cohesion, revisions to family structure, and the future of the Jewish race itself.

This book is organized both thematically and chronologically, moving from the transnational to the local but with elements of each throughout. This is a transnational story in three registers: it traces the flow of people, the circulation of ideas, and the evolution of multinational organizations with important local implications. The term "transnational" can also be interpreted as fundamentally about mobility itself, rather than dispersal from or settlement in particular sites.[83] This book illuminates transnational mobility through analyses of networks, serial migrations, and the mechanisms of navigating regulatory systems, such as forgery, bribery, and strategic marriage. The first three chapters situate the victimized female white slave and darkened Jewish master in a global map of discursive and migratory flows as they evolved from the late nineteenth century through the interwar period. This framing begins at the broadest level, with the development of the international discourse of white slavery and the ramifications of responses to this moral panic. The following chapters situate Jewish sex workers and their managers in this discourse and lived experience. The book then focuses more tightly on Buenos Aires, tracing the dialectical development of the Argentine capital's mainstream Jewish community and the institutions of the "unclean."

Chapter 1 considers the narratives of white slavery that circulated in the press and popular publications and through national and transnational organizations for a half century. These stories served sensationalist and persuasive ends and refracted racial and sexual anxieties in an era of massive population shifts. The white slave concept presumed the subject's victimization, which allowed multinational reform organizations to position themselves as rescuers. The racialization of both the white slave and the presumably nonwhite slave master helped to sharpen the boundaries between groups as racial and national categories evolved. Even as the language of trafficking replaced the widespread use of the language of white slavery, the danger of racial mixing remained a potent element of the phenomenon's threat. During the interwar period, the League of Nations ran an elaborate investigation into sex trafficking, which when visualized on a world map demonstrates the fundamental concern of entities in the United States and northwestern Europe with border control, the possible loss of productive population, and the dangers of undesirable foreigners. As a migrant-receiving nation with a larger European population than most, Argentina became an important battleground in the global interwar struggle for racial and sexual order.

The second chapter centers the figure of the Jew on this discursive and experiential map. Ashkenazi Jewish men, whose racial categorization was slippery, became more tightly associated with sex trafficking than did men of other ethnic groups. The moral threat supposedly posed by such Jews became an excuse for limitations on Jewish migratory mobility. Paradoxically, the work of Jewish moral reformers to curb trafficking drew further attention to the Jewish presence in the field. While antisemitic stereotypes exaggerated the phenomenon, Jews actually did play a significant role in organized transnational sex work between the 1890s and early 1930s, the structure of which is a distinctive aspect of this study. The antisemitic narrative of the Jewish trafficking conspiracy thus incidentally overlapped with—even as it obscured—the temporary flourishing of a hierarchical system of coordinated labor among Ashkenazim along certain migratory routes.

Chapter 3 explores a particular aspect of the white slave narrative, the *shtile khupe*, a Jewish religious marriage ceremony lacking a civil component, which was often denounced by reformers as a key trafficking recruitment technique. In stories of trafficking that involved Jews, such sham marriages often trapped naïve young women into crossing the Atlantic. While opponents saw sex workers' marriages as a nefarious method for traffickers to exploit women, women sometimes entered voluntarily into these contracts for their own purposes. Marriage was in fact a common element of the transnational movement of women for sex work, but was often used strategically by prostitutes as well as by male and female managers. Ironically, anti–white slavery activism tightened border surveillance of single female migrants and thus increased women's incentive to marry in order to gain international mobility. Analysis of the particular dyadic relationships among Argentine sex workers and managers suggests that these were sometimes business arrangements, sometimes genuinely affective, and often both—as in the overall history of marriage. Among the tmeim, the quest for respectability on the very same terms as mainstream society facilitated evasion of legal restrictions, strengthened underworld networks, and could even help create satisfactory lives.

The fourth chapter enters into the daily workings and structure of the Varsovia Society at the peak of its power in the 1920s. This mutual aid organization managed a cemetery, synagogue, and social welfare services, while supporting the management of hundreds of brothels in the capital and provinces. Although the organization was often excoriated as a false charitable institution with a make-believe synagogue, its complex organizational structure mirrored that of other voluntary immigrant associations and its members engaged in public and private displays of Jewish religious identity. Society members acted like other immigrant businessmen, protecting their economic and religious interests, claiming respectability, and strategically identifying as Argentine. The range of community activity perpetuated by the Society also undermines the victim/ exploiter dichotomy, as women accessed certain forms of power and security.

Chapter 5 visually maps the evolution of Jewish organized sex work in Buenos Aires from the 1890s through 1930 alongside the evolution of the boycott against it. These maps highlight the scale, density, and visibility of prostitution in the heart of a nascent and insecure community.[84] The discursive visibility of Jewish prostitution was not simply a result of antisemitic exaggeration or mainstream Jewish anxieties: the ostentatious "impure" were among the most powerful and visible members of a new community with few options for upward economic mobility. A disproportionate number of Jewish men and women in the 1890s were involved in legally registered brothels, clustered in the area that was then just beginning to become the primary Jewish residential and business neighborhood. In the 1920s, the homes and brothels of the "impure" continued to permeate the primary urban Jewish area. Although many Jews moved out of the city center, the heart of the Jewish underworld remained in the core downtown neighborhood that continues to this day to be associated with its Jewish past.

The conclusion connects this history of international prostitution and the language of trafficking to current debates over marriage, migration, and trafficking. The process by which a young naïf from the countryside is overtaken by confusing urban customs and characters and beguiled or forced into degradation can be traced with little variation from these earliest tales of white slavery to contemporary stories of human trafficking.[85] While incongruent goals and assumptions make this a challenging conversation for historians to have with current activists and policy makers, lessons of the past can also be fruitful for present efforts.

CHAPTER 1

# White Slaves and Dark Masters

*People in Europe speak with indignation of the traffic in negroes. It would be just as well if they would open their eyes to what is going on much nearer . . . the exportation of white slaves. . . . The greater number are probably engaged for Montevideo and Buenos Ayres.*　　　　　—Josephine Butler, 1888

*There is not, and apparently has not been in recent years, a single well-tested case in which a girl has been trapped into the white slave traffic.*
　　　　　　　　　　　　　　　　　—William Leonard Courtney, 1913

White slave narratives starred an innocent woman of European descent taken far from home by a foreign or racialized man. In the eyes of moral reformers, popular press and fiction, and international Jewish community leaders, the transportation of women from Europe to South America produced an ugly stain of sexual criminality on the world map. Buenos Aires became a metonym for trafficking. Given that the Argentine capital was only one of many cities with legally regulated prostitution and a thriving underworld, why did Buenos Aires loom so large in the public imagination? The power and contours of white slave narratives reflected unequal global power relationships and uncertainty about the postcolonial world order, the effects of mass migration, and the consequences of interracial interactions.[1] Concern with the movement of women across the Atlantic between the late 1800s and the interwar era was about not only sexual commerce but migration more broadly. This became particularly apparent in the League of Nations' massive antitrafficking investigation of the mid-1920s, which unevenly assessed different nations in accordance with racialized fears and an abolitionist approach to prostitution in general.[2] The story of the white slave was used to draw hard lines between white and nonwhite, desirable and undesirable immigrant, victim and exploiter, bystander and rescuer.

## RACE, CLASS, AND THE GENEALOGY OF THE WHITE SLAVE

In the late nineteenth and early twentieth centuries, voyeuristic tales of seduction, betrayal, and syphilitic death encouraged European and North American newspaper readers to fear for their daughters' safety.[3] Spurred by "yellow journalism," the explosion of mass migration, and the interests of social reformers, mobilization against white slavery succeeded the movements for the abolition of African slavery as a major international social cause. Feminists in London, Berlin, and New York rallied against the evils of the "white slave trade," and organized conferences and rescue missions on behalf of innocent European maidens coerced across the Atlantic by swarthy pimps. However, several decades of historians have demonstrated that white slavery did not actually exist on this enormous scale, and even many contemporary observers expressed doubt.[4] For example, a Boston theater critic in 1913 questioned the credibility of a recent white slave novel, calling it a "lurid tale," "a revival of a somewhat ancient legend," and a "tract . . . to support the agitation against the white slave traffic" and praised British suffragette and founder of the Women's Freedom League Teresa Billington-Greig's recent debunking of the hysteria.[5] In the same year, the *New York Times* excoriated reformers for mounting "shocking public exhibitions" despite having "reformed nothing" of "this so largely mythical white slave traffic."[6] Given the relatively few proven cases of innocent women abducted across national boundaries for the purposes of forced prostitution, why did white slavery provoke repeated moral panics on both sides of the Atlantic for more than half a century?[7]

Part of the ongoing appeal of the story was doubtlessly pornographic, an excuse to allude to sex and even show images of women's naked bodies.[8] The titillating spectacle of beautiful young white virgins coerced into having sex with men, often of other races, while lamented, also helped to sell newspapers. Stories of older women working as doorkeepers or madams rarely elicited such interest. The white slave story also contributed to assumptions and proposals in the realm of public policy, in this era of transnational organizational efforts. Framing sex traffic as a form of migration suggests that antitrafficking projects shared in broader anxieties and regulatory projects related to race, foreignness, and national identity. The particular historical evolution of the transatlantic concept of white slavery reconstituted the prostitute as a victim of a racialized or foreign male exploiter, thus sharpening ethnic distinctions and policing morality in an era of mass migration and national reorganization.

The application of "white slavery" to cross-border prostitution appears to have spread in influence following a March 1870 letter from Victor Hugo to British feminist Josephine Butler that linked African chattel slavery to prostitution in an attempt to bring together the causes of abolitionists and feminists. In this letter, Hugo argued "the slavery of black women is abolished in America, but the slavery of white women continues in Europe and laws are still made by men in order to tyrannize over women."[9] Josephine Butler played a primary role in connecting the successful movement for the abolition of chattel slavery to the development of a movement in opposition to sex trafficking. In 1875, she was instrumental in founding the organization that became the International Abolitionist Federation, a driving force in opposition to the state regulation of prostitution.[10] One of her main concerns was that regulation focused on women's bodies rather than men's: prostitutes were forced to submit to regular examinations, forbidden to work if infected, and branded as prostitutes in a way that often forced them to remain such for life. Meanwhile, clients were ignored.[11]

By the late 1880s, discussion of white slavery on both sides of the Atlantic took on the key defining elements that would remain essentially unchanged for the next half century. The first *New York Times* article to discuss white slavery and prostitution explicitly linked the trade to Jews, which would continue to be an underlying theme among broader immigration-related anxieties concerning both North and South America.[12] Also in 1886, Josephine Butler wrote about the transportation of girls from Hamburg to Montevideo and Buenos Aires for the same purpose, which was already becoming synonymous with international prostitution.[13] The varied aspects of white slave discourse, focusing on racialized men, allowed female social purity activists to shift their target from the general category of all men and potentially make common cause with male reformers and politicians.

Before the term "white slavery" came to refer to sex trafficking, other international reformers deployed the term "white slave" to criticize racialized masters. Abolitionists critiqued chattel slave owners, Orientalists targeted Barbary Coast traders and harem keepers, and those concerned with the dangers of U.S. Western expansion underscored Indian barbarism. British advocates of African chattel slavery in the West Indies from at least the 1780s used the language of white slavery to justify the continuation of the institution with the claim that West Indian slaves lived and worked under conditions far superior to those of English child laborers and short-lived miners. Their abolitionist opponents at first ignored the equation between chattel and wage slavery, focusing on the legal definition of human beings as property as civilization's foremost evil.[14] After the abolition of chattel slavery, reformers found the comparison useful as rhetoric; the discussion of industrial white slaves was laced with references to black slaves, regularly implying that white workers suffered under the same brutal conditions, which would be even crueler to whites than to blacks.

European concern with the inversion of the natural order in which white Europeans were masters of darker races extended to Barbary captivity narratives, which Paul Michel Baepler argues were among the most popular publications in the nineteenth century. His analysis of these tales in *White Slaves, African Masters* shows that they are intimately intertwined with the American slave narrative and the Indian captivity narrative, which he claims American literary historians have overemphasized, while the three should be considered together.[15] One such text, Charles Sumner's 1853 *White Slavery in the Barbary States*, compares the abolitionist movement against African chattel slavery to European outrage at the sixteenth- to eighteenth-century enslavement of European and some American Christians in Algiers and the surrounding area.[16] In North America, the related genre of Indian captivity narratives generally featured a female victim and shared Barbary Coast tales' anger at the inversion of the natural order. Argentina had a similar nineteenth-century Indian captivity narrative genre, featured in fine arts as well as poetry and other forms of literature.[17] Captivity narratives on both sides of the Atlantic, like later white slave stories, outlined the capture of a white innocent by racialized strangers, followed by resistance, acceptance or assimilation, and eventual redemption.[18]

Captivity, Barbary Coast, and white slave narratives emphasized the cultural gap between captor and captive, between Native American or French Canadian and Anglo, between Muslim and Christian, and between more and less desirable immigrant ethnic groups.[19] Before Italian immigrants were considered white and desirable in the United States, they were stigmatized as exploitative masters in terms almost identical to the white slave narrative. An 1873 *New York Times* article describes the well-fed, fur-clad, gold-chain-covered Italian "owner" of white slave children kidnapped and brought across the Atlantic for factory labor, a "ruffian" reminiscent of the "rufianes" (pimps) populating the Buenos Aires underworld.[20] Thirty years later, a *Los Angeles Times* European correspondent reported on the circumstances of rural Italian parents duped into selling their sons into wage slavery by duplicitous "contractors for white slaves" in language very similar to the common story of small-town parents inadvertently selling their daughters into sexual slavery: "A well-dressed man, usually an Italian, appears in the poorest and most wretched district he can find and casually displays much money and volunteers his history, which usually runs on the lines that he was once as poor as any of his hearers, but went abroad with a kind friend and returned in affluence as all can see. To the poor parents in the village he offers golden prospects for their children, out of love of mankind, if they will only turn them over to him: comfort, little work, all the money they want, and $40 or $50 a year to the parents."[21] This narrative differs only from those of female sexual white slaves in the gap between this trafficker's "love of mankind" and a professional "suitor's" love for a daughter. Even more dangerous than the Italian immigrant was the eternal wanderer and dubious trader, the Jew. Italian and Jewish immigrants both arrived in large numbers in Argentina in this era, but only the latter group became associated with the traffic in women.

The most common use of "white slave" in the nineteenth century, in fact, was in critiques of wage labor exploitation, with the term "slave" leveraged to argue that European-born child and adult workers in the industrial North were treated even worse than Africans in the American South. Critics of white slavery often referenced the ideals of the movement for abolition of African slavery to plead for similar consideration of other exploited workers, and occasionally weighed in against the termination of the chattel trade. In 1833, the year of the British Factory Act, which for the first time placed significant legal restrictions on child labor, the poem "The Factory Child," penned in Britain and republished in U.S. newspapers from Charleston to Boston, described young children suffering under exhausting hours, tyrannical factory overseers, and pitiful wages, fated for premature death.[22] "White slave" was used both for children working on British textile looms in the 1830s and for garment workers on New York's Lower East Side seventy-five years later.[23]

White slavery was understood in this sense on both sides of the Atlantic, and extended to the situation of other exploited workers, such as Russian serfs in the 1840s and English domestic workers in the 1850s.[24] The term appeared in the streets as well as off the presses, as exemplified by an 1863 broadside addressing workers as white slaves in a New York City labor organizing effort.[25] For example, in the 1890s, some strands of Protestantism claimed that "for every black man emancipated by Abraham Lincoln there is a white slave in America today in a worse plight" and that "the American black slave had, as a rule, a better time than the American white slave is having. Cane fields and cotton fields had their drawbacks, but it was not a sweatshop."[26] In the early twentieth century, "white slave" was also used to criticize the tyranny of both labor unions and business monopolies.[27]

The concept of whiteness itself was in flux during this period, and discussion of industrial workers often highlighted the slippery racial categorization of immigrants to the United States. A 1907 New York Sun article republished in Life described garment workers on New York's Lower East Side as industrial wage slaves, who, although "by some they are called 'white slaves.' But they—the 'slaves'—are nearer black than white. All of them are foreign-born and most of them are females."[28] David R. Roediger has argued that the metaphor of white slavery as industrial wage labor allowed workers to condemn new inequalities while distinguishing themselves from African chattel slaves.[29] The use of "white slavery" to protest the exploitation of immigrant labor thus became a part of the whitening of Italian, Irish, and Jewish immigrants.

### THE UTILITY OF WHITE VICTIMS AND DARK MASTERS

The white slave always dragged the black slave as a shadow. Even as the "peculiar institution" was dismantled in the nineteenth century, African chattel slavery remained the primary referent such that "white slave" would have had the jarring quality of an oxymoron, juxtaposing two inherently contradictory terms.[30] Reformers harnessed both abolitionist and retrograde sentiments: while some critics of white sexual slavery drew on popular opposition to black slavery to create sympathy, others implied that the injustice of white slavery was magnified in comparison to black slavery by the skin color of its subjects, who could not be "natural" slaves.[31] A 1913 social purity sexual education manual argued about the coerced prostitute, "No other form of slavery which has ever been devised can equal her condition."[32]

The boundaries of race are always bound up with sexuality, as the prevention of racial mixing is key to keeping races separate and making racial identity easy to parse.[33] Fear of racial mixing often appeared in white slave narratives, as a call to protect the sanctity of white womanhood, as demonstrated in this 1913 social purity text: "She was ravished . . . and taken to a house of ill fame . . . and there confined and compelled to receive foreigners and turn the earnings over to the master to whom she was sold by her captors."[34] The protection of white womanhood from black or foreign Others was a common trope with a range of political uses, from cartoons published in William Randolph Hearst's newspapers justifying the Spanish-American War to *The Birth of a Nation*.[35] White women could be dragged into debauchery by Near and Far Eastern men as well, as Orientalism saturated Western visions of the world.

In addition to reflecting racial anxieties connected to chattel slavery, white slave narratives often refracted Orientalist fantasies of European women imprisoned in Eastern harems. Visions of the harem, and ideas of white women forced therein to engage in sexual adventures with darker-skinned men, fascinated Europeans in the colonial period.[36] In 1822, a London newspaper reported the sale of ten thousand women from Greece to Ottoman harems and derided the lack of British response: "What a howl would have been set up if so many hundred negroes had been disposed of in the same manner! . . . The English government is now upholding the system which produces the white slave trade in the east, and affecting great indignation that it should be carried on by other powers of the west."[37] A work of pornography widely circulated in the Victorian Era, *The Lustful Turk*, detailed the deflowering and subsequent voracious sexual appetites of European women sold into the harem of the Dey of Algiers, whose foreignness and extreme sexual appetites were underscored.[38] Art critics and other Orientalists were fascinated by the servitude of the odalisque and her "aggregated knowledge of the arts of pleasing."[39] These images were both erotic and moralizing, implicitly critiquing racial mixing and promiscuity. Concern with Chinese involvement in prostitution, sometimes claiming the entanglement of white women despite little evidence, was particularly prevalent in California, where Chinatown symbolized brothels and opium dens.[40] As in Orientalist descriptions of sexual excesses in harems, East Asians were implicated as sexually deviant, thus elevating European morality: "The sexual immorality of these people is horrifying . . . [while] in America woman stands on a pedestal far above the status of her sisters in any other land."[41]

This Orientalist legacy intertwined with chattel slavery references continued into the late nineteenth-century white slave panic. In 1886 the *New York Times'* first mention of white slavery as explicitly sexual describes "Slaves Sold to the Turk" for the supply of harems, and while this is described as a "mild and rather human form" of slavery in comparison to the chattel form, it also points out that "truly not even in America's palmiest days of slavery was human flesh held so cheap as it is to-day in the land of the Crescent!"[42] Comparable newspaper stories about the Middle East and North Africa published in the late 1880s and 1890s made similar comparisons to African chattel slavery and references to the British abolitionist movement, as well as demonstrating slippage around the terms "white" and "Caucasian," then in definitional flux.[43] According to some critics, Orientalism continues to influence today's antitrafficking work, as "the figure of the 'suffering Third World prostitute' serves to symbolize the excesses of the global march of capital, and its negative effects on women" and activists in the global West/North often treat Eastern/Southern prostitutes as though they are unable to speak for themselves.[44]

As forced cross-border prostitution became the dominant definition of white slavery, new targets included foreign panderers, corrupt police, regulatory systems of prostitution, and the lack of effective international law. Anti–white slave diatribes took on different tones: William T. Stead's 1885 British exposé criticized traditional aristocratic sexual privilege, while French authors tended to defend their system of regulated prostitution and reformers in the Americas expressed concern with the ramifications of mass immigration and legacy of African chattel slavery.

Concerns with race and racial mixing underlay much of the local and international conversation and policy around white slavery. In the United States, the 1910 White Slave Traffic Act, or Mann Act, which prohibited interstate travel for "immoral purposes," was famously used against the African American boxer Jack Johnson for bringing his white wife across state lines, and its broader enforcement helped consolidate the power of the FBI.[45] In 1912 and 1913, Georgia representative Seaborn Roddenbery introduced a proposal in the House of Representatives to add the prohibition of miscegenation to the U.S. Constitution, in direct reaction to Jack Johnson's multiple marriages to and affairs with white women.[46] A Harlem Black Jewish sect leader, Elder W. Robinson, was convicted in 1926 under the Mann Act for having multiple wives.[47] Beyond black–white relations, journalism blaming white slavery on foreigners called for the protection of the superior Anglo-Saxon race.[48] Overall, through white slavery sensationalist journalism and activist debates, sex literally constructed the boundaries of race as race policed the boundaries of sex, and sexual purity crusades supported racial purity.

While "trafficking" began to supplant "white slavery" in the 1910s, in an effort to broaden the narrative, the racialized dynamics of white slavery continued to suffuse popular and political discussions. White slavery differed from its foreign counterparts *la trata de blancas, la traite des blanches,* and *der mädchenhandel* in the term's close historic association with African chattel slavery and its abolition, industrial labor abuses, and Orientalist fantasies. Germanic language terms erase race and slavery entirely, literally referring to the traffic or trade in women and girls. The Spanish and French terms specify "white" females, but do not contrast as pointedly with slavery. International discussions of these terms also shaped debate within Argentina, as evidenced by a Buenos Aires city councilman's consideration of international semantic arguments.[49] The connection between the *trata* (trade) in *blancas* (whites) and *negros* (blacks) was pervasive enough that the 1910 international congress at Madrid encouraged the alternative term *trata de mujeres* (trade in women).[50] Racially explicit language continued to adhere to these discussions both in Argentina and internationally, as evident in the coverage of the 1930 court case against the Varsovia Society that frequently used "trata de blancas" rather than "trata de mujeres."

More than a metaphor, the concept of white slavery reflected social critiques and both concrete and abstract proposals for social change. Although by the eve of World War I "white slavery" was generally understood in the English-speaking world to refer to coerced prostitution, this sensationalistic phrase continued to reflect the nuances of several distinct meanings that had been deployed to various ends for at least a century prior. The genealogy of "white slavery," as it evolved into meaning coerced prostitution and then transformed into trafficking, contributed to the believability of its central victim narrative. Pre-prostitution definitions of white slavery, particularly as chattel slavery, Barbary Coast slavery, and wage slavery, later amplified the resonance of the innocent inveigled prostitute with other racial, national, and labor-related anxieties.[51] The coercive element of the traffic was the central shared concern of representatives from the many interested countries who met in international conferences from the turn of the century and later through the League of Nations. International collaboration on the issue tended to reduce white slavery to the particular narrative of a young white Western European female forced into sexual immorality by a man of foreign, racially ambiguous nationality. This transference of guilt from prostitute to trafficker and removal of agency from the blameless victim allowed antitrafficking activists to place themselves in the position of rescuer.

The victim narrative and rescue of purported white slaves created a range of opportunities for women, both victims and redeemers, to take on positions of moral superiority over men.[52] Both whiteness and victimhood allowed the previously bad girl to be good. Early feminists used the Victorian discourse of women's moral virtue, based on natural maternal tendencies, to justify their forays into the public sphere.[53] Women's natural moral purity would serve better than men's superior intelligence in the realm of social service, they slyly answered their critics. As massive immigration stirred nativist fears in the United States, imperial fears of racial deterioration and decline shook late Victorian Britain. Arguments against women's work in factories and meeting halls amply exploited both sets of anxieties. Many feminists defended their ongoing fulfillment of their domestic duties and even positioned themselves as "mothers of the race," as the literal vessels guaranteeing the future purity of the Anglo-Saxon race.[54]

This was certainly not a challenge to the Victorian mythology of women's natural role as custodian of sexual purity, although feminist activists such as Josephine Butler had different goals and motivations from the social purity activists. Butler and other feminists worried about regulation as yet another way for men to control women's behavior, and certainly antitrafficking organizations such as the JAPGW's Gentlemen's Committee fit this shoe. Women's organizations and women as individuals led the fight against prostitution in the United States and Europe, due not only to the increase in women's education but also to their desire to loosen men's tight grip on women's public behavior to make way for the New Woman—if a defenseless immigrant girl could be safe on the streets, so could anyone.[55] Defense of female industrial workers and shop-girls, sometimes also called white slaves, paralleled these concerns.[56] Some narrators of white slave stories, from "gentlemen" like William T. Stead to Butler and other feminist activists, explicitly incorporated the reformer as savior. This resonated with earlier stories of other kinds of white slavery, such as captivity narratives.[57] As journalists and moral reformers took the place of ministers, they similarly shaped stories for their own didactic purposes.

White slavery or trafficking was often conflated with prostitution as a broader phenomenon, and provided a useful answer for the question of why women became prostitutes. In contrast to the depictions by religious and conservative observers who emphasized sin and corruption, portraits of prostitutes as victims were intended as an alternative to condemnation.[58] Some reformers highlighted economic necessity; an example is Teresa Billington-Greig, who put at the center of her campaign poverty and family coercion, while critiquing both reformers and the church for disallowing the possibility that women could be responsible for their own decisions about their sexuality.[59] Economic causality was both broadly accepted and challenged.

On the eve of World War I, the public outcry against sexual exploitation prompted investigation into women's working conditions. The hypothesis that low wages drove women into prostitution inspired the proposal in 1913 that a minimum wage be established for female workers in the United States.[60] One critic of this proposal insisted that if women's wages were raised, women would be fired from their jobs, creating greater deprivation, as men could then do more work for less pay due to their greater strength. This author was careful to note that the situation would unfold in this way not because of employer preference for men, but because women had been hired due to being cheaper workers, and these calculations were all purely economic.[61] Other respondents in this debate held that "the low wage scale is scarcely ever a direct cause for the downfall of young women."[62] Prostitutes themselves weighed in with letters to the Vice Investigation Commission. One prostitute signing her letter K. R. L. agreed with the latter perspective, blaming male seducers rather than low wages: "Girls don't go wrong because they are hungry or because they need clothes. They go wrong because they are tempted by lies and overpowered by the evil in men."[63] This version of the victim narrative pushed back against the accusation that women's love of luxury might drive them into prostitution, as in the common story of the shopgirl tempted by her wares but unable to afford them on her salary.[64]

Just as K. R. L. strategically blamed manipulative men for the downfall of herself and other women, many reformers deployed narratives of women's victimization to shift blame from women to men, from prostitutes to traffickers. This shift was also racialized, as female victims were framed as white while their exploiters were not. White slavery implied a dark-skinned master, an inversion that fed the vitriol against traffickers and pimps, always figured as foreign and racialized.

This racial dichotomy correlates with reformers' usual simplification of the structure of prostitution into male pimp exploiters and female prostitute victims. In fact, the management of sex work on the ground in Argentina and transnationally was far more complicated than a clear gender split, with clients' money ultimately trickling up to doorkeepers, brokers, commission agents, and landlords, as well as police and immigration authorities and a range of businesspeople, from manufacturers of clothing to those producing condoms. While prostitutes had to thus give away at least half of their earnings, the profession was among the most lucrative available at the time, certainly for women. Buenos Aires, especially, became a transnational sex work center.

## The Reputation of Buenos Aires as a Trafficking Hub

As "white slavery" became associated with the transport of women across national borders, generally from the Old World to the New World or from the Global North to the Global South, the destinations were usually left vague and terrifying, but when specified, they more often than not turned out to be on the Río de la Plata. The French journalist Albert Londres's 1927 exposé *The Road to Buenos Ayres* sufficiently indicated the subject matter of white slavery in the title for the theme to go unsaid in newspaper coverage of the internationally popular work, published in multiple languages and as a play.[65] This connection had begun several decades earlier: in 1888, Josephine Butler appealed to the women of the United States to join British women in the combat against "the enforced movement . . . of these youthful victims of human cruelty . . . [of whom] the greater number are probably engaged for Montevideo and Buenos Ayres."[66] In the same year, a *New York Times* article about a market in Constantinople where

"European girls . . . imported for the purpose . . . are publicly sold as slaves" mentioned Buenos Aires as the prime destination across the Atlantic.[67] The British National Vigilance Association, it was reported, was already aware by 1891 that "a very large trade is being carried on in European girls for the purposes of prostitution in Buenos Ayres."[68] Most European nations and many others signed on to international agreements that attempted to control the traffic in women by modifying national policies, from the late nineteenth century through the League of Nations' massive efforts of the 1920s. But Argentina refused to cooperate, provoking complaints by abolitionist forces that the nation promoted global exploitation.[69]

The U.S. press in the 1910s and 1920s often referred to South America as the most popular international destination for white slave traders bringing women across the Atlantic and as a common refuge for those fearing prosecution in the United States who hoped to continue their occupation elsewhere.[70] In the generally uncorroborated mappings of the trade routes and interconnected criminal associations of purportedly internationally organized white slave traders, Buenos Aires always appeared as a key hub or destination.[71] Although unsubstantiated, an "organized trade to South America" emerged from a U.S. federal case in 1917, in which witnesses claimed that the defendant belonged to "a band engaged in kidnapping girls, taking them to South American ports, and selling them to confederates in South America."[72] Buenos Aires sometimes served as a synecdoche for the entire continent of South America. Similarly, Evelyn Waugh's 1928 *Decline and Fall* described the Latin-American Entertainment Company as a cabaret recruitment front and evoked in its name the connection not only, as one critic observes, "between music halls and white slavery," but between the entire region and white slavery.[73]

Buenos Aires maintained this international reputation through the 1930s, no doubt strengthened by the international press coverage in 1930 and 1931 of the trial that broke up the Varsovia Society. In a 1930 Polish novel, *The Ravishers: A Novel of White Slavery in Its Heyday*, a Warsaw vice squad director denies passport clearance to Argentina to a beautiful young applicant, telling her, "If you wished to emigrate to North America, to the United States for instance or to Canada, I shouldn't put any obstacles in your way. But I know too well what South America has in store for a young, pretty girl."[74] A British traveler in 1933 mentioned white slavery as the first negative association with Argentina that might pop up in the foreign reader's mind.[75] Theater demonstrated interest in the subject, as evidenced by a play produced in New York in 1935 featuring "the snaring of a virtuous girl by an Argentine white slave band."[76] Some sensationalist sources continued to promote the association between Buenos Aires and white slavery into the 1960s and 1970s, as in a 1979 work that conflates all prostitution with trafficking and describes Buenos Aires as the principal destination of "the overseas trade in girls [that] proved to be one of the most remunerative criminal enterprises of the twentieth century . . . an international spider's web along whose threads 'parcels' . . . were dispatched with all the efficiency of a well-run export business."[77]

Argentine officials, journalists, and businessmen were deeply concerned by the late 1920s with how the rest of the world viewed the republic. Commissioner Alsogaray's memoir bemoaned the fact that at the International Congresses against White Slavery in 1895, 1899, 1903, 1904, and 1906 in Paris, London, Budapest, Berlin, Amsterdam, Zurich, and Frankfurt, as well as in the League of Nations' Committee on the Traffic in Women and Children in the 1920s, Buenos Aires was considered the principal center of this commerce, the "Athens of La Plata."[78] The defense of the nation's reputation became a crucial part of the publicity around the 1930 court case against the Society. Argentine defensive concerns were economic as well as patriotic. The publication of *The Road to Buenos Ayres* happened to coincide with the run-up to the Argentine presidential election of Dr. Hipolito Irigoyen for his second nonconsecutive term. Irigoyen was reputed to resent the book's popularity in the United States, at least in part because a nationalist campaign against U.S. oil interests had been central to his reelection.[79] As Argentine leaders competed with the United States for European import markets, they hoped to remove the traffic in women from common perceptions of the Argentine international trade circuit. The identification of traffickers as foreigners assisted in this distancing effort.

Argentina's infamous reputation in Britain in particular may have been shaped by the unique relationship between the two countries. As Europe and the United States sought neocolonial relationships with Latin America in the wake of the region's independence from Spain and Portugal, Argentina ended up in the British sphere of influence, in what some scholars have called a relationship of "informal empire."[80] Britain was Argentina's largest export market from the 1880s, buying from 20 to 40 percent of its exports before the First World War, particularly meat and cereals.[81] The dominance of European immigrants flooding into the Río de la Plata also pushed industrializing Argentina to identify more with Europe than with the rest of Latin America. However, the legalization of prostitution in Argentina allied the country with French-style regulationism rather than British-style abolitionism. This, in addition to British economic involvement in the country, doubtless raised British concerns about prostitution in Argentina. Technological changes and migration continued to make the world smaller, and new trade relationships spurred anxiety about the potential dangers of intercultural interactions.[82] Some concerned observers conflated the ideology of free trade with a laissez-faire response to the traffic in women.[83]

British and U.S. beliefs about Argentina's centrality on the world map of sexual vice mattered. It was in Britain where the white slave as sex slave connection exploded in the 1880s and the world's largest international antitrafficking organizations were based. Even though the United States was not an official member, the two English-speaking nations were the most powerful forces in the League of Nations in the 1920s. The League's Committee on the Traffic in Women and Children became instrumental in coordinating international activity around this issue and attempted to shift the tone of conversation, beginning with the rejection of the sensationalistic term "white slavery" in favor of the more progressive "traffic in women." Its antitrafficking work adopted earlier abolitionist positions of international anti–white slavery conventions and networks spearheaded by the International Bureau for the Suppression of the Traffic in Women (IBSTW) and the JAPGW. The Argentine government was implicitly blamed by the League for regulating rather than abolishing prostitution, and took up a disproportionate amount of researchers' attention.[84] Argentina also housed core underworld figures who introduced undercover investigators to other contacts in a transatlantic network—Jewish figures based in Buenos Aires were key to their "snowball" research technique.

This attention to Buenos Aires provoked a defensive reaction: A group of Latin American delegates led a protest against the League of Nations in 1927, charging that its expensive international investigations into the traffic in women were carried out by investigators who spoke only English and were biased against non-Anglo countries.[85] In what the New York Times described as "one of the heaviest emotional gales that has ever swept the buildings housing the Secretariat of the League of Nations," objections stalled the final publication of the already-ratified second volume of the Report of the Special Body of Experts on Traffic in Women and Children.[86] Uruguayan feminist leader Dr. Paulina Luisi charged the trafficking committee's chairman William F. Snow with having handpicked investigators who overlooked the severity of conditions in Anglo-Saxon nations while shaming Latin nations and effectively withdrew from her leadership role in protest, boycotting several meetings and refusing to ratify the final report.[87] Although a number of references to Buenos Aires in the final reports, perhaps in response to this protest, were somewhat disguised as unnamed sites or generic South American locations, the Argentine capital was described explicitly "as a sort of Golconda"—the source of the Hope Diamond, which in that era signified a site of great wealth—for traffickers and prostitutes, who flocked there "as if they expected to find gold in the streets."[88]

## Antitrafficking as Migration Regulation

White slave discourses did not merely float in the ether of media and popular culture but had real policy consequences, particularly in the realm of immigration. Women's mobility was often restricted in the name of preventing them from being trafficked. One of the first historians to analyze antiprostitution organizing in the United States compellingly described two distinct campaigns against prostitution, one nativist or xenophobic and the other antinativist or defending the rights of immigrants.[89] The association between prostitution and immigrants created particularly among nativists a call for the deportation of immigrant women of suspicious moral character. Reformers more friendly to aliens argued against this approach. Entrenched elites in Europe and the United States, anxious about a new social order threatening to emerge from this era of mass migration and shifting labor patterns, conflated women's migration with inevitable sexual slavery, encouraging foreign women to remain home in their own countries—an argument echoed in today's trafficking debates.[90] Opponents to the nativist connection between prostitution and immigration included social workers such as Frances Kellor, Jane Addams, Grace Abbott, and Lillian Wald. This perspective erases women's agency in desiring and seeking mobility. Within Argentina as well, displacement of blame for prostitution onto foreigners served the interests of various parties, while ignoring the decision-making potential of sex workers themselves.

A visualization of the interconnection between trafficking and migration can be constructed from the massive research and policy program sponsored by the League of Nations in the 1920s. The League's Advisory Committee on the Traffic in Women and Children sent "expert" investigators to 112 cities in twenty-eight countries to interview police, immigration authorities, social reformers, and government officials. Field reports, correspondence, and official publications provide rich detail of conditions on the ground in each locale, as well as overall dynamics between countries and around regulatory efforts. Undercover investigators infiltrated underworld circles, pretending with apparent success to be pimps or aspirational traffickers in women. The League's investigators were publicly led by attorney Major Bascom Johnson, who had previously shut down San Francisco's "Barbary Coast" red-light district working for the American Social Hygiene Association and openly used his position to conduct interviews in Argentina and the other countries with local police, border and immigration officials, and those considered "respectable."[91]

Paul Kinzie, the chameleon, led the League's undercover investigations. According to field reports that named him only in code, Kinzie was able to alter his appearance, style, and language to be perceived as a number of different races and nationalities, from a Yiddish-speaking Jew in Argentina to a Muslim in North Africa.[92] The confidential reports combined interviews with and observations of sex industry figures, networks, tactics, and spaces. The investigators' codes for informants categorized them with anonymized numbers, using "DH" for disorderly house owner, "P" for pimp, "M" for madam, and "G" for girl (prostitute). The category "R," for "respectable" informants, included President Theodore Roosevelt and his wife, as well as businessmen, actors, politicians, and other local officials. For interactions with underworld figures, Kinzie built on his experience and underworld contacts from previous U.S. operations to disguise himself as a novice trafficker seeking advice and connections. He reported secrets gathered in this guise from South America to North America, sometimes moving abruptly to maintain his subterfuge. His cover story varied, but generally included past accumulation of capital through bootlegging in the United States, which he was trying to use to either transport a young woman out of Europe or place one in a brothel. In Tunis, Kinzie wore "a fez (cap) and [was] represented as a Turk" as "according to the Mohamedan custom . . . these women will not trade with nor permit anyone but a member of their own sect to enter their homes."[93] In Buenos Aires he posed as a Jew, to follow up on international connections linked to Max "Mortche" Goldberg, a powerful brothel owner whom Kinzie knew from the New York City "vice trust" investigations and arrests a decade prior.[94] Kinzie sometimes included nationality and linguistic markers when describing individuals but did not label any as Jewish. Jewish identity appeared through language and self-identification in conversations between underworld members.

Kinzie's field reports of his interactions with prostitutes, pimps, madams, and other underworld figures were circulated only among a limited group of League of Nations officials and trusted collaborators. If considered as a genre of writing, they share many similarities with the confidential reports he and other undercover investigators produced in New York City twenty years earlier for the American Social Hygiene Association and the Committee of Fourteen.[95] The way in which these investigations were conducted and written about also echoes the published and widely circulated trafficking exposés of the period, particularly Stead's muckraking work and Londres's *The Road to Buenos Ayres*, which shortly followed the publication of the League's Experts' Reports and was accused of using them as unacknowledged sources.[96] In all of these accounts, the chameleon-like investigator implicitly heroized himself, both for his success at convincing hardened underworld characters that he was one of them and for resisting the imperative to prove his commitment by accepting any of the frequent sexual offers or producing the women he claimed to traffic or manage. Whether their reports were intended for small- or large-scale circulation, the investigators underscored their masculinity by highlighting the frequency of these sexual offers, the risks of their adventures, and their ability to move between "respectable" and "disreputable" circles, both out-pimping the pimps and out-copping the cops.

Because Kinzie and other investigators engaged mostly with other men as peers, from higher-status brothel owners to street-level pimps, women appear even in these behind-the-scenes reports at a distance magnified by objectification. The physical appearance of both male and female subjects is frequently detailed for identification and ethnographic purposes, but the tone of women's descriptions more frequently slips into details verging on the pornographic, with detailed descriptive images of women's bodies as well as clothing and facial features.[97] Men's speech is reproduced more often, and women are generally spoken to only when men are also present. Perhaps because investigators' goals were to understand organizational systems, sex workers themselves are usually observed rather than interviewed, and most reported conversations occur with brothel owners, pimps, and madams. These reports rarely describe prostitutes as unwilling victims, and sometimes take a judgmental tone toward women's sexuality, particularly among lower-class prostitutes, often characterized as depraved instigators of perverse sexual acts or hardened, hopeless lost souls.[98] The perspectives of sex workers themselves are thus far less clearly reflected than the opinions of others who profited from their labor or sought to reform it.

Even taking these limitations into consideration, the League's international field reports, corroborated with the previous decade's investigations in the United States as well as police and immigration data, suggest transnational linkages between Ashkenazi Jewish men and women who supported one another in the business of sex over several decades. While not as formally structured as anxieties about "vice trusts" and "white slavery rings" suggested, trusted relationships were maintained through ties of marriage and kinship, language and ethnicity, and collective experiences of risk and exclusion. Between the 1890s and 1920s, certain transit routes predominated, though particular routes between cities and across national borders shifted with local conditions. Because investigators moved between underworld connections through referrals, the usual limitations of the snowball sample technique shaped their findings: individuals outside of these networks were not visible. The use of this technique and the relative interconnectedness of Jewish sex work managers meant that other ethnic and national groups who worked in more competition and isolation appeared to be less significant to overall trafficking patterns.

Decisions about where to focus these investigations and the general conclusions drawn predominantly reflected U.S. and Western European concerns with the postcolonial global balance of power leading to the increased policing of national borders. Despite the League's central role in promoting the language of trafficking over that of white slavery, the racialized norms and victim trope of the earlier model persisted. Investigators focused on seeking out coercive practices, particularly the transport of minors and women who had not previously practiced prostitution. The exploitation of women from northwestern Europe to countries where they would presumably have clients of other races was the central concern.

In the 1927 published report distributed to the members of the League, the relative strength of incoming and outgoing traffic of each country under review is assessed.[99] Each country is described as basically a sender or receiver of women, with some serving more as transit through routes. These three groups fall in a bulls-eye pattern, with three rings moving outward from Europe. In the center are the primary sending or recruiting grounds, the countries of Southern and

Eastern Europe plus France—though France also had a bustling and internally organized local sexual economy, as did Italy. In the middle ring, the countries that are generally just passed through are positioned as gateways between regions of the world. Turkey, for example, serves as a conduit with the Near and Far East, regions that were not studied in depth by the League until the following decade. The language of transmigration, as a term used frequently in discussion of the transnational movement of people, can be applied to these countries. In the outer ring, the endpoint countries of the traffic are mostly colonial or postcolonial societies.

This overall pattern underscores the primary concern of the European-dominated League that white European women would be forced into less civilized zones, there to be degraded by forced intercourse with non-European men. "Native" women practicing prostitution were mentioned only in passing as "in keeping with the filthy huts in which they reside," and women of African descent characterized with uncensored racism.[100] The hierarchy of valuation of women of different nationalities was dramatically illustrated in June 1930, when the story broke and then quickly faded—perhaps because not entirely factual—that an English madam and trafficker residing in Paris provided clients who wanted to buy women to bring to Argentina with a price list that valued English women at £120–£150, and up to 25 percent more if "of the rosebud type"; French at £110–130; Russians at £30–35; and Poles, Czechs, and Latvians at £25–30. According to the English-language Argentine newspaper, "Owing to the 'dirt cheap' prices of girls from Eastern Europe and Russia, the agency could not undertake anything but bulk orders for the supply of these."[101] This hierarchy, roughly corresponding to the ethnic valuation of eugenicists and scientific racists at the time, also coexisted with the grosser racial distinctions made between white and non-white.[102] Women from Northern and Western Europe were considered more purely white, followed by those from Southern and Eastern Europe.

The hierarchies on this map relate as well to enforcement efforts. Reformers carved up a longer list of countries based on their cooperation with the 1904, 1910, and 1921 international agreements and conventions on the "suppression of the white slave traffic," and whether or not governments responded to the League's 1924 questionnaire. For example, while Argentina did respond to the questionnaire, it did not agree to adhere to any of the international conventions.[103] Although police from seven South American countries agreed at a 1920 local convention to share information from their lists of known traffickers, the League investigators complained that this information was never actually shared and South American police forces would not cooperate with the League's work.[104] The work of the League in the interwar period, like that of other European-based international antitrafficking associations such as the JAPGW and the IBSTW, thus reflected broader Eurocentric chauvinism as well as resistance by nations seeking greater sovereignty.

Johnson, Kinzie, and the other League investigators spent between a week and four months in each of the twenty-eight countries. While longer stays might be assumed to indicate greater scale of traffic, the final Experts' Report provides the disclaimer that "the investigation was of longer duration in certain countries, not necessarily because they were regarded as specially important as centres of traffic, but because they revealed sources of information both official and from the underworld which were of particular interest in regard to the methods employed by procurers in recruiting and transporting their victims."[105] The defensive tone of this disclaimer, along with other modifications to the final report, was prompted by extensive complaints from various governments, organizations, and other interested parties in reaction to earlier drafts and reports that their particular group was being assigned disproportionate blame.[106] Argentine newspapers also complained that the League gave Argentina "the first place of honor in the market of human flesh."[107]

Despite the report's disclaimer, the number of days spent in each country did correlate to the significance of that region to the League's vision of the international traffic. The top four countries, in descending order of days spent investigating there, were the United States (187), France (136), Italy (118), and Argentina (84), with the next lowest investigated for a month less.[108] The field notes on Uruguay and Brazil reveal that research in those countries was substantially devoted to discussions of conditions in Buenos Aires. The relative significance of countries can also be weighed by the number of pages devoted to each in the final report. Based on the committee's narrative analysis alone, Argentina tops the list with nine pages, followed by Poland's seven, then Egypt, France, Italy, and the United States with six each. When each country's pages of appendices (mostly local regulations) are added, Argentina still tops the list with sixteen pages, followed by Poland (eleven), Italy (eleven), and Uruguay (ten). The overall report thus gave readers the impression that Argentina was the site of greatest concern, followed by Poland, which was the sending country with the largest Jewish population. The Jewish traffic to Argentina thus received particular weight in the investigation.

As figure 1.1 illustrates, League investigations focused on borders, particularly on weak points between neighbors. They concentrated not on the entire country but on certain cities, nearly all of them along national borders. Pairs of cities on either side of national borders, particularly around the United States, emerge on this map as of central interest: San Diego and Tijuana, El Paso and Juarez, Detroit and Windsor. All of the sites investigated in the Americas and other receiving countries were at borders or ports, with the exception of the Mexican and Canadian capitals and San Antonio, Texas, which was the first major railroad stop after the border towns.[109] A number of sites hug the newly enforced U.S.-Mexico border, for which the Border Patrol had only just been created. Three of the national analyses in the Experts' Report featured maps showing the routes

Buenos Aires,
Argentina

Figure 1.1. League Experts' 1920s Americas' trafficking investigation sites. Source: City list from League of Nations, *Report of the Special Body of Experts on Traffic in Women and Children, Part Two* (1927), 195.

by which regulated border crossings were most frequently evaded: along the Argentine-Uruguayan border by crossing the river between Salto and Concordia; around the Panama Canal Zone to evade U.S. authorities; and out of Poland through the Free City of Danzig.[110] Some of these places, such as Salto and Concordia, had small populations, but were crucial nodes in networks of illicit migration.

Traffickers and prostitutes were not the only ones to cross at these points. A Jewish broker at the Salto-Concordia crossing assisted both poor immigrants who could not reach relatives in the capital and others without police papers, aware but unconcerned that some were prostitutes: "Sometimes I see that they are not Kosher (clean) but what business is it of mine? They pay well. . . . You could see Koorve (prostitute) written on their faces, but what difference does it make."[111] He also assisted other marginal individuals, such as deserters from the Polish Army.[112] The distinction between prostitution and trafficking thus appears as a migration issue: landlocked cities with large-scale prostitution, such as Chicago and Rosario, Argentina, were generally not visited, unless also significant in transnational population flows.

From the early Travelers Aid and antitrafficking associations' dock and railroad station inspectors, efforts to fight white slavery focused on national points of entry. As immigration restrictions tightened in the 1920s, inspired by the new quota system in the United States, official monitoring of poor and suspicious new arrivals increased. On incoming steamships, first-class travelers were minimally scrutinized, but those in second and particularly third class had to meet ever-higher standards of moral character and labor utility. In Argentina, a new 1923 law empowered officials to bar those engaged in "vice or useless activity."[113] Migrants without sufficient references, skills, money, or paperwork would frequent the same circuitous routes as sex workers and their managers. Organizations and networks of sex work managers, however, kept abreast of changing restrictions, and shared resources in order to evade surveillance, while other migrants were more likely to suffer from policies aimed at stopping sexual commerce.[114] Blaming foreigners for white slavery and tightening border control enabled governments to wield greater moral force in restricting entry to poor and otherwise undesirable supplicants, including Europe's Jews, who would soon become increasingly desperate.

Mapping the uneven world of trafficking discourse underscores how the long shadow of the white slave continued to shape international discussions and policies. Though transnational organizations shifted their language from white slavery to trafficking in women, old assumptions about race, sexual purity, and victimhood continued to drive decisions. In an era of massive demographic movement, the sex slave's forced sexual contact with presumably nonwhite men also reflected the fear of white women engaging in sexual relations with nonwhite men, as populations increasingly came into contact in growing urban areas. Framing traffic as migration also illustrates the effect of international anti-trafficking efforts on migrants more broadly, extending Donna Guy's argument that regulated prostitution in Buenos Aires restricted the mobility of all working-class women. The discourse of white slavery framed all prostitutes as victims and blamed foreign and racialized Others for their exploitation; prevention became intertwined with a new migrant regulation regime. Antitrafficking activism inspired many national governments to restrict the entry of single and minor women—a condition that women could evade with strategic marriages and other tactics.[115]

The figure of the Jewish trafficker of innocent women intersected with long-standing discourses of racialized Others. The racial liminality of the Jew made him a convenient scapegoat for transnational anxieties about sexuality and population mobility. But Jews themselves were the most concerned. Yiddish literature and other forms of cultural production reflected well-known associations between prostitution and the road from Eastern Europe to Argentina, warning young women away from well-dressed suitors. Jewish communities around the world, with particular urgency in Argentina, pushed back against popular perceptions of Jewish overrepresentation in the coordination of sex trafficking. They worried that punishment of Jewish traffickers would further restrict broader Jewish mobility, a fear sharpened by the new U.S. immigration quota system of the early 1920s, which was copied by governments decreasingly interested in open migration policies.

CHAPTER 2

∼

# Jewish Traffic in Women

*"I wanted to ask what your business is. What exactly do you deal in?"*
*The man from Buenos Aires: "What do I deal in? Ha, ha! Not in citrons, my*
*friend, not in citrons!"* —Sholem Aleichem, 1909

These lines conclude one of the beloved Yiddish author Sholem Aleichem's Rail-road Stories, a series of humorous monologues narrated by a salesman traveling through the fin-de-siècle Jewish Pale of Settlement. In "The Man from Buenos Aires," an international businessman chronicles his financial success to the narrator and reader without explicitly revealing the nature of his merchandise. While the narrator does not recognize the attributes of the Jewish trafficker in human flesh, the reader would have immediately interpreted his business description: "I provide a commodity that everyone knows about but no one ever talks about . . . all over the world: in Paris, in London, in Budapest, in Boston—but my headquarters are in Buenos Aires."[1] This allusion to Buenos Aires would at the time have signaled to readers throughout the Yiddish diaspora that the eponymous merchant dealt in women and was traveling back to the Old Country searching for new recruits.

Yiddish literature frequently referenced and reinforced the connection between sex trafficking and the Argentine capital. Sholem Asch's 1916 novel *Motke Ganef (Motke the Thief)* is partially set in Warsaw's Jewish underworld, where local pimps did business with Jewish international traffickers. These travelers were particularly famed for bringing women to Buenos Aires and Argentina, where supposedly "girls were free, made lots of money from the 'blacks,' then acquired a husband and they themselves became proprietresses of establishments."[2] In the particular racialized worldview of many Eastern European Jews, with their own form of Orientalism, native-born Argentines were taken for "princes and black sultans," sheiks from Arab harems. The connection permeated the expanding Jewish diaspora: A young Jewish immigrant to New York reported later of her 1918 arrival at Ellis Island, "You've been told that any man . . .

you don't know, is going to take you to Buenos Aires to a brothel, that was the favorite source of terror to young girls traveling alone."[3] The link between Jewish traffic and Argentina was also promulgated in the international Yiddish press, as in a September 1930 story in the Warsaw Yiddish press republished in Buenos Aires, of a trial against a trafficker who had been reputed to transport women into Russia during the First World War and then to Argentina.[4] Even several decades later, Isaac Bashevis Singer referenced Jewish Argentine prostitution in multiple works including his novel *Scum*, in which the main character moves between the underworlds of Buenos Aires and Warsaw in the early twentieth century, a milieu supported by the traffic in women, document forgery, and illegal alcohol production.[5]

As these references suggest, Ashkenazi Jews around the world in the mass migration era between the 1890s and World War II were well aware of the infamous linkage between members of their community and sex trafficking routes out of Europe, particularly to South America. Beyond Jewish sources, often in a more hostile tone, Jews frequently appeared in press, literature, and reformist discourse as disproportionately involved with the white slave traffic. As immigrant populations reshaped the modern city, the charge of trafficking reflected anxieties about the Jew's liminal racial and national identity. While resonant with antisemitic images of the Jew as greedy exploiter, this story also responded to the actual existence of international networks and associations of Jewish managers of transnational sex work. Members of many national and ethnic groups were involved in this era's traffic in women, but Ashkenazi Jews were even more visible than the sexualized French. Antisemitic tropes, in conjunction with the particular business and organizational methods of these individuals, further increased public controversy around their semilegal work.

In 1927, in the League of Nations' international trafficking report and in Londres's international best seller *The Road to Buenos Ayres*, networks of Ashkenazi Jews and the Golconda of Buenos Aires bore disproportionate responsibility for the global scourge of prostitution. The League's investigations revealed a transnational network of Ashkenazi Jewish traffickers, brokers, and pimps who cooperated in moving Jewish women for commercial sex across national borders from Eastern Europe to points across the globe. Although not as tightly coordinated as antisemites imagined, these networks incorporated such local institutions as the Varsovia Society, as well as family, kinship, and business structures, and thus dominated certain routes in these decades.

Driven by self-protective fear and moral indignation, sectors of the Jewish community responded by condemning Jewish trafficking in internal and public arenas. Self-protective Jews struggled to defend their community's reputation without paradoxically drawing further attention to the "impure." Despite their efforts, organizations such as the JAPGW inadvertently shone greater light on the problem even as they tried to eradicate prostitution from within the Jewish world. The popular linkage between Jewish-led trafficking and the particular endpoint of Argentina initially developed with the high visibility of the tmeim in Buenos Aires's burgeoning Jewish community in the 1890s, and persisted internationally for several decades. This connection underscored the racial ambiguity of Jews as nations sought to define their citizenry in a period of major demographic change.

## White Slavery Racializes Men and Whitens Women

The antisemitic construct of the Jew as hidden conspirator and unscrupulous economic exploiter of white Christians has a long history and persists today.[6] Exclusion from higher education and the professions steered Jews into concentration in capital in early modern Europe, where they could be blamed for industrial labor exploitation and property mismanagement, providing a target for disenfranchised workers living in substandard housing. Accusations of parasitism, mistreatment of workers, and slumlordism resonated with the image of the Jewish pimp and brothel owner. The idea of the Jew as trafficker thus fit neatly with existing ideas about economic exploitation.

The image of the Jew as seducer of innocent young women, often presumed to be Christian, also had roots in an earlier era. The satiric graphic images in Hogarth's 1732 "A Harlot's Progress" portrayed the Jew as a "lascivious reprobate, willing to lay out significant sums to entice young gentile women into prostitution," while also being mocked as a cuckold.[7] One literary critic notes that Hogarth thus consolidates this "image of the Jew as Sissy: effeminate, educated, wealthy—in sum, the badge of modern, tolerant society."[8] Such representations emasculated the Jewish man to alleviate his threat. Representations of the Jewish man's seductive capacity and the emphasis on his reliance on financial incentives rather than physical attraction allowed for the expression of anxiety about predatory Jewish male sexuality while simultaneously reducing its threat. As Sander Gilman writes on late nineteenth-century forensic science: "The madness of the Jews is a sexual madness."[9] Jewish racial ambiguity was magnified by this forced liminality and pathologization.

Both the concepts of whiteness and Jewish racial identity were in flux in this period, as Jews fled Eastern European poverty, restrictions, and violence to cross the Atlantic with many others reshaping the modern New World.[10] Jews and non-Jews debated the racial character of Jewishness, and Jews in various international contexts were treated both as white and as Other. While Jews served as fundamental racial Others in Europe, their position was less clear in the Americas, where the legacy of African chattel slavery generally positioned blacks as the paradigmatic Other. Jews, however, were not allowed to be consistently or fully white as the concept developed between the late nineteenth century and the mid-twentieth century.

Racial ideas about whiteness and Jews varied across Latin America. Earlier migrant communities of German-Jewish immigrants held a higher social status than the more racialized Eastern Europeans who flooded into the Americas from the 1890s through the closing of the gates in the 1920s. In Brazil, resident Jews were considered nonblack and allowed to climb the social hierarchy, while later-arriving Jews were considered nonwhite and undesirable.[11] In the late 1930s and early 1940s, although Jews were then considered nonwhite in Germany and some other Latin American countries, such as Bolivia, Dominican dictator Rafael Trujillo encouraged Jewish immigration to whiten the population and distract international attention from his 1937 massacre of racialized Haitians.[12] Jews could thus shift their status from white to nonwhite by crossing international borders but were generally granted the higher social status in places that had minimal Jewish populations and larger black and brown populations, places that were more desperate to grow their lighter-skinned populations as part of elite whitening projects.

Racial categories in Argentina, as in other parts of Latin America and the Caribbean, have emphasized racial gradations rather than the traditional binary of U.S. racial conceptualizations. However, the Argentine population from the late nineteenth century onward was less black, indigenous, and mixed-race than populations in other regions of the hemisphere and increasingly dominated by new arrivals from Europe. While the Argentine government hoped to attract Northern European migrants to help civilize the indigenous and mixed-race population, the Southern and Eastern Europeans who came were then considered less desirable in the hierarchy of racial science. Immigration and population demographics have not been theorized in terms of race in Argentina as elsewhere, perhaps because Argentina has had lower black and indigenous population percentages than other areas. Jewishness in Argentina was considered both a race and a nationality in this period, called "raza y nacionalidad" in the final 1931 legal decision on the Varsovia Society.[13] As Argentine nationalism evolved, antisemitism mingled with anticommunism, as rightist factions conflated all Jews with Russians and all Russians with communists.[14] Argentine racial identity continues to be somewhat unstable into the current era, particularly among middle-class residents of Buenos Aires, as porteños have struggled with the conflict between their privileged position in Latin America and their marginal position in the world.[15] Within and beyond national borders, policy and cultural arguments about prostitution framed as white slavery were also about race and national inclusion.

The association of Jews with white slavery provides a rich site for examining the complexity and instability of Jewish racial identity and racial identity more broadly in times of demographic change. Considerations of Jewish criminality and other socially undesirable behavior, as for other groups, often returned to racial—and thus immutable—characteristics. In the Committee of Fourteen's 1908 investigations into the New York City underworld, both Jewish and Italian subjects and districts were frequently racialized and, when possible, assigned investigators "of the race."[16] League of Nations investigators often referred to Jewishness as a race, as in Kinzie's report of his interactions with the internationally known Yiddish theater star and writer Boris Tomashevsky, whom Kinzie referred to as "a noted man of his race and profession" engaged in researching and combatting "the part the people of his race are playing in the commercialized prostitution of South America."[17]

When Jewish men became the archetypical masters of white slaves, their nonwhiteness was reinforced, along with the whiteness of their victims. For example, Reginald Wright Kauffman's 1910 anti–white slavery morality tale *The House of Bondage* plays up the racial contrast between swarthy Jewish procurer Max and fair subject Mary.[18] Ironically, on the ground, it would have been very rare for Jewish pimps or traffickers to be involved with women who were not Jewish. However, these women's Jewishness was generally overlooked or not encoded as racially Other. Because the darkness of the white slaver highlighted the whiteness of his victims, and vice versa, the racial identity of the women involved often fell out of white slave narratives that circulated about Jewish traffickers except in Jewish internal conversations. Newspaper stories that accused "white slavers" with Ashkenazi Jewish names, leaders of a "white slave mart" and their own synagogue, leaving their female victims nameless, allowed familiar images of innocent white, non-Jewish women to fill the reader's imagination.[19] Although Raquel Liberman herself was often named in coverage of the 1930 court case, sometimes distinguished as a "Polish Jewess," much of the non-Yiddish discussion of the case implied the Jewishness only of the men involved, with the women nameless victims of the "wiles of the white slave trader."[20] The imagined white slave victim of the Jewish trafficker was whitened by her victimization.

On the ground, however, the sex workers managed by Jewish men were also Jewish and ambiguously racialized. The race of Ashkenazi Jewish women, like that of Jewish men, was not stably white, and sexuality, like other aspects of morality, could nudge groups up or down on the racial hierarchy. Price differentials for sex workers of different nationalities suggest that Jewish women were often considered whiter than black or mixed-race women, but less white than women from Western Europe. Immigrant women in general commanded higher prices than local, often darker-skinned women in the multiracial capitals of Rio de Janeiro and Buenos Aires. A well-connected madam in Rio testified to the undercover League of Nations' investigator that "the men who spend money in this city,—real money I mean, not like those bums on Moraes de Valle Rua (cheap houses), don't want Brazilian girls; they want girls from Europe, French girls, Russians, Germans—not these half-niggers."[21] Russian women here would have implied Jewish women, grouped with other European immigrants as more valued by wealthier clientele than anyone of African descent, following the racial hierarchy promoted by that era's liberal politicians and experts.

In New York City, investigators collected data on individual sex workers between 1927 and 1931 that suggest that the prices that Jewish women charged for sexual acts overlapped with the lower part of the white women's hierarchy and the higher part of the black women's hierarchy. Women labeled "colored" but denoted as "very fair," "mulatto," or "high yellow" usually charged five dollars for a standard sexual act, while "Americans" charged from ten to twenty dollars and "Jewesses" from five to ten dollars.[22] In Buenos Aires at the same time, an unverified but widely referenced newspaper report published as part of the media flurry around the 1930 court case claimed to reproduce a chart found in Paris of "the current market prices of young girls in the world's vice market," which valued Northern and Western European women the most highly, with Jewish women in the lowest categories.[23] Jewish sex workers held whiteness tenuously.

## THE KINGDOM OF THE JEWS

Albert Londres's *The Road to Buenos Ayres* was probably this era's text most responsible for solidifying internationally the linkage between Jews, sex trafficking, and Argentina.[24] First published in French as a newspaper series in 1927, Londres's work circulated in South America in Spanish in the same year, and the 1928 English translation became a best seller in the United States.[25] In this memoir-style exposé, the author shared more than a little camaraderie with French procurers, whom he seemed to respect. He emphasizes the clannishness of the Jewish pimps and procurers in the Argentine capital, who he says regarded him suspiciously. In contrast, he describes their French and Argentine counterparts as accepting him without question into their midst, teaching him the tricks of the trade to the point at which he begins to procure women himself—an investigative precedent set by William T. Stead in the 1885 exposé that launched the British-based anti–white slavery movement.[26]

Londres's presentation of the Jewish trafficker reflected the image by then standard in international portrayals of white slavery, in which white slave masters reflected racialized, Oriental, or explicitly Jewish characteristics. Racialization and antisemitic associations emerge in his descriptions of the Jews, whom he describes as "dark Levites, their filthy skins making the strangest effect of light and shade, their unwashed locks corkscrewing down their left cheeks, their flat round caps topping them like a saucepan lid . . . turning their heads all the time to look after me, just as savages do."[27] These "dark" and "filthy" Jewish "savages" stood out from their French counterparts in their physical and behavioral characteristics. Londres dubs Buenos Aires's infamous brothel-filled port neighborhood of La Boca "the Kingdom of the Polacks," meaning Jews.[28] Londres was blamed by interested parties both for giving Buenos Aires a bad reputation around the world and for exaggerating the role of the Jews in trafficking.[29]

Ashkenazi Jewish women, like their male ethnic counterparts, also played a major role in popular images of prostitution in this era. Within South America, particularly the great prostitution capitals of Rio de Janeiro and Buenos Aires, Eastern European Jewish immigrant women were broadly associated with prostitution.[30] The term *polaco* or *polaca* (Polish man and Polish woman), like *ruso* (Russian), was synonymous with Jew, as few non-Jews emigrated from Eastern Europe in this period.[31] "Polaca" became a synonym for prostitute, and continues to be used today to reference prostitution in Argentina and Brazil, as in the 2002 play *Las Polacas* and 2003 novel *La Polaca*.[32] In some cases, "polaca" has been used to refer to any prostitute whether or not of Jewish or Eastern European descent.[33] A Polish university graduate and decorated Red Cross nurse "found it such a handicap to be known as a Pole that she Latinized her name. She told [the investigator] that to own yourself a Pole in Rio was to brand yourself as a prostitute."[34] Women often claimed other nationalities if they wished to be viewed as respectable. Among women in sex work, just as many might state they were French for the higher status and price French women could command, many denied they were Jews. A researcher in Rio reporting to the League stated: "In my opinion, practically all those listed as Polish, Russian, Austrian and Roumanian are really Jewish. A large percentage of those listed as Brazilians were probably not born in Brazil, many of them are without doubt Jews."[35] This language also reflects the preoccupation of both local elites and European reformers with the plight of European-born women, to the exclusion of women of indigenous or African descent, who were also well-represented in sex work but rarely considered victims.[36]

The Argentine popular lexicon related to the underworld, including the Buenos Aires slang language of Lunfardo, usually tied prostitution and its management to foreignness, and particularly to Jewishness. In Argentine popular culture, reflected in tango lyrics, *sainetes* (plays), and cheap pamphlets, Jewish women from Eastern Europe appeared only as prostitutes, driven by misery in their country of origin. A mass-produced pamphlet described twenty women playing the violin in a bar, but only three had rosin on their bows—suggesting that the others' playing made no sound, as it was a ruse covering their true work. The potential client could choose from among the fake violinists and was told they were tired from their recent journey from Warsaw.[37] References to the port zone of La Boca often mentioned polacas as residents of the local *casitas* (brothels, literally little houses). One pamphlet of tango lyrics depicted a melancholy dancer with the polaca and the low cost of the polaca's services.[38] Another traced the source of the polaca's tragedy to the *pocilgas israelitas*, the Jewish pigsties of Poland.[39] Roberto Arlt's then-contemporary underworld fictions also featured similar characters, and Jorge Luis Borges carried the trope later.[40]

Male managers of prostitutes in Argentina and their importers were also entirely associated with foreignness. The French words *maquereaux, alfonsin,* and *souteneur* and the Italian *rufian* were sometimes used to refer to pimps and traffickers. In more common use was *tenebroso,* literally meaning shadowy and thus implicitly racially inflected. A song published in a 1912 pamphlet called *La trata de blancas* (The white slave trade) tells the common story of "rusos" and "polacos" seducing and entrapping women from their homelands to bring back to the brothels of Buenos Aires, pretending to be businessmen and thus deluding poor local families.[41]

Representations of Jewish managers of sex work often emphasized widespread bribery and influence. Local contemporary observer Victorio Luis Bessero argued that they were "often respected people who enjoyed influence in official spheres. Owners of grandiose brothels and of enormous sums of capital, all was achieved with money."[42] Commissioner Alsogaray claimed that many members of the Society penetrated important social circles, curried friendships and favors with ministers, legislators, judges, and other high-level administrators, and stood out with particular prominence at the Hippodrome.[43] He also reported that high city functionaries communicated with the society's leaders using formal address, even "Don," as in the case of Mauricio Caro, the last treasurer of the Society, inspiring others, such as police officers, to imitate their superiors in such signs of respect.[44]

This common image of the Jewish trafficker resonated with vitriolic interpretations of Jewish racial identity and danger in Argentina. Several famous Argentine novelists of the time wrote explicitly antisemitic books; the most well-known are Julian Martel's 1891 *La Bolsa* and Manuel Galvez's 1913 *Nacha Regules.* Martel blamed the stock market crash of 1890 on speculation spurred by international Jewish capital interests and accused the 2,400 Jews then residing in Argentina of exploiting their wealth and their role in the white slave trade to attack and undercut Christians. He drew on imagery from French antisemitism to portray a hidden cabal of Jewish men dominating Argentine politics, polluting the country with their foreign and decadent ways.[45] Antisemitic tracts could also be found in local kiosks and newspaper stands, such as Tiberio Lolo's 1919 *El peligro semita en la República Argentina.*[46] Argentine popular theater in this era often denounced Jewish migration.[47] Exaggerated physical characteristics of Jews were often associated with stereotypes in the popular press.[48] Antisemitic publications in Argentina continued into later periods to combine stereotypes with references to Jews as pimps or white slavers, exaggerating the actual historic involvement of Jews in prostitution.[49]

Jews organized and fought more intensively against being associated with prostitution than any other national or ethnic group. "Respectable" Jews may have found this identification acutely disturbing because of the historic antisemitic connections between Jews and the immoral acquisition of wealth. In the wake of the 1930 court case and publicity around the Varsovia Society, Victorio Luis Bessero described members "prowling impudently through our streets, insolently flaunting regal automobiles and valuable jewels, without any protective measures against these subjects that live a life of luxury and of pleasures at the expense of the lucrative market in white flesh."[50] Bessero emphasized the free flow of money, "lent to anyone," which these men used to secure legal impunity, reflecting stock antisemitic associations of Jews with dirty money. Mass migration instigated the collapse of many traditional boundaries of social class and produced anxiety among traditional elites. In addition to his moral critique of the corruption spread by Jewish traffickers, Alsogaray emphasized that the source of their capital was unclean, in contrast to the clean fields and factories of modern Argentina.[51] This analysis implicitly defends the nation's old social order and critiques the displacement of the land-owing aristocracy from their traditional place by new money of dubious origin.[52] Opposition from inside and outside the Jewish community thus reflected concern with not only morality but also Jewish economic mobility and social respectability.

Prostitution and pimping stood out among limited avenues available for economic advancement; the work did not require education and could be very lucrative. A certain parallel can be drawn with Jewish money lending in medieval Europe: both professions grew from limited economic options, restricted landholding, and demand for a service that others were not inclined to supply due to social stigma.[53] It should be noted, contrary to antisemitic propaganda, that Jewish religious law forbids both charging interest and prostitution. If given more freedom to choose an occupation, Jews would surely not have concentrated in moneylending or prostitution, and the widespread blame placed in particular historical periods on the Jews for following these stigmatized occupations would not have taken root.

## DID JEWS ACTUALLY DOMINATE ARGENTINE PROSTITUTION?

International literary and media references to Jewish women in Argentina in this period generally presumed they all worked as prostitutes and that all pimps and procurers were Jewish men. Possible antisemitic distortions of this correlation preoccupied both contemporaries and later analysts. Sandra McGee Deutsch's history of Argentine Jewish women bemoans the invisibility of Jewish women in this era who were not prostitutes, but she concedes the necessity of writing about the phenomenon. Pinpointing the precise scale of the Jewish role as sex workers and managers, however, proves no easy task. Demographic data on immigrant nationality and religion, as well as on prostitution beyond the limited scope of municipal registration, vary to a frustrating degree. Estimating the numbers of Jews historically resident in Argentina has been a matter of debate among historians, in large part because the country had only two national censuses in the main period of Jewish population growth (1900 to 1960), in 1914 and 1947, and only the latter inquired about religion, although many of those surveyed did not declare one.[54] The city of Buenos Aires, where the majority of Jews lived, took censuses in 1904, 1909, and 1936, of which the last was the most detailed.[55]

Bolesao Lewin, author of one of the first studies of Argentine Jewry, initially published in 1971, vividly describes the "bitterness that invaded [him]" when he discovered that the first chapter of Alsogaray's memoir was dedicated to the history of the Jewish people, making the unfounded assumption that the evolution of Argentine prostitution was intrinsically linked to the Jews.[56] Lewin critiques several demographic sources in his attempt to rescue Jews from outsized responsibility for Argentine prostitution. He wrestles with one set of statistics on registered prostitutes between 1899 and 1915 gathered by Carlos Bernaldo de Quiros, which implies that between 4,000 and 5,000 of the 16,468 women registered in that period were Jewish, approximately 25 to 30 percent.[57] Lewin acknowledges that until 1930 Jewish involvement in the local control of prostitution was very visible, but he relates this to the social phenomena driving massive immigration rather than to any particular aspect of Jewish culture; he underscores that over 75 percent of registered prostitutes had been born across the Atlantic Ocean, reducing Jews to a subset of all immigrants.[58]

Ashkenazi Jewish men were certainly disproportionately visible as managers of sex work from the initial establishment of the Argentine capital's Jewish community. If there were only 753 Jewish residents in Buenos Aires in 1895, as that year's census reported, then the 164 Jewish men arrested for pimping or trafficking in the city in 1893–1894 made up a truly notable percentage of that population, and some of these men had arrived in earlier decades, when there were even fewer Jews.[59] When the Argentine Jewish version of the *Mayflower*, the SS *Weser*, arrived with 820 immigrants in 1889, the capital's 1887 census had found only 366 Jews out of a total population of 429,558.[60] The 1895 national Argentine census counted 6,085 Jews out of a total population of 3,954,911, or 0.15 percent, with only 753 Jews among the 663,854 residents of Buenos Aires, or 0.11 percent.[61] The small numbers of Jews in the overall population would have made their visibility in brothels and other sites of sex work even more striking.

The same 1895 census data show 229 Jewish prostitutes in the city's registered brothels, noteworthy given how few Jewish women were in the city. Jewish women's visibility continued: between 20 and upward of 30 percent of registered prostitutes in Buenos Aires across the period from 1899 to 1924 came from Central and Eastern Europe and would have been presumed to be Jewish. Based on available data, following shifts in national boundaries, Russian, Austro-Hungarian, Polish, Rumanian, Ukrainian, and Czechoslovakian women composed only 1.1 percent of the total Argentine population in 1909, but 29.9 percent of registered prostitutes in the period encompassing 1899–1915, 20.3 percent of those registered 1910–1923, and 33.3 percent of those registered in the first half of 1924.[62] Thus, greater percentages of Jewish women were registered as prostitutes than would have been had their numbers mirrored the percentage of Jews in the capital's overall population.

Although Jewish women made up a very high proportion of registered sex workers relative to their total numbers in the population, they certainly did not constitute an absolute majority of sex workers. Similar numbers of registered women in these data were identified as French, in growing numbers across these periods, which might have been overinflated in self-reporting, as French women were purportedly the most valued prostitutes. Italian and Spanish women were registered at rates between 5 and 12 percent, substantially lower than their proportional representation as the predominant immigrant nationalities in the city. Negligible numbers of British women (less than 0.3 percent) throw into relief the ongoing significance on the global stage of British-led organizations against white slavery or the traffic in women: these international institutions were most concerned with the fate of British women and others from Northern and Western Europe, though these groups were minimally represented in foreign brothels. International and local Jewish antiprostitution organizations, on the other hand, reacted not only to antisemitic distortions but also to several decades of Ashkenazi women's disproportionate involvement in the municipal system of regulated sex work.

## COMMUNITY SELF-DEFENSE

Just as organized opposition to trafficking became the largest international women's issue besides suffrage in the half century before World War II, Jewish women and men around the world took leadership in multinational antitrafficking organizations. A central goal of Jewish reform organizations throughout this period was to dissociate Jews from blame for the traffic and thus reduce the antisemitism that this connection might worsen. From the earliest years of the JAPGW, leaders worried privately, as in this 1901 letter from the head of the JAPGW to the Jewish Colonization Association (JCA), that "the trading and trafficking of girls is so greatly in the hands of Jews . . . in nearly all the centres, the Committees are aware that a very large proportion of the traffickers are Jews . . . in some of the countries the antisemitic feeling occassioned by this is very strong. . . . We are assured that our long continued endeavor to check the evil has had the effect of softening the antisemitic feeling to which the traffic naturally gives birth."[63] The JCA's ongoing engagement with (and funding of) the JAPGW reflected its fear that the local and international reputation of Jewish immigrants be bound up with prostitution. Financial appeals from Jewish antitrafficking organizations drew on these victimization tropes familiar from white slave stories and were careful to continually distinguish Jewish vice from the "respectable" lifestyles of the majority of the population.

Jews were the most organized national or ethnic group against prostitution from the beginning of this period and visible as such. Jewish organizations appear to have been the first in the Americas to establish the precedent of employing women to work at the docks to meet arriving boatloads of immigrants and warn young women who appeared to be particularly vulnerable to be on their guard against the appeals of those who might trick them into prostitution. The National Council of Jewish Women (NCJW), founded during the Chicago World's Fair of 1893, quickly became involved in immigration issues at the behest of the U.S. government, and took on the exploitation of immigrant women as the organization's major concern. The NCJW tried to disassociate the issues of prostitution and immigration from one another and to discourage deportation for girls who did fall into it, stating it "is not a question of immigration if an immigrant girl is so unfortunate as to become the victim of some evil man who has traded on her credulity to put her to shame [but] a purely local and American and social question, and we must be careful not to confuse the two."[64]

NCJW delegates went to international conferences on white slavery, and their Ellis Island dock workers "set an example that other organizations would later follow."[65] These pioneering dock workers wore obvious badges, could speak several languages, and distributed and posted placards and leaflets at various ports of entry. Dock workers were employed in this work at ports around the world, including those from several organizations stationed at the piers in Buenos Aires. Many reports indicate, however, that few women were actually rescued in this way, suggesting either that this was not generally the actual first moment of contact with traffickers or that a dock worker speaking a young woman's language was not as appealing to a new arrival as the elegantly dressed man of the sort she was warned against.

Jews around the world worried about both perceived and actual involvement of Jews as traffickers and prostitutes. In Warsaw in 1905, Jews turned violently against the managers of prostitution in their community in what was publicized as the Alphonse (Pimp) Pogrom.[66] Some reformers tried to blame the existence of Jewish trafficking on antisemitism and its social and economic effects. British Chief Rabbi Dr. Hermann Adler made this case at the 1910 JAPGW conference: "We can trace this deplorable change directly to the recrudescence of active Russian persecutions in 1881. We are deeply grieved, but we cannot be surprised if ill-treatment, oppression 'that maketh a wise man mad,' defective education, persistent exclusion from honourable pursuits and consequent fear of starvation drive men and women to reprehensible means of earning a livelihood . . . the vile traffic which results from the wretched economic conditions among our brethren in Eastern Europe."[67] The limited success of most rescue efforts was also sometimes attributed to the traumas inflicted on Jewish women by Russian authorities, making them afraid of appealing to government officials, as U.S. representative Sadie American testified at the same 1910 conference: "A well-intentioned man, who means nothing but good to the girls, finds it hard to understand that many of these girls have learned, by their experiences, to fear and distrust men, particularly those who come from Russia, where even the official uniform causes them to tremble."[68] Among Jewish reformers, as suggested in these comments, explanatory causes for the involvement of both Jewish men and women in the condemned traffic tended to highlight antisemitism, economic desperation, and externally imposed professional limitations.

Jewish communities and institutions did not respond monolithically to the Jewish trafficking problem. Solutions ranged from greater policing of women's sexuality and marriage decisions to lobbying for universal international standards around prostitution regulation. In transnational organizations, leaders such as Sadie American and German feminist Bertha Pappenheim as well as lesser-known figures created space for Jewish women as political actors and equal public members of the Jewish polity. Some Jewish men opposed the work of women's organizations in this arena, claiming that the publicity would be bad for the Jews, but perhaps also concerned about the visible role of female leaders.[69] Conflicts and cooperation also reflected local concerns. Dozens of Jewish organizations large and small joined the Argentine boycott of the tmeim, speaking out with particular unity around the 1930 court case against the Varsovia Society.[70] Ezres Noshim spearheaded these efforts.[71] However, just three years after the Varsovia Society's destruction, Buenos Aires daily Yiddish newspaper *Di Prese* published missives from both sides of a conflict between the powerful Union Israelita Residentes de Polonia en la Argentina or Poilisher Farband (Jewish Union of Polish Residents in Argentina, or Polish Union) and Ezres Noshim, in which several other organizations took sides in a debate over who got to determine and voice the Jewish community's standards of morality and respectability.[72] This fight between male-dominated institutions reflected competition for leadership of Buenos Aires Jewry. Despite such internal conflicts, fears of the intensification and spread of antisemitic violence and restrictions on Jewish mobility tended to push Jewish organizations into public agreement.

The very dedication and visibility of Jewish opposition to the role of coreligionists in international prostitution may have strengthened the connection between Jews and trafficking in the popular imagination. Parallel to Uruguayan feminist Dr. Paulina Luisi's public protest of the emphasis on South America in the League of Nations' Experts' Reports on international trafficking, Jewish leaders who were and were not involved in the shaping of these documents spoke out against their portrayal of Jewish involvement. Samuel Cohen, head of the JAPGW, was also a part of the League's Traffic in Women Committee, which sponsored the Body of Experts' investigations and reports. During a visit to

Buenos Aires in June 1930, in the immediate wake of the Varsovia Society arrests, he gave public presentations as well as worked with his organization's local branch. In a talk to delegates from fifty local organizations, Cohen said that the League's Experts' Reports had "tried to present the problem of the traffic in women as a purely Jewish problem and he had to bring it into the general perspective."[73] His request to the League that the detailed information behind the reports be shared with member committees was refused by the League's secretary general, Sir Eric Drummond, and head of the Social Questions Section, Dame Rachel Crowdy (who oversaw the traffic committee).[74] As League representatives struggled with the competing demands of various concerned parties, they did not want to risk according Jewish organizations privileges over others.

Non-Jewish committee members did not necessarily understand or sympathize with specifically Jewish concerns. Crowdy reported back to the League about her attendance as the only non-Jewish participant of the JAPGW's 1927 London Conference, at which the majority of the attendees argued that volume 2 of the Experts' Report was "deliberately anti-semitic," even "the most anti-semitic document produced during the last hundred years . . . [which] might even create such a public opinion against the Jews as to induce further massacres."[75] Conference president Claude Montefiore calmed this debate, disagreed with this characterization, and urged members "not to be over sensitive and not to mind what the Christians said about the Jews when they remembered what the Christians said about each other, but to do all they could to rectify the state of affairs among their own people by maintaining as far as possible the sanctity of the Jewish home and by educating their boys and girls to the highest aims of morality."[76] This tone of internal moral policing mirrored the tone of much local community leadership, including Argentina's. Crowdy expressed gratitude for this position and "said that if the Experts had quoted a certain number of instances of Jewish traffic, it was because the Jewish Associations had been extremely vigilant in their work."[77] Jewish antitraffic organizations were thus blamed for drawing additional attention to Jewish trafficking, and ongoing internal community moral policing was encouraged.

Although the sensationalist narrative of the Jewish white slaver suggested swarthy Eastern men trafficking in Western Christian virgins, business networks on the ground concentrated men and women of the same cultural and linguistic groups. Despite the suggestion in white slave narratives that Jewish men were overrepresented in the exploitation of white, non-Jewish women, Ashkenazi Jews in the transnational sex industry generally kept their business relationships within their own ethnic and linguistic group, as did others. This standard of "procur[ing] girls of a nationality that can work in harmony with the pimp for whom she is procured" smoothed transit through the many possible danger points on the international journey and daily life in the destination.[78] Many

women were previously involved in sex work or made at least some of the decisions along this journey. However, the story of the unscrupulous Jewish trafficker
persisted from the late nineteenth century through the interwar period, as it
proved useful for antisemites, for nativists, and for advocates of immigration
restriction. Jews served a useful purpose as ur-Other on multiple sides of this
period's immigration debates.

Jewish organizations engaged in self-protective publicity also made use of this
narrative to underscore the victimization of Jewish women and separate the
"respectable" majority of Jews from a few bad apples. Their vigorous efforts to
stymie both the actual Jewish involvement in trafficking and popular perceptions of Jewish overrepresentation paradoxically highlighted the significance of
Jewish involvement, as no other ethnic, racial, or national group organized collectively on this scale or with as coherent a sense of group identity.

CHAPTER 3

~

# Marriage as Ruse,
# or Migration Strategy

The popular narrative about white slavery was so iconic that it was often referred to in shorthand as "the marriage ruse." It went like this: The white slave's journey began with her wedding. A well-dressed young man would arrive in a village and sweep the beautiful young woman and her naïve parents off their feet. After a rapid wedding, the newlyweds would depart for a bright future overseas. Once out of familial reach, however, the trafficker's true intentions would become clear. Far from home, bound to her husband, the young woman would have to submit to sexual exploitation. The marriage itself would prove to provide no legal protections to the bride. Variations on this story in the press and among reformers might emphasize courting, deflowering, or the multiple agents along the journey from village to brothel. Jews, more than other groups, were associated with this strategic usage of marriage. Because a Jewish marriage contract (*ketubah*) had no civil weight, reformers—Jewish and otherwise—feared religious marriage could be exploited as a tactic by traffickers. Eastern European authorities and Jewish community leaders were particularly concerned with the risks of what was generally referred to as the *shtile khupe*, literally, "discreet wedding canopy" or "silent marriage" in Yiddish. The Jewish wedding that complied with rabbinic but not civil law was debated on both sides of the Atlantic, as men could "marry" a woman—or several—in Europe, take her to the other side of the world, and be free of any binding legal responsibility upon arrival.

As Jewish populations and patterns shifted in the nineteenth century, religious and secular authorities, along with cultural producers, reflected and grappled with popular fears about sexual maturation. Stories of the dangers of the shtile khupe reflected modern changes in courtship, marriage practices, and family economies in the Ashkenazi diaspora and secularizing societies. Naomi Seidman's work on Jewish literary representations of "sexual secularization" argues that Jewish modernization entailed more than a shift from arranged marriage to romantic love, as the Christian roots of the idea of romance exacerbated Jewish suspicion of the concept.[1] Civil marriage was not common in Eastern Europe in the nineteenth century, and thus Ashkenazi Jews rarely considered this option. Jews in Eastern Europe followed different marital patterns then their non-Jewish peasant neighbors, often marrying earlier.[2] Bourgeois German Jewish families changed marriage norms in early nineteenth century to more closely fit non-Jewish norms, though economic factors often continued to outweigh romantic attraction well into the twentieth century.[3] In Eastern Europe, matchmaking ended earlier for the upper classes, and the Jewish lower classes had not routinely practiced arranged marriage, although the liminal figure of the matchmaker persisted in multiple literary genres.[4] Affection and choice thus long played a larger role among the masses than the concerns of *maskilim* (Jewish disciples of the *Haskalah*, or Jewish enlightenment movement) and high Yiddish literature would suggest, which tended to depict the love match as a new turn.[5] In Eastern Europe, poorer Jews usually married in a short ceremony in a private house, sometimes but not always in the presence of a rabbi or other religious officiant. The minimal religious requirement was that the groom put a ring on the bride's finger while saying a ritual consecration phrase in Hebrew, in the presence of two adult Jewish men. The witnesses would sign the ketubah, but it would not be put on any official record. Although Eastern European governments tried to engage rabbis as agents of the state, they had little effect on Jewish marriage practices in the period covered by this study.[6]

The principal source for most historians who link Jews and prostitution has been Edward Bristow's 1983 transnational historical analysis *Prostitution and Prejudice: The Jewish Fight against White Slavery, 1870–1939*.[7] Scholars have cited Bristow's work as proof that the shtile khupe made women vulnerable not only to desertion but also to being trafficked as white slaves.[8] However, examination of the primary sources for Bristow's discussion of the shtile khupe as a tactic of white slavers shows that his argument reflects the concern of organizations such as the JAPGW and the IBSTW rather than any hard data on causal connections.[9] While Bristow's book is based on an impressive range of multilingual and multicontinental archival materials and was transnational before the term was coined, he cites no documentary evidence that the phenomena of prostitution and unregulated marriage are causally linked. Despite extensive concern over unregulated Jewish marriages in general and potential links to sexual trafficking in particular, Jewish social welfare organizations presented anecdotal evidence of causality, with few incidents of rescue to show for their extensive efforts. Instead, frantic warnings about the risks of the shtile khupe can be understood to encapsulate broader anxieties around migration and changes in the institution of marriage itself as well as a different kind of causal connection between marriage and cross-border prostitution.

Reformers worried that in addition to facilitating the entrapment and international transit of women, marriage could keep unwilling women in prostitution, due to the power of a husband over his wife. Local and international antiprostitution activists advocated for harsher punishment of men who lived on their wives' immoral earnings, particularly as this might mean a wife working to support an unproductive husband. Argentine reformers tried to prevent immigrant women arriving alone at the port from disembarking to meet suspicious "'bridegrooms-to-be,' accompanied as a rule by venerable-looking but temporary parents."[10] When Raquel Liberman denounced the Varsovia Society to Argentine authorities, she claimed that she was brought back unwillingly into prostitution through marriage, tricked by a man she did not know was a member of the Society. The particular association of the marriage method with Jews was so tight that the Argentine Yiddish press sometimes referred to local-level Jewish pimps as "grooms" and their associated prostitutes as "brides."[11]

Marriage was in fact a common element of the transnational movement of women for sex work, but was often used strategically by prostitutes as well as by male and female managers. Women in Eastern Europe sometimes chose a quick religious marriage as an emigration strategy, even if aware that they might end up in prostitution. In some cases they were already sex workers and were looking for a more lucrative market. Marriage helped single women and minors cross international borders and continued to facilitate the business of sex on the ground. The Varsovia Society supported marriage and marriage-like relationships throughout the hierarchy of prostitutes, pimps, madams, doorkeepers, and property owners and upheld a form of serial monogamy that looked more like the culture of other Jews than like the non-Jewish circuits of commercial sex. While this structure maximized profit, it also created spaces for some women to make more extensive choices around work, love, and sexuality than would otherwise have been available.

## PROSTITUTION AS A BUSINESS DECISION

This analysis of women's limited labor and marriage options fits with the position of many activist and academic advocates of rights for sex workers over the past several decades, who argue that while prostitutes should not be seen as helpless victims, their life choices are fundamentally constrained by hierarchies of race, sex, and class, and thus they do not operate with total freedom.[12] The "modified choice" position seeks to avoid the pitfalls of both "radical feminists'" insistence that all prostitutes are passive victims of patriarchy and sex workers' rights advocates accused of ignoring structural violence. The move from victim to constrained agent maintains a trace of the moralism that has long shaped responses to prostitution: just as the trafficked, seduced, or duped victim has not chosen the life of a prostitute, neither has the person with "modified choice," if other employment and relationship options are so terrible and social hierarchies so rigid that a rational actor could do little else.

Even beyond economic necessity, some women might have chosen to engage in sex work and live in related circles because they wanted the same sexual freedom commonly enjoyed by men. In Rio, Rosita Steinman, age twenty, told the League investigator in Yiddish that she was born in Warsaw and while she had not practiced prostitution there, she had engaged in premarital sex with multiple partners—or as the investigator put it, she had "indulged in promiscuous intercourse."[13] She said she had no pimp and that a female friend who worked at the "Glue Pot" brothel had inspired her to join in the profitable opportunities there. She hoped to return home to her parents in Warsaw in less than a year and was careful to keep her occupation a secret from them.[14] Her version of her own story emphasizes the influence of female peers, with the central goals of earning money followed by a rapid and respectable return home. As for other immigrants from Europe to South America, the postage stamp serves as a crucial immigration agent: "Her friends write home how well off they are. A girl here wants to help a friend, so she sends her a ticket."[15] This was the battle that the "respectable" Jews from London to Buenos Aires fought, to prevent women from going down dangerous paths and prevent them from returning unmarked once they had done so. New immigrants must be shown the difference between the wealth of the pimps and madams and the less visible advantages of their "respectable" neighbors. The "unclean" must not be allowed to purify themselves and return to the fold, endangering Jews' hard-fought and shaky social acceptance.

Unfortunately, the perspectives of the women themselves often fall out of the sources here, smothered by male interpretations of their behaviors and motivations. League of Nations undercover agent Kinzie glosses his interviews with women "admitting" they "indulged in promiscuous intercourse" before getting paid for sex, but does not provide women's words or meanings.[16] He does not leave room for women to understand themselves as anything other than fallen women. His own moral judgments and preferential treatment of male interlocutors erase women's opportunities to voice their own perspectives. He is more likely to repeat the stories of women who fit the victim narrative, a central goal of his investigation, and usually gives economic necessity as the shorthand for other women's descriptions of their motivations, occasionally quoting examples such as this French prostitute: "I tried to get work, but the most I can make is 6 francs to 15 francs a day sewing. So I go out three or four times a week and do business."[17] This articulation of prostitution as work, and of the workers themselves as businessmen and businesswomen, seems to be shared by everyone

Kinzie quotes, on both sides of the Atlantic and from the lowest to the highest levels of organization. Contrary to the victim narrative, most women engaged with prostitution in a range of ways, not as the degrading life sentence imagined by moral reformers, but to different degrees at different times and in a range of settings.[18]

## THE MARRIAGE RUSE: NARRATIVES AND RESPONSES

The marriage ruse featured prominently in public discourse around the 1930 breakup of the Varsovia Society as an explanation for how the group had coordinated the importation and ongoing exploitation of woman on such a large scale. Captions below newspaper photographs of the group's synagogue during the May raids implied that the synagogue's true central function must have been the performance of these false weddings. The legal summary of the 1930 court case against the Society summarized the organization's use of the marriage ruse succinctly: "The majority of the traffickers went to Europe, especially to Poland where they contracted religious-only marriages, with young women, to whom they made all kinds of promises of well-being in order to bring them to this Capital, which are agreed to by their parents in the belief that they are actual merchants."[19] Seduction stories of young women and their parents hinge on both good looks and displays of wealth. The latter echoes the tradition of arranged marriage. This articulation of the idea that poor families might be literally unable to resist the temptation of money manages to erase their decision-making power. Ignorance and need are equally emphasized. Some narratives explicitly argued that money was more important than physical attraction for impoverished young women: "Chosen members of Zwi Migdal made a regular practice of visiting Europe. . . . Having infatuated the girls (as a rule with their money rather than good looks), they took apparently regretful departures to return to Argentina."[20] The idea that money could charm young women spoke to their desire for a better life rather than a love match.

The Argentine province of Santa Fe's newspaper, *El Orden*, widely advertised a sensational serial interview with Arnold K. in the first weeks of the police raids against the Society's members. Supposedly a former member of the Society, Arnold K. describes this entrapment method and elaborates on the role of "bridegrooms" in facilitating victims' transatlantic journeys:

> There suddenly arrives in a village a compatriot who has made a fortune in Argentina and who travels with a certain indifference for all the economic anxieties that mark the majority of the households of his fatherland. This man deludes the humble people. Argentina must necessarily be a great country, luminous and rich, where life is easy and where fortune is available in the streets to anyone who wants to enjoy it. One week is sufficient to select his prey

and lock down a relationship with her. The family vacillates. But the same suitor makes a donation to the father or the mother so that they can equip the girl and she can marry him without shame at their difference in fortune.... And the wedding is arranged without difficulties.[21]

Money thus rapidly overcomes all possible doubts and difficulties and families and village functionaries are too naïve to question its source. The bridegroom's manners and generosity enflame fantasies of the New World's easy fortunes. Local authorities are as easily swayed.

The young woman's desperation to escape known drudgery through romantic fantasy proves her downfall. "For the girl, the arrival of the traveler symbolizes the fulfillment of all her dreams and illusions forged while she devoted her days to heavy labor. This is her liberation.... In many cases, the victim brought to Argentina continues being for her relatives a young girl of good luck, well married to a wealthy man, and who sends monthly support to elderly parents or younger siblings, because her fortune permits it."[22] Limited local options thus drive the naïve young woman into falling for a deception. Even when she discovers how her Argentine fortune is actually to be made, her pride and desire to realize that dream push her into maintaining the illusion in her letters and remittances sent home. The marriage ruse narrative thus implicitly condemns women for their aspirations, even as it underscores their victimhood. Young people's romantic dreams were fed by reading secular literature—while boys' reading was channeled into religious realms, girls were more openly able to read novels in Yiddish and European languages, feeding modern relationship ideas.[23]

Arnold K.'s story expands the deception method to include a set of equally naïve bridegrooms, enlisted in ignorance to travel with a group of still-deluded brides. "Sometimes, the [Varsovia Society] auxiliary ... befriends some young countryman and proposes to him, without explaining to him why, a good business deal. He will give him a sum of money (quite swollen), and the friend has to do nothing more than get married also, with an indicated young woman, and then to make a trip in her company.... The director of the action returns to Argentina with five or six such couples. The husbands return to their country when they are no longer necessary. The women stay to be exploited."[24] Arnold K. then details how these women would be groomed for big-city life through European "honeymoons" and taken through elaborate border crossing journeys disguised as tourist nature adventures. The deception of the marriages would not be revealed until final delivery into brothels, abandoned by their "husbands" and trapped by distance and language.

The naïveté presumed in these narratives on the parts of brides, their families, and temporary bridegrooms was probably less common on the ground than the weight of financial incentive. The correlation between Jewish religious marriage and transport to Argentina for the purpose of prostitution had been made for decades before 1930, particularly in the Eastern European Jewish milieu. Anxiety about the risks of the Jewish wedding without a civil component permeated many arenas. While familiarity with particular texts would have varied, the frequency of cultural association between places and phenomena suggests wide popular awareness. The common beginning of the white slave story, in which a woman is fooled into marriage by an attractive man, in part reflects concerns about the broader shift in marriage from an arrangement between families to a love match chosen by young people, with the implication that youth could not be trusted to select their own mates.

Jewish antitrafficking reform organizations raised the dangers of the shtile khupe across several decades. At the 1910 international JAPGW conference, Secretary Samuel Cohen reported to the assemblage:

> Many cases have come under my observation during the last six years of girls who have been led astray by looking upon the "Kesubah" [Jewish marriage contract] of the "Stille Chupe" as a legal document, and one man will make use of such a "Kesubah" with different girls for his nefarious purposes. I was at Southampton a few weeks ago, watching a steamer which was to sail for South America, and there I saw a Jewish girl sitting in the corner of a second-class cabin, which was not her proper place, as she should have been in the steerage . . . a man appeared, producing the "Kesubah," and saying "This is my wife, here is the Kesubah." . . . I was quite satisfied from his contradictory answers that he was trafficking her.[25]

Cohen reflected the reform organization's tendency to monitor women outside of their "proper place," policing poor women's mobility and sexual agency for their own good.

Twenty years later, as portrayed in the Argentine Yiddish press, the same Samuel Cohen, still in his leadership position with the JAPGW, visited Buenos Aires in the wake of the Varsovia Society court case and spoke on the subject with members of the JAPGW's Argentine branch and the Immigrant Protection Society. He complained that the shtile khupe was one of several religious idioms commonly deployed by traffickers, but the particular visibility of Jewish religious modalities, Cohen claimed, fed the League's inaccurate perception that the entire worldwide traffic in women was controlled by the Jews.[26]

Muckraking journalists around the world implicitly identified marriage as a technique of Jewish traffickers in particular. In *The Road to Buenos Ayres*, Londres describes a trip to Poland in which he explains how Jewish procurers negotiate false marriage contracts with the families of attractive, impoverished girls in their late teens and early twenties, often on the recommendation of matchmakers whom they pay year-round for the privilege.[27] In 1907 and 1909 a series of widely read articles published in *McClure's* emphasized the Jewish role in organized prostitution, particularly in Chicago and New York City. Attractive

Jewish men lured young women with "promises of an easy time, plenty of money, fine clothes and the usual stock of allurements—or a fake marriage. . . . In some instances the hunters really marry the victims."[28] The *Los Angeles Times* repeated news from the Jewish press under the title "Jewish Girls Are Sacrificed": "Some [procurers] seek the company of Jewish maidens with avowed intention of honorable marriage. Others actually marry the girls and then force them to lead dissolute lives. Many of the latter class of men, declares the Jewish Courier, have married dozens of girls under various names and disguises."[29] The U.S. government's immigration report of 1911 also cited marriage as a method of entrapment among Jewish procurers in particular: "There are large numbers of Jews scattered throughout the United States who seduce and keep girls . . . by the methods already indicated—love-making and pretenses of marriage—they deceive and ruin."[30] Charges of immorality and criminality against Eastern European Jews and other suspicious immigrant groups could encourage popular hostility as well as migration restrictions.

One response to some of the risks uniquely faced by women was to encourage civil marriage. Marriage had been a longer-standing solution to the problem of prostitution. In a letter of January 8, 1915, to William Alexander Coote (head of the IBSTW), the Argentine Committee for Public Morality bragged of "the work we have done for the benefit of the culture and of the good customs of our society, having intervened and brought to fruition various marriages."[31] Civil marriage was one of the key tools used by Jewish antiprostitution reformers. The international JAPGW Report of 1928 described cooperation between the Warsaw and Buenos Aires branches in responding to a shtile khupe case by adding the civil component to the ritual marriage: "The Warsaw Committee asked our assistance concerning a young woman who had gone to Buenos Aires to join her husband. . . . She was met on arrival by our officer, who found that she was only married by a Ritual marriage. Steps were taken to get the marriage civilly legalized."[32]

This story shares with others the emphasis on the primary problem with the shtile khupe being the lack of legal protection for the woman thus married: although she could not legally divorce at this time in Argentina, civil marriage would prevent men from marrying multiple times, saving numerous potential female victims from entrapment. Jewish social welfare agencies focused on marriage responsibilities as a solution to women's poverty. For example, the Progressive Era New York Jewish legal aid agency the National Desertion Bureau conceived of its work as helping women in general through its particular focus on abandoned wives.[33] The problem of the *agunah*, or abandoned wife, was frequently linked to the shtile khupe, and Jewish antitrafficking organizations also assisted in tracking down missing husbands and fighting bigamy.[34]

Polish authorities, concerned with their region's reputation as a recruiting ground for the traffic, highlighted Jewish religious marriage practices as a causal factor, thus shunting responsibility to other realms.[35] The shtile khupe became a rhetorical focus for efforts to increase state control over religious authority, an effort parallel to that previously made by the imperial Russian state. In a proposal submitted to the 1927 International Congress on the Subject of the Suppression of Traffic in Women, the Polish National Committee for the Suppression of Traffic in Women and Children argued that religious marriage gave Jewish traffickers an advantage over other groups in recruit women for prostitution:

> It consists in the giving of a symbol (a ring or even a coin) by the man to the girl on reciting a sacramental formula. Even the presence of a Rabbi or another official representative is not required; any Jew can be a witness. . . . The Jewish ritual secret weddings are conducive to the traffic in women . . . the unscrupulous husband in order to get rid of his wife, can take her abroad and sell to some brothel without losing the possibility of contracting new religious weddings, because for the aforesaid reasons, his private documents do not mention any previous marriage. As it is, the traffickers, especially in Jewish communities, have more opportunity for carrying on their trade than in other communities, due entirely to the ritual weddings.[36]

Marriage as a recruitment strategy was articulated by the Polish government as a Jewish practice and Jews implicitly blamed for Polish involvement in international sex trafficking.[37]

Polish reformers thus proposed to solve the problem created by Jewish marriage practices through increasing state oversight. Beyond vulnerability to trafficking, Jewish women married in this way would be legally considered concubines, not wives. While not a violation of Polish (or other European) law at the time, this did expose women to financial and social risk. Reformers argued this would be easily solved if "Jewish clergy and intellectual classes" would give up this custom and Rabbis register all weddings with civil authorities.[38] This proposal thus called for an increase of the penetration of the Polish state into Jewish life. Tighter Rabbinic control over individuals' lives was also proposed, as the danger was partially caused by the sacramental formula being performable by "any Jew in the street."[39] Rabbis should formalize all Jewish marriages and be responsible for registering them with civil authorities. In 1929, Polish authorities arrested and imprisoned two Rabbis in Warsaw for drawing up "false marriage certificates" in collaboration with two brothers and the three young women whom they were collectively trying to bring to the United States through "bogus marriages with American nationals." The investigation expanded internationally and resulted in a "whole band" of accused traffickers being sentenced.[40]

Globally, Jewish community leaders deployed related strategies to police these issues. The formal recommendations proposed at the 1927 London international conference of the JAPGW urged all rabbis around the world, including the Chasidim, the ultra-Orthodox who generally kept themselves more separate from secular matters, to become more involved in the prevention of shtile khupe marriages: "It is to be suggested to Rabbis and others holding responsible positions in the Jewish communities to discourage the continuance of such marriages to the utmost of their powers. . . . [They] should require young men and women, who come to them for the purpose of marriage, and who have been born in a foreign country, to produce evidence that there is no legal impediment to the proposed marriage. It is also desirable that the Rabbis should themselves institute enquiries."[41] Religious authority would thus be more powerfully brought into family decisions. Parents and guardians were also to be more strongly warned "of the grave dangers which may threaten their daughters' future welfare unless strict enquiries are made concerning young men who propose to marry them, and of whose antecedents they know but little or nothing."[42] This work was to be done through existing local JAPGW branches or committees, who "should seek the cooperation of Rabbis and others to warn parents against such marriage brokers (Schadchen), whose object may be only to make money, and who are often the accomplices of the traffickers."[43] The risks of unknown men and marriage brokers from outside local community networks would be counterbalanced by greater involvement of Rabbis and reformers in families' decisions.

On the ground in Argentina, these and similar strategies were attempted. In 1924, League of Nations investigators reported on Argentine efforts to regulate the entry of women being brought to the country with promises of marriage to men met for the first time at the Buenos Aires port. "Girls coming to be married are not allowed to leave the docks until the marriage has taken place and this marriage is only solemnized when an investigation by the police reveals the fact that the man in question is a respectable person."[44] By 1932, Ezres Noshim collaborated with the Polish consul and other organizations in Argentina to "safeguard young girls arriving for the purpose of marriage. Every application for a permit of entry for a fiancée must be accompanied by a sum of money to enable the civil marriage to take place immediately on arrival, and in the presence of our officer . . . [to prevent the possibility] that the young man suggests cohabitation without marriage, for the purpose of driving the girl to a life of immorality. The new arrangement will assist our Committee to safeguard the girl."[45] Later in the 1930s, this organization required that prospective brides and grooms provide rabbis with premarital morality certificates to try to protect the reputation of the local Jewish community's future generations.[46]

Efforts to control the shtile khupe through tighter religious leadership could not necessarily be successfully implemented. Jews in Argentina faced a particular crisis in the area of rabbinic authority. There were few rabbis in Argentina before 1930, and even those "did not enjoy the respect of the community."[47] Rabbis still in Eastern Europe were consulted on important matters, while Ashkenazi rabbis in Argentina struggled for economic survival and often fought with ritual slaughterers for jurisdictional authority, while Sephardim created a new "Grand Rabbi" position and tried to build a closer relationship with the government.[48] Issues of marriage and divorce became particularly contentious, and the broader community began to restrict rabbis' authority to preside over marriages and grant divorces.[49] The consolidation of community leadership was in flux as the Jewish communities expanded rapidly in interwar Argentina. Potential community leaders jockeyed for power, and the balance between civil and religious authority was unstable. Debates around the shtile khupe must thus be situated in the larger context of modern changes in Jewish marriage and family patterns and changing relationships between religious and civil authorities.

In Eastern Europe, a young Jewish woman's decision to marry a man she knew or suspected might be a trafficker should be interpreted as linked to broader trends in youthful defiance of parental authority over partner choice, as marriage ages rose and youth exerted greater decision-making power.[50] Poor women seeking to raise their economic status through marriage would have found limited options, while the Americas promised limitless opportunities. A Rio madam arranging a "kept woman" situation for her niece defended her role to Kinzie: "What could she do in the marriage line? Marry a schnorrer (beggar) in Warsaw? She's better off here."[51] When Kinzie asked this aunt "'Do you think she will like the man?' she replied 'Like? What's the difference? Anybody who gives you everything you want, you have to like!'"[52] This conversation reflects both limited possibilities and the uneasy coexistence of two relationship models: the family-arranged match and the love match.[53] Young women unsatisfied with the arranged marriage options available within their social group or denied the option of a love match might prefer the possibilities of an unknown land.

## MARRIAGE AS A MIGRATION STRATEGY

"Girls always believed that the fairy prince had come and they would not realize the dangers until they were told openly about the white slave traffic," argued Lemberg deputy Madame Melzer at the 1927 JAPGW international conference. The fight against the shtile khupe must be "not only against the dealers but against old prejudices," by which she meant young women's marriage fantasies and families' reluctance to address prostitution openly.[54] The marriage ruse entrapped parents unwilling to squarely face the possibility that their daughters might be at risk of being trafficked. Young women's unrealistic hopes for perfect husbands and rescue from poverty contributed to their vulnerability.

While some women and their families certainly may have been tricked by some version of the marriage ruse or other methods, it is also probable that other families and young women knew that a foreign brothel might be the journey's end point but that choices closer to home were worse. Poor women seeking to raise their economic status through marriage would have found limited options at home, while the Americas promised limitless opportunities. Depending on the time and political regime, a woman interested in leaving her parents' house to emigrate would have had no legal right to do so without getting married, as women held the nationality and thus citizenship rights of their fathers or husbands. In contrast to the narrative of the shtile khupe as a trap for naïve virgins, religious marriage without a civil component was also deployed intentionally by women to gain mobility in the face of unappealing alternatives. Women sometimes chose non–civilly binding marriages in order to have the temporary legal right to move. Radical political groups in the Russian Empire assisted single female members in contracting fictitious marriages in order to garner internal passports and the legal right to live away from the home of their parents.[55] A sensationalist 1925 *Los Angeles Times* article about a Latvian "slave band" supposedly involved in trafficking hundreds of young women to Argentina and Brazil notes in passing that "some couples by mutual consent agreed upon obtaining a divorce upon their arrival either in Buenos Aires or Rio de Janeiro, the girls expecting positions with friends of their temporary husbands."[56] This suggests that it may have been a not-uncommon practice for women to voluntarily contract non–civilly binding marriages in order to have the temporary legal right to migrate.

The use of sham marriages in this period as a way for immigrants to Britain to gain British citizenship and thus avoid deportation upset authorities there as well. Jewish authorities in the London Ashkenazi community expressed concern from the turn of the century through the interwar years with such illicit marriages among the poor, and the London Metropolitan Police in 1921 fretted that these "apparently can be annulled at any time," leaving women vulnerable to desertion, as they had no civil claim on their husbands, and their children would be officially illegitimate.[57] The issue also dovetailed with immigration restriction efforts. In the early 1920s, Home Office officials and police blamed Jewish religious marriages without a civil component for enabling criminal immigrant women, particularly prostitutes, to evade deportation. In response to this and related cases, the Jewish Marriages Bill in Britain made shtile khupe marriages a felony, like other irregular marriages, but the Jewish community generally refused to cooperate with enforcement.[58]

International activism around white slavery increased the scrutiny placed on young single women at many border crossings and ports. The League's investigation paid particular attention to enforcement at these points, criticizing both local officials and national governments for insufficient action. Although the undercover experts sought evidence of corrupt officials knowingly complicit in the traffic of underage and coerced women, they generally found women who had already been in prostitution working together with men to deploy both legal and counterfeit travel documents.

Immigration laws and border enforcement enacted in the first decades of the twentieth century often responded to international antitrafficking activism by restricting entry of single and minor women.[59] The French and Spanish governments would not grant passports to minor women unless they were married.[60] Investigators frequently focused on minors as unequivocal victims of exploitation.[61] Marriage, or documents reflecting this status, became the predominant strategy for evading this surveillance focus. It smoothed the travel of minor women to and from many locations; as a madam in Marseilles told the League investigator, "All the bunch that I know, marry their girls. If the girl is young, you then have no trouble."[62] While minors, defined in Argentina as under age twenty-two, were discouraged from entering the country and could not legally register as prostitutes, marriage essentially granted minors majority status. The Varsovia Society was accused of a brisk trade in documents with inflated ages as one work-around, in addition to the marriage strategy.[63] Short-term marriage as a border-crossing strategy for minors did have limits, however, as men who traveled the same route repeatedly with different women became known to officials. A larger network might then be enlisted, as described by a French pimp: "I know a lot of boys who left for Brasil, but they got friends to marry the gals first. Married women even under 21 they got to give a pass to" as the "boys [themselves were] already married or too well known themselves."[64] If multiple routes were traveled or officials less observant, many young men appear to have married a half-dozen women at different times.[65]

During the mid-1920s immigration policies tightened in many receiving countries. Argentine officials became increasingly strict about passports and other paperwork at the end of 1923, in part inspired by newly restrictive quotas in the United States that aimed to reduce immigration from Southern and Eastern Europe.[66] Argentine law 817 targeted the entry of those involved in "vice or useless activity," suggesting a crackdown on known underworld characters.[67] The mainstream Jewish community argued in the Buenos Aires Yiddish press against the public association between Jews and the traffic in women in part out of fear that restrictions would be further tightened for all immigrants.[68] The English-language business community newspaper *Buenos Aires Herald* bemoaned the "paper barrier" to entry upheld by the "Grand-motherly Government," complaining that desirable immigrants are kept out by the expense and inconvenience, while anarchists, white slavers, and other undesirables manage to manipulate the system to their own advantage.[69]

Ironically, the very immigration and border control restrictions designed to prevent trafficking by scrutinizing women traveling alone pushed women into strategic marriages in order to avoid notice. The details of immigration restrictions inspired various bypass methods. The effort to exclude from entry to Argentina women registered in other countries as prostitutes resulted in women finding ways to get their names off the books before getting their passports, making the common shift from registered to clandestine work for the necessary period.[70] Others unable to get required documents attesting to good character entered Argentina over land at less secure borders, disembarking at the less stringent ports of Rio de Janeiro and Montevideo.[71] As Argentine law 817 required a judicial or police certificate and a health certificate for entry, relationships with local police in particular sending locations would be exploited to produce required entry forms, in addition to the creation of false documents.[72] Marriage facilitated the passages of majority-age women as well as minors. Ezres Noshim knew by late 1923, even before the increased restrictions of that year's law, of the commonplace practice that women who had already worked as prostitutes often arrived with husbands, perhaps justifying the focus of their dock inspections on single women as more likely to be sex work novices.[73] In the 1930 court case, prostitute Lea Rossman and an additional witness testified that in order to travel from Poland to Argentina without being scrutinized as a single woman, she had made an arrangement with Society member Aaron Wiernik, whom she had known for several years, to travel with him under false names and documents as his wife.[74]

Antitrafficking activists from the League of Nations to the JAPGW spent years at the local level hunting down evidence of involuntary traffic, with disappointing results. According to over a hundred League undercover interviews in Buenos Aires with prostitutes, brothel owners, and others in sex work as well as police and officials, "There was agreement, practically amounting to unanimity, that the vast majority of alien women who are now practicing prostitution in Buenos Aires were prostitutes in their home countries and that they came or were brought for that purpose without deceit, fraud, or force being used."[75] Aware of the legal restrictions on trafficking, none of the one hundred prostitutes interviewed "would admit having been brought by a man or having had their passage paid."[76] All insisted that they chose to migrate in search of better earnings, the same story told by their madams and pimps, who added that the women did repay over time those who had assisted in facilitating their transit.[77] So-called regular business girls already in the life in Europe would cooperate with a strategic marriage—or the documentation thereof—with a member of the traffickers network in order to make the trip across the Atlantic.[78] Evidentiary limitations make quantification impossible, but these data suggest that involuntary traffic was less the norm in the global flows of women engaged in sex work in this period than constricted choice, in which women and their families might have hoped to make use of some of the skills and resources available through underworld connections, with or without clear intentions for employment after transit.

## MARRIAGE AS A BUSINESS PARTNERSHIP

Some versions of the marriage ruse story continued beyond initial seduction and transatlantic journey into local brothel imprisonment. As the news cycle ramped up in late May around the 1930 court case, the *Buenos Aires Herald* reported on legal testimony on the role of marriage in the Society's practices of entrapping and keeping women prisoner: "The trail led to the society's synagogue in [the Buenos Aires suburb of] Avellaneda, and as a marriage ceremony was performed, no action could have been taken, even supposing suspicion to have been aroused. Once 'married,' the white slavers told their victims what their future occupation would be, and the girls had to choose between possible starvation in a strange land, with a strange language, or careers of infamy."[79] In this version of the ruse, marriage tied the victim to her exploiter upon arrival. The existence of married women engaging in prostitution often disturbed reformers more than the presence of single women. The husband was often blamed as the exploiter. The existence of marriage among prostitutes and pimps was considered by mainstream Ashkenazi Jewish culture to be a sham, for example as represented in Sholem Asch's play *God of Vengeance*, in which Schloyme the pimp proposes to the rather more sympathetic brothel owner to marry his oldest prostitute in order to set up a brothel of his own.[80] The legal summary from the 1930 case asserted that most of the Society's members forced their own wives into prostitution.[81]

This critique gained power from deeper messages around men's and women's breadwinning and familial responsibilities. The husband-pimp is criticized for his own laziness, while his wife works to support him: "The individual satisfies his vices with the 'WORK' done by his wife whom he has placed in a Brothel or whom he compels to walk the streets. If he places her in a Brothel, he takes her earnings or, if he leaves her in apparent freedom, he compels her to give him the money earned from her 'CLIENTS.'"[82] This capitalization in the original also calls attention to internal descriptions of prostitution as sex work, albeit by framing the idea as ridiculous.

Despite these narrative assumptions about women's victimization by husband-pimps, women's desire to choose their own partners does appear to have played a role in the transnational circulation of sex workers. Women's desires may even have been supported by the Varsovia Society, particularly if the women wanted to change partners in their primary relationship. Although the court case against the Society framed it as obligatory for prostitutes to always have a pimp within the Society, League investigators acknowledged that the Varsovia Society mediated "if any of them did not wish to live with the men."[83] Wealthy Buenos Aires brothel owner Max Goldberg explained to Kinzie how the Society would support transfer of a prostitute's primary attachment from one man to another: "You know women; when they are whores, or when they are respectable they are all alike. They like a change too. Of course, the girl must like the man."[84] This suggests that women at least occasionally had some choice in changing their managers and primary partners. Experienced traffickers routinely warned Kinzie to be sure his girl would stay with him before making the large investment in bringing her across the Atlantic, underscoring the frequency with which women would move from one man to another.[85] While a marriage in the Old Country might not have been chosen freely, with divorce rare, prostitutes in South America had the option to change their primary partner, free of stigma within the underworld. Women were probably less naïve than the dominant narrative suggests and sought opportunities to switch to preferable partners.

The victim narrative did have a connection to the seduction strategy suggested to the League of Nations' investigator for finding a "fresh recruit," though the usual advice was that entrapment would not be worth the time, money, and effort, when plenty of women would not need to be fooled. To encourage even experienced women to join forces with male managers in the dyadic structure that the marriage migrational strategy required, attractive younger men played a critical role in the international network of sex importers. As one older trafficker articulated: "A young fellow can always get a girl to hustle the streets for him. . . . The young girls don't want an alter cocher (old man) [literally 'old shitter']."[86] Police archival photographs of dozens of Ashkenazi Jewish men arrested as pimps in Buenos Aires in the 1890s capture many nattily dressed young men with carefully groomed hair and moustaches and elaborate ties and cravats, who can easily be pictured as seductive bait for young women seeking love marriages.[87]

The standard shtile khupe variation of the white slave narrative emphasized marriage as the initial entrapment method, suggesting that these false unions would be dissolved after transport and deposit into brothels. Relationship patterns in local underworlds, however, indicate that marriage facilitated sex work well beyond recruitment and transit. Just as marriage proved to be a useful workaround for evading border restrictions, it also expanded work and life options on the ground, in the face of local regulations. For example, in Marseilles, married prostitutes working in hotels and cafés were not required to register with the authorities, unlike their unmarried counterparts, giving them more freedom in how and where they worked.[88] A form of monogamy between working girls and pimps seems to have been enforced by both police and other members of the underworld. As a madam articulated to the League investigator, "The only ones the [police] pick up are the girls who annoy people. Anyone could hustle in Marseilles for years and not get into trouble as long as she don't go from man to man like some of those 5-franc girls do down the street."[89] The dyadic unit would thus become strategically useful from the Old World, through the transatlantic journey, and on into the Americas.[90] Both the pragmatic goals of the arranged marriage and the sentimental goals of the love match could be met in relationships between sex workers and others who both benefited from and facilitated their labor.

As in the transit phase of trafficking, marriage had multiple functions in the sex industry in Buenos Aires, which varied considerably from the published marriage ruse. Once on the ground, prostitutes' relationships with pimps were generally described by others in the business as relationships between "sweethearts." Kinzie encountered prostitute Fanny with her pimp Harry Kratzenbloom at Goldberg's boarding house when the "boss" wasn't home. The relationship dynamic described between this prostitute and her "sweetheart," despite Kinzie's quest for evidence of coercion, was one of a normal romantic relationship: the two invite Kinzie out for an afternoon walk; they stroll for a mile and enter a café, where the couple brainstorms what to purchase as a present for her nephew in Warsaw, before finally deciding on a signet ring.[91] Kinzie says he and the pimp then compared their signet rings. Fanny appeared content with a romantic partnership that could provide handsomely for her family back home. Kinzie appeared content with his signet ring and acceptance as an underworld member.

Kinzie does not record asking the prostitute for her perspective, but asks Kratzenbloom the pimp if it was difficult to persuade her to enter the trade. He responded, "Naw, ven der tivel iss hungery, er fress flegen! (When the devil is hungry, he eats flies)."[92] The pimp thus denies his own culpability and blames economic circumstances instead. In a Rio brothel, pimp Herschel or Hirsch told Kinzie that he had married twenty-two-year-old prostitute Fanny Rodoshik three years prior in Warsaw, from where they went to Paris and she voluntarily practiced prostitution, continuing to do so in Rio.[93] Although framed differently in the story of Arnold K., Herschel's claim that "the victim brought to Argentina, continues being for her relatives, a young girl of good luck, well married to a wealthy man, and who sends support monthly to elderly parents or younger siblings, because her fortune permits it" corresponded to an aspect of cross-border prostitution that the victim narrative generally elided.[94]

Unaware that their interlocutor is a researcher, the prostitutes Kinzie interviews rarely articulate their story as a narrative of victimhood or entrapment. Some stories barely feature men at all. Yvonne, a French prostitute in Naples, indicated that she had been able to use a network of madams and agents to work very profitably in Marseilles, Paris, Genoa, Rome, and Palermo, without relying on a man. In response to Kinzie's reaction to her success, "'Your boy friend (pimp) must be riding around in a Rolls-Royce!'; she replied 'No! No pimp for me! I had one once. He sent me to Panama and made me give him all my money. I ran away and since then, no pimp for me! My mother has ten kids and instead of me giving my money to a pimp, I am sending mine home!'"[95] Transatlantic travel and migration restrictions might have required women to pair up with men, but those relations could be temporary once the pair arrived in Argentina. This case also underscores the responsibility many of these women upheld, like other migrants, to send remittances to family in the Old Country. In Rio more broadly in this era, several informants describe a system in which managers had less power than in Buenos Aires, despite the goal of the 1919 Buenos Aires municipal ordinance to reduce their power, and many prostitutes operated without pimps. Madams there seem to have had higher-level roles, including working together as business partners, owning multiple properties, bringing women temporarily into second-class hotels, and dealing directly with importers, all tasks generally done by men in Argentina.[96]

In Argentina the organized Jewish underworld promoted dyadic relationships between prostitutes and "sweethearts." Other nationalities there and in other locations maintained alternate work structures, but acknowledged primary dyadic relationships.[97] In Naples, Kinzie pretends to complain about the Italian system of rotating women every two weeks between brothel "branches" in different cities, telling a brothel owner, "'If it were not for that damn system I would be here with my girl! Or at least we would be together.' He said 'Oh, I see . . . it's *your* girl!'"[98] Both men understood that Kinzie would want to be in the same location as his chosen girl, although he might have business relationships with other women kept on longer leashes. This exchange highlights an understanding of the fundamental dyadic relationship between a pimp and a primary prostitute, his girl, versus any other women who might also turn over to him a percentage of their earnings. Obviously these attachments, and even marriages, did allow for a woman to have clients, and would not even preclude her from becoming a "kept woman" of a "sucker," common in Rio de Janeiro, where one steady wealthy client might exclusively maintain a young woman, as Benjamen Morteh described: "That's how my wife got her start. When she came here with me twelve years ago she got a sucker from Sao Paulo and he lined her with diamonds."[99] This husband and wife maintained their relationship far longer than the woman and her sucker.

In a parallel to the priority that Jews outside the underworld place on in-group marriage, sex work managers strongly promoted partnerships only between Jews. In Constantinople, a suspicious manager discourages Kinzie, who speaks Yiddish and pretends to be a Jew, from attaching himself to a non-Jewish girl: "The schicksers [sic; a *shiksa* is Yiddish for a non-Jewish woman] are no good. They are all right for goys [non-Jewish men] but not for our kind." Very few examples appear in the Argentine legal or investigative reports of Jewish pimps, traffickers, or property owners working with non-Jewish women. Unlike the justification given among mainstream Jews, for the continuation of the culture, the explicit explanation is one of profit maximization. In Rio, Jewish brothel owner Morris Gold tells Kinzie, in relation to young Brazilian-born prostitutes: "They're dumb, and they're not for us! They all have Brazilian boys (pimps)."[100] Jewish men should stick with Jewish women, and leave other groups to men of their own kind. The importance of shared nationality and language between pimps and prostitutes is thus constantly underscored. This reiterates the necessity of good communication and a stronger bond between pimp and prostitute and contradicts the implicit racial or national divide between white slave and nonwhite or foreign master.

Relationships ran the gamut from prostitutes and their sweethearts at the lowest level to property owners and madams at the top. The network of underworld Jews helped to facilitate matches.[101] In Buenos Aires, at least according to the stories gathered by the League investigator, the structure of both sex work regulations and the Ashkenazi Jewish underworld culture seemed to require that every prostitute be paired with a man. In general, perhaps unsurprisingly, the lines between legal, religious, and common law marriage do not seem as significant to these individuals as they do to legal and immigration authorities, but the dyadic nature of relationships is strongly supported.

Police Commissioner Alsogaray brings evidence of these dyadic relationships to court in the 1930 prosecution of the Society, although he shares the usual victim-exploiter narrative that if a man lived with or had a relationship with a prostitute he must be exploiting her. Cohabitation or marriage between men and prostitutes or madams becomes evidence for their prosecution for corruption of women. Women known to be prostitutes or madams are listed in pairs with men. Alsogaray tracks who is married to whom, if the legal or religious status of the marriages is known, and who is cohabitating, and even submits who visited whom in prison as evidence of association.[102] Out of the ninety-three partnerships submitted by Alsogaray or discussed elsewhere in the court records, thirty-seven are defined as cohabitation, twenty-two as marriages (without specifying legal or religious), eight as legal marriages, and two as religious marriages. Of the remaining twenty-two partnerships, five are managerial, meaning the man is described as exploiting or renting property to a prostitute, and seventeen are circumstantial—one man has clothing belonging to a prostitute in his residence and sixteen are visited in jail by prostitutes, one of whom says he is her mistress and several others of whom say the men are their clients or friends.

While the norm thus appears to be cohabitation rather than legal marriage, some slippage between categories is evident. Of the ten couples with shared last names (of which three have one deceased member), two are described as cohabitating, two as legally married, four as married, one as religiously married, and one as a prison visitor, claiming to be a sister-in-law. Others refer to cohabitation as a "married state" or living "as husband and wife."[103] None of the men appear to have concurrent relationships with more than one woman, or vice versa, with the exception of one man who appears to cohabitate with two madams. The only pairings of men with an additional woman or vice versa follow death or separation. Of the ten relationships described by one or the other as having ended due to separation, many of the endings are an unconvincing part of a general denial of all knowledge that the Varsovia Society was a group of traffickers and pimps. In addition to these marriages and marriage-like relationships, many other connections appear among the tmeim, from blood relations and shared housing to various forms of business partnership.

## Green Girls and Lovers

The League's failure to find true victims paralleled reformers' generally fruitless search in receiving countries for "green girls" or "greenies," women who had not previously practiced prostitution. Traffickers from Cairo to Paris to Panama City disavowed the entrapment of greenies as unnecessary, dangerous, and, most significant, not cost-effective. The League investigator's summary of the transit route between Uruguay and Buenos Aires affirmed, "Professional prostitutes already trained are regarded as better money makers than amateurs."[104] Individuals involved at all levels of the transatlantic movement of women for sex work certainly had self-protective incentive to disavow practices targeted by transnational anti–white slavery agreements and lied egregiously when taken to court about all aspects of their business dealings.[105] However, Kinzie, through the network of highly respected references cultivated over decades in addition to his language, dress, and demeanor, seems to have convinced most of his interviewees that he was indeed one of them. His queries about how to best induce minors and greenies into the life were nearly always met with the candid suggestion that he marry the minor and forget about the green girls, as their low profit potential and the risk of their escape would not guarantee a return on his investment in transit costs.

Goldberg told Kinzie, "You are mersugar [sic] (crazy)! Green girls you can't get here! A green girl is twice as much trouble as a wife."[106] Or as he put it more succinctly: "It's 100 per cent. better to get one who has done business on the other side."[107] When Kinzie insisted to a pimp "I don't want any old stock," he was told, "Fresh girls [new to prostitution] are too much trouble and pretty dangerous too."[108] Violent coercion, which was the usual explanation reformers used for their low success rates in saving women from white slavers, was particularly discouraged by the Argentine cooperative association of Jewish sex work managers: "That kind of a girl [green] is no good. I'll tell you why: Suppose you give up a couple of thousand pesos for a nice-looking French girl. You put her into a house and after a little while she packs up and runs away! This aint Russia, you know! You can't stop her! If you beat her you have a fine chance of getting into trouble!"[109] When women had not previously practiced prostitution, the rarity of their status as green girls was heavily emphasized by both Kinzie and his informants.[110]

The commitment to marriage or marriage-like relationships between pimps and prostitutes was repeatedly articulated as a point of pride for the Jewish men interviewed by the League inspector. Goldberg thus distinguished their practices from those of their French rivals in the Argentine capital: "The French pimps are different. Some have two and three women. They beat their girls to make them bring in money. They make *real slaves* out of them! Our boys (pimps) treat their women right, and they never have more than one at a time."[111] This form of monogamy and lack of violent coercion, in explicit contradistinction to the dominant white slave narrative, paralleled other claims to respectability. Goldberg also supports these dyadic relationships through the kind of boarding house he runs in the heart of Buenos Aires's downtown Jewish district, where at the time of the interviews, four pairs of "girls and their men" live as couples, and do not bring clients there.[112] This serves as a way of getting around registration restrictions, as if a woman lives in a place that does not function as a brothel and finds clients on the streets, she is not required to register with the Health Department.[113]

As further evidence of morality, Goldberg describes "boys" as not making much money from pimping, with one example living hand to mouth—although he contradicts himself by calling Buenos Aires "the one town in South America for the boys (pimps) . . . [as] there is no law here against pimps."[114] The French, on the other hand, might get illegitimately rich from practicing white slavery, such as "the Frenchman [Carl Charlot]; he's a susicher (White slaver)! That's different! Naw, our agents don't do that!"[115] This distinction is a moral claim to superiority over less scrupulous business rivals, and perhaps a defense against antisemitic associations between Jews and unscrupulous business practices. The members of the Varsovia Society define themselves through word and deed as respectable businessmen, giving charity and supporting their own. Even more convincing than these moral claims are the repeated arguments that converting a green girl is more expensive than keeping an experienced girl happy.

Love was also described as the only possible profitable way to recruit a green girl, particularly a virgin. In a parallel narrative to that of the standard white slave story, in which the handsome and wealthy stranger inveigles the naïve local girl into marriage with his good looks and cosmopolitan promises, many interlocutors dissuade the League investigator from his supposed quest for a fresh recruit, as this kind of romantic seduction would be the only possible, profitable way. Goldberg warns him: "There is only one way, and that is to get a girl who likes you, and who will do as you say. . . . [Green girls] fall only for love, and then it takes time to introduce them into our way of living, and to get them to bring in a dollar."[116]

Although many madams and brothel owners advise against taking the financial risk of recruiting "greenies," some pimps and traffickers point out and make use of the slipperiness of the slope between women's premarital sexual activity and prostitution. "Charity girls"—often referred to in more explicit language—women willing to have sex with men for free, could be easily enticed into prostitution, and if willing to engage in the full menu of acts, could be just as profitable and reliable as experienced prostitutes.[117] The two categories draw a bright line at virginity: green girls are maidens, while charity girls are not.[118] As Goldberg explains to Kinzie: "'If a fellow loses his girl he goes to France or Russia and brings himself back a greeny (an inexperienced girl).' I said, 'Do you mean an absela (maiden)?'; he replied, 'No, a charity c—. This girl was a charity c—. He brought her here and when she got here she couldn't get work and neither could he; so, rather than starve to death she listened to reason."[119] The fundamental distinction is made between women who do and don't have sex, or who have and have not, then secondarily if they have had sex for money. From the perspective of the men profiting, if women are willing to have sex with multiple partners, why would they do it for free if they could get paid for it? The pimps and brothel owners thus articulate women's sexuality as a commodity that can be improved under certain conditions and would be irrational to give away for free.

The trope of the rural virgin tricked into a sham marriage by a flashy seducer bore the same relation to the continuum of practice as did the white slave narrative more broadly: absolute victimization occurred far less than constrained choice. The story was useful, however, for many groups. Concern about the lack of civil documentation of marriages meshed with state and religious authorities' desire for greater control over and information about individuals and families. Proposed solutions to the problem of the shtile khupe generally involved greater rabbinic and civil control over marriages, just as interwar governments sought increasing control over mobile populations. Fears about the shtile khupe underlined patriarchal reaction to the ascension of the love match: young people cannot be trusted to make wise partner choices on their own, and rejecting parental guidance would tear apart family and community structures as well as leave women vulnerable to exploitation and abandonment.

Marriage was in fact a common element of the transnational movement of women for sex work and was often used strategically by prostitutes and managers. It served as a cover for the movement of sex workers, helped minors cross international borders, and continued to facilitate business on the ground because antitrafficking laws assumed a dichotomy between wife and prostitute, between pimp and family man. While authorities expressed great concern about the difference between civil and religious marriage, the legality of marriage mattered in the underworld predominantly to the extent that it could facilitate mobility across borders. Marriage enabled evasion of border restriction. Legal marriage was the exception rather than the rule, although many couples lived "as husband and wife." In practice, underworld members sought respectability on the same terms as mainstream society. Marriage facilitated evasion of legal restriction, tightened organizational structure and services, and shaped the meaning underworld members made of their own lives.

To summarize, the best way to make money in prostitution in this period, according to its Ashkenazi managers, was to own houses conforming with brothel regulations; to get women to give you their best work and a share of their earnings for love; to allow women some say in trades between men; to refrain from mistreating women or forcing them to do what they don't want to; to maximize profits with stigmatized practices; and to work in a collective group to invest in property and bribe the police and other officials. Familial relationships of blood and marriage as well as shared religion facilitated the trust that enabled sharing of resources and successful competition against less tightly organized ethnic and national groups.

From the perspective of the women who worked in the brothels and other spaces of commercial sex in Buenos Aires, some chose to increase their life choices by marrying for purposes of transnational and economic mobility. Some remained in these or other relationships for business purposes or romantic connection. While migration and labor shifts certainly presented new risks for women, possibilities also opened to escape old problems. Life away from families of origin could permit new freedoms of leisure, interaction, and sexual expression. Women's lives in sex work could also involve violence and coercion, but little evidence supports the extremes of white slave narratives. Given the limits of other possibilities, prostitution might not have been as devastating a fate as reformers feared. For both international antiprostitution reformers and mainstream Jewish activists seeking to combat antisemitism and establish community respectability, however, the white slave victim narrative and marriage ruse story worked far better than the more ambiguous reality. Especially when comparing this model to antisemitic stereotypes, it is clear why the victim narrative of white slavery and quiet marriage has been the one recirculated in popular culture.

CHAPTER 4

# Immigrant Mutual Aid among Pimps

In 1910, the Jewish Association for the Protection of Girls and Women organized an international conference in London to strategize against Jewish prostitution on a global level. Although none of the invited Argentine representatives could make the journey, European and American coreligionists discussed the Buenos Aires tmeim and the local Jewish community's excommunication strategy. Israel Zangwill, British leader of the Jewish Territorial Organization, questioned the efficacy of the boycott, as the already infamous Varsovia Society members operated with sufficient audacity to "have a Synagogue of their own, and at the same time conduct houses of ill-fame!"[1] Rabbi Hermann Adler responded with an uncommonly optimistic perspective, arguing that the Society's synagogue represented "very extraordinary evidence in favor of orthodoxy. The orthodox congregations boycott these people, but they are still anxious to offer up prayer, and we should be glad to know that they are not lost to all sense of religion . . . we have the chance of appealing to their better nature."[2] While Adler took the religious engagement of the Argentine tmeim seriously, press and reformers in the following decades, and scholars in later decades, generally shared Zangwill's interpretation, that the Society's religious and mutual aid activities were duplicitous.[3]

During the first days of the arrests of Varsovia Society members in May 1930, the *Buenos Aires Herald* reported that provincial authorities had granted legal status to the organization from 1906 onward, including a 1921 withdrawal and renewal, because they had been "duped" by its members, who "disguised their true vocation under the pretext that their activities were purely of a charitable nature."[4] Police Commissioner Alsogaray insisted that the Varsovia Society's legal status as a mutual aid and burial society was merely a front for a nefarious cabal of criminal Jews, which could not possibly function as a true mutual aid society, as "absolutely no human sentiment or sense of solidarity exists" among its members.[5] Although most historians have agreed with Alsogaray's assessment of the group's legal status as a transparent deceit, close analysis of the association's own 1925–1926 annual financial report—the only document produced by the Society that appears to have survived in publicly accessible archives—suggests that the priorities, structure, and benefits of the Varsovia Society closely resemble the voluntary associations created by other immigrants.[6] In court, members universally stated that they joined for mutual aid, burial, and/or religious functions, while generally denying that they knew of other members' involvement in prostitution.[7]

Analysis of previously untapped primary sources reveals the behavior of the members of the Varsovia Society to be similar to that of immigrants in other voluntary associations. Setting aside the stigma of their profession, the group's members resemble other new arrivals in search of community ties, financial security, peer recognition, and religious familiarity. Jewish sex workers in Buenos Aires modeled their social organization on conventional Jewish marital and communal life. They both imitated and exploited marriage to their professional ends and provided social support and communal resources that paralleled those of the "respectable" Jews who repudiated them. They claimed their own form of respectability through displays of wealth, religiosity, and charity, and proclaimed themselves to be different from other ethnic groups in the sex industry by shunning violence and prioritizing cooperation. Mainstream Jewish leaders, afraid that the entire population would be tarred with the same brush, were more outraged that the tmeim practiced endogamy and had their own synagogue and burial society than if they had shunned religious practices and institutions.

## THE VARSOVIA SOCIETY AS AN IMMIGRANT VOLUNTARY SOCIETY

In late May and early June 1930, during the height of national excitement around the arrests of Varsovia Society members, a regional daily newspaper in the province of Santa Fe published a series of tell-all interviews with Arnold K., a supposed disgruntled ex-member of the Society. Arnold K.'s description of the organization and operations of the Society is fairly similar to the picture that emerges from court records, reform organization archives, and undercover investigations. He laid out a rigidly defined structural hierarchy. At the bottom, the exploited women were moved around at the will of their exploiters, given a fraction of their earnings, fed at a lower quality than the men, and unable to select between clients. Their hope: to become *patronas*, boss-women, called doorkeepers or madams in other sources. Patronas collected money from clients and shared responsibilities with male managers. Men occupied several tiers: Arnold K. and other agents acted at the will of those above, with incomplete information, he claims not directly involved in the actual entrapment or movement of women. Then there were the "auxiliaries," who traveled back and forth to Europe, bringing fresh recruits.[8] They had to travel in steerage, were several levels removed from decision making, and brought women back to be exploited directly by other men, who were one level above the auxiliaries.

At the highest level, Arnold described the most powerful members of the Varsovia Society as generally over age fifty, deploying "enormous" "mental labor and responsibilities. . . . As they get older, they are more rich and more fearsome, raising the number of their women and possessing establishments each time of greater importance."[9] These fortunes are kept in the independent "Bank of the Society," which offers rotating credit for travel and the purchase of new properties.[10] Arnold contrasted this elaborate structure and the behavioral norms of the Varsovia Society with the lack of cooperation and tendency to physical violence among non-Jewish traffickers and pimps. The Varsovia Society members do not hit women because "to hit them is to damage them . . . a loss of money."[11] If violence is required, another racial group is called in to do the dirty work, generally French or native-born Argentines, who are the other principal groups involved in the underworld. The broad reach and long-standing success of the Society can be attributed to "the spirit of solidarity. Helping each other mutually, shoulder to shoulder, they complete all their plans."[12] Thus the organization in fact functioned as the Mutual Aid Society it was legally incorporated to be in 1906.

Most of the omnipresent voluntary mutual benefit societies in Argentina in the early part of the twentieth century provided support for health and burial services, as well as pensions, emergency expenses, and cultural benefits such as education.[13] Although the Varsovia Society's operations provided these functions as well, neither contemporary nor later observers of the institution classified it with the broader category of immigrant associations. In terms of the structure and activities of the Varsovia Society, however, it can be interpreted as more similar to other immigrant voluntary associations than to criminal associations.[14] Critics considered it to be a criminal society, but the group's self-definition, legal status, and organizational apparatus suggest that the Varsovia Society functioned more like any other mutual aid society.[15] Scholarship on Jewish immigrants in the late nineteenth and early twentieth centuries tends to emphasize associations created around place of origin, called *landsmanshaftn*, the Yiddish term for immigrant aid societies based on birthplace, with analyses often grounded in labor history and engaged in questions of class identity formation.[16] Many of the early members of the Varsovia Society hailed from Warsaw, the location after which the society was named, suggesting that the organization's founders deliberately referenced this model.

Warsaw was a key hub at both the beginning and end of this period. Of the Jewish men arrested as pimps in Buenos Aires in 1893–1894, Warsaw was listed as the city of origin more than any other city but Constantinople, which was listed for fifteen and Warsaw for fourteen, with the latter as a more plausible birthplace rather than transit point.[17] The establishment in the following decade of the Varsovia (Warsaw) Society in Buenos Aires appears to have followed the model of the *landsmanschaft*. The organization's first president, Luis Migdal, hailed from Warsaw, as did cofounder Bernardo Gutvein and three other members in these early police records and still active in 1926.[18] Other important members in the 1920s were also born in Warsaw, such as Max Goldberg, born in Warsaw fifty-six years before his 1923 conversations with Kinzie, and his colleague Harry Kratzenbloom, with eighteen years working in Buenos Aires at that point.[19] The possibility that the Society's members saw it as a landsmanschaft was underscored at a May 1929 meeting of 107 members, at which the reason the president expressed for changing the name from Varsovia to Zwi Migdal was in part that nearly all the members had become naturalized Argentines.[20]

## THE HEVRA MEN'S INTERNATIONAL NETWORKS

The characterization of sex industry collaboration as parallel to other immigrant associations corresponds to the portrait of the international "hevra" discussed in the undercover archival records—but not in published League of Nations reports. The Yiddish term *khevre* means club, society, or noncriminal gang of friends and was spelled *Hevra* in the League records, which recorded the term being used by Kinzie's Ashkenazi informants to discuss their relationships.[21] This transnational network of managers and transporters of sex workers bridged Eastern and Western Europe, North and South America, and the Middle East and intersected with the Varsovia Society, which was not named in these records, but some of its members appeared. Jews along multiple branches described themselves and others they knew as "hevra men," associated with this club that seemed to lack a formal name or structure—standard Yiddish orthography would be *khevre-man*, meaning not only a member of an organization but also a fellow, good guy, or tough guy. Kinzie's informants and internal Varsovia Society records portray a world of business coordination in which those involved saw themselves and one another as businessmen like any others, though facing greater stigma and risk, against which they often strove collaboratively to assert their legitimacy as well as to profit.

Men and women who worked to move prostitutes across national borders and situate them in local brothels helped one another through formal and informal networks. League of Nations' confidential field reports gathered by undercover agents provide the clearest available window into how members of these networks conceptualized the structure and nature of their work. Spread as far as Johannesburg, Cairo, Constantinople, Rio, Paris, and Detroit, Yiddish-speaking Eastern European Jews affiliated through personal and familial relationships assisted one another in navigating shifting local and border restrictions. Connections through personal reference and gossip about shared acquaintances seem to have facilitated collaboration beyond any formal group membership.

Coming out of the Eastern European Jewish Pale of Settlement, one main route went east, to Constantinople and Cairo.[22] The other went west, through Paris, to South America.[23] These two routes were also connected by individuals who traveled on multiple circuits or served as hubs. Some of his international informants introduce Kinzie to one another as a fellow hevra man, bolstered by letters of introduction that he carries. In Constantinople, for example, an English-speaking prostitute introduced Kinzie to a pimp as a hevra man just arrived from Rio; the pimp asked him to prove himself by providing information about several mutual acquaintances and to show a "grease,"[24] which Kinzie explains in his report is "a letter usually given to hevra men traveling in a strange land to friends. This letter also serves as an identification, and at the same time is the carrier of salutations between individuals in this network."[25] Trust also had limits among these business associates. When Goldberg referred Kinzie to a key contact in Paris, he suggested a system of payment that ensured that no money would change hands until after a woman actually was delivered.[26]

Prompted by exclusion from mainstream occupations and social networks, Ashkenazi Jewish men seem to have created particularly robust business networks in the international sex industry along the Eastern axis, similar to and somewhat earlier than the transatlantic route. The League of Nations' maps produced in conjunction with its investigation highlight trafficking routes out of Warsaw toward Vienna, Italy, Constantinople, and beyond.[27] Narratives of interconnected Jewish traffickers highlighted connections between Warsaw and Odessa, Paris, and Buenos Aires.[28] These routes generally conform to the larger trafficking patterns discussed in the League's reports, mapped in chapter 1. European women—Eastern and Western—moved to countries with formerly colonized and racially mixed populations.

These transnational linkages between Ashkenazi men involved in organizing international sex work appear to have been established in the late nineteenth century. Buenos Aires police mug shots of suspects arrested for pimping in 1893 and 1894 are nearly entirely Ashkenazi Jewish men.[29] Each has a city, region, and/or country of origin listed along with other identifying data, but some of these geographic locations might indicate their immediately prior residence or source of papers rather than their birthplace. Out of 210, 48 percent came from Poland, Russia, or Romania; 17 percent from Austria, Galicia, or Vienna; 16 percent from Turkey or Constantinople; and 15 percent from England, Germany, or France. When compared to the demographics of Jews living in and leaving from these places in the period, the most striking number is the third. Constantinople was a Sephardi not Ashkenazi capital.[30] These data suggest regular Ashkenazi trafficking routes extending from South America into the Near East, with prominent hubs of supply and transit in between.

In Constantinople, Kinzie's key contacts are linked to the hevra men in Western Europe and South America. He meets there with a group of Yiddish-speaking pimps in a Kosher restaurant, where the men he describes as Roumanian and Russian are fascinated with his South American experience, imagining more successful business prospects there.[31] Their current most frequent trafficking routes, according to their conversations, stretch from Bucharest and Chanowitz to Cairo and Constantinople.[32] Their acquaintances also travel for business into other parts of North Africa, to Western Europe, and across the Atlantic.[33] The prevalence of Ashkenazi Jews in Sephardi zones working as managers and distributors in the sex industry had been noted for decades.[34] Ashkenazi women were brought as prostitutes to Constantinople and other parts of the Ottoman Empire.[35] German-Jewish feminist and antitrafficking activist Bertha Pappenheim reported a significant presence of Jewish women in Constantinople brothels.[36]

Explicit discussions of shared Jewish identity do not appear in these sources, but shared cultural references, Jewish contacts, and use of language underscore this link. Kinzie appears to speak Yiddish, referencing conversations in Yiddish without the presence of a translator, although according to his reporting at least one of his interlocutors expressed suspicion that he was a Yiddish-speaking non-Jew: "Maybe you are a goy. Who knows: Say, I met many goys who speak Yiddish."[37] Yiddish terms abound in the reports, including *balaboss*, or boss, used for both madam and brothel owner; *mocher* (respectable business man); *naphers* and *nekayvers* (prostitutes); *schnorrer* (beggar); *gelt risser* (gold grabber); *yold* (dunce); and *Roumanischer schickers* (Roumanian Christian girls).[38] In Rio, the investigator asks a madam directly about a lawyer with whom those in her circle work: "'Is this lawyer a yehuda (Hebrew)?'; she replied 'No'; I said 'His name sounded like a Jewish name'; she said 'No, he is a Brasilian. [Continho] is a real Brasilian name.'"[39] This exchange highlights the connection between names, language, and national identity. Although many of those in the underworld used multiple names, particularly those who moved frequently across borders, ethnicity often continued to be signaled through naming. Ashkenazi names were sometimes partially Hispanized, as in José Zysman, Abraham Jacobo Grosfeld, Jaime Lopachin, and other examples of those arrested in 1930 (see figure 4.1).

In describing their values and operations, these Jews also defined themselves in opposition to their main rivals, the French. Hevra members claimed to act like businessmen, unlike others who acted like criminals or white slavers: "They just work among our people, the same way as if a man in business wants a good clerk; he might know of one who works in another store, and he sends someone to see him, and to make him an offer."[40] When arrested in 1930, most of the Varsovia Society members wore suits and ties, as reflected in their published mug shots.[41] Members' self-conception is thus reflected as nonviolent, ethical, and

Figure 4.1. Varsovia Society arrested members. Source: "Los socios de la Zwi Migdal," *El Ideal* (Buenos Aires), May 27, 1931.

cooperative businessmen, in opposition to unethical others, particularly the French who "are always cutting each other's throats! They stool (spy and inform) on one another all the time!"[42] Other sources suggest that the French also had their own organizational structures, but the press, internal discussions, and League investigators disagree.[43] The informal overall League summary of the Buenos Aires investigation highlights the difference between each national group's approach: "The French kaftens are not so cautious or considerate of their women, but keep them under control more often by force and fear than do the Jews. . . . We could find no evidence of organization among the French kaftens or kaftens of other nationalities besides Jewish. In fact, the evidence is that the French and Spanish particularly are extreme individualists and often fight to the death amongst themselves over their women."[44] Through language, endogamous business ties, and collective definition as nonviolent in opposition to other ethnic groups in the sex industry, hevra men asserted their identity as Ashkenazi Jews.

## THE 1926 VARSOVIA SOCIETY

The Varsovia Society's 1925–1926 financial report is silent on the infamous business of the Varsovia Society's members, with little text and no description of mission or values. The president's two lines of introductory framing present this as the first time such a document has been created, with the goal of "exposing with the greatest possible clarity the economic state of our Institution, and accentuating to the extent possible its always ascendant progress."[45] The next section thanks the members of their Directive Commission for their "publicity and activity" in recruiting thirty-four new members over the prior year.[46] The report's overall tone proclaims financial expansion and vitality, and suggests that some aspects of members' participation, such as in-kind contributions to the Cordoba mansion and its synagogue, were entirely voluntary. Particularly generous members are featured as key benefactors for the larger community, with all of its members named and their precise contributions listed by category.

Aspects of the association's life are thus made transparent, a message underscored by the president's statement of personally vouching for the balance "with a calm conscience" and reference to financial details backed up by records in the group's headquarters and available for interested members to consult.[47] The central exhibit in the case for the group's commercial success was the collaborative purchase and outfitting in this period of a mansion on Cordoba Avenue, for the substantial sum of 150,000 pesos with a 45,000-peso mortgage. Notably, the financial report makes no mention of sex work or relations with either Jewish institutions or civil authorities. Instead, claims to legality and moral legitimacy reappear: the Society was legally incorporated and paid taxes on its land in Avellaneda and to the municipality of the city of Buenos Aires as well as interest on the mortgage for the Cordoba property.[48] As in the marriage ruse narratives, the combination of wealth, certain manners, and silence on income source suggests sex work.

The Varsovia Society's formal administrative structure resembled that of a typical voluntary society.[49] According to the lists of officers' names in Yiddish and Spanish on the front and back covers of the financial report, the institutional structure of the Varsovia Society comprised a board of directors with five officers and twenty-seven members, a five-member judicial body, and several functionaries devoted to bookkeeping, the synagogue, and the burial society. Directive Commission officers held positions of president, vice-president, secretary, subsecretary, and treasurer. The judicial body, referred to as a *geshvoirene*, Yiddish for jury, also had a president, a secretary, and three judging members. Other titled positions included an inspector, two *revisadores de cuentas* (accountants or bookkeepers), a *gabay* (beadle or synagogue warden), and two *mlotshes* (burial society administrators). These forty-three office holders combined contributed a third of the organization's total funds collected from members for this period. Group officers and possibly the entire membership body participated in a voting system; a "carved mahogany ballot box" was donated for *escrutinio*, the counting of votes.[50]

Varsovia Society members paid an entrance fee and monthly dues. New members can be identified in the report, as they are the only ones to pay *cuotas de ingreso*, or entrance fees, which according to this internal source ranged from 5 to 205 pesos. The last president, Simon Bruskevich, testified in court in 1930 that the regular entrance fee of 205 pesos could be paid in monthly installments, and the monthly fee of 5 pesos could be reduced to 3 pesos in case of a member's poverty.[51] Other members testified that monthly dues from an earlier era, before the 1920s, were 2 and later 3 pesos, eventually raised to 5.[52] Some membership contributions seem to have been required and others voluntary. Monthly pensions paid for a form of health insurance, credited with the treatment and recovery from illness of "various" members over the prior sixteen months.[53] President Bruskevich testified that an additional sum could be donated to the organization to be used for "benevolent purposes"; and the internal report shows that Directive Commission members contributed on average substantially more to the organization than other members, ranging from 1,000 to 3,400 pesos, with the largest amount going toward the real estate fund. This provides further evidence of the significance of the Society's role in supporting shared real estate ventures, particularly in new brothel development in response to changing regulations.

Combined analysis of this annual report and immigration records, police and legal summaries, and other primary sources reveals group members' ages, nationalities, arrival dates, purported professions, and relationships to one another. Of the Varsovia Society's seventy-five active members in 1926 for whom age information can be found, the average age was just below forty-six. Fifteen were under the age of thirty-five, and a dozen were age sixty or older. Most members arrived in Argentina when they were in their twenties, like the young single male majority of all immigrants in the period, but their involvement in the Varsovia Society generally corresponded with their later working lives.[54] Most of the nationalities of the 1926 Varsovia members recorded at entry to the country correspond to the Eastern European Jewish Pale of Settlement (sixty-six available): 35 percent Russian, 22 percent Polish, 18 percent Argentine (these twelve included those naturalized as Argentines), and the remaining 25 percent from other areas of Eastern and Western Europe. The distinction between Russia and Poland was one of shifting boundaries around the same region, rather than shifting places of origin, and by 1930, Argentine court records classified as Polish many of the same individuals earlier identified in immigration documents as Russian.

The rate of arrival in Buenos Aires of 1926 Varsovia members closely mirrors the overall pattern of Jewish immigration, as can be seen in the similarities between the two lines in figure 4.2.[55] The main period of Jewish immigration to Argentina is generally agreed to have begun with the 1889 arrival of 820 Jewish settlers on the SS *Weser*, generally increasing from that point until the beginning of World War I. Immigration resumed after the war, averaging around 7,000 Jews a year until 1930, when the international depression and immigration restrictions of the new Argentine government began to cut off this flow.[56]

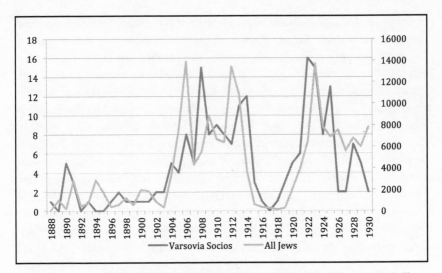

Figure 4.2. Annual immigration to Argentina, Varsovia members (left scale) and all Jews (right scale). Sources: Varsovia members: Ships' manifests at the Centro de Estudios Migratorios Latinoamericanos (CEMLA), Buenos Aires. General Jewish migration: Ricardo Feierstein, *Historia de los judios argentinos*, 3rd ed. (Buenos Aires: Galerna, 2006); Simón Weill, *Población israelita en la República Argentina* (Buenos Aires: Bené Berith, 1936).

Suspected Jewish pimps and traffickers came to Argentina from as early as the beginning of the 1870s (not included in this chart), which indicates that the tmeim became established when few other Jews were there, and even if they were not working in the field before the 1890s, their relatively large numbers in the small early Buenos Aires Jewish community affected the development of communal identity and mainstream institutions.

For 1926 Varsovia members, out of a total of 217 arrivals portrayed in figure 4.2, the peak immigration frequencies occurred in 1890, 1908, 1914, and the early 1920s. The steep decline during the war, with peaks before and after, reflects larger immigration rates of both Jews and non-Jews.[57] The 1908 peak suggests a phenomenon particular to this subgroup, possibly related to the law passed in that year by Buenos Aires city officials that changed brothel regulations and effectively benefited owners and managers, making it possible for younger women between the ages of eighteen and twenty-two to register and allowing unlimited recruitment for downtown brothels.[58] This may very well have encouraged a temporary increase in traffic, which might then have been reduced in response to public protest and resulting legal changes. Also, 1908 was the year in which another Jewish sex work organization, the New York Hebrew Benevolent Association, was broken up and a large number of Jewish brothel owners and traffickers were forced out of the city, at least some of whom came to Buenos Aires.[59]

Many Varsovia Society members shared familial relationships before their arrival in Argentina. Twenty-three last names are shared by two members, five names by three members, six names by four members, and two names by five members. Shared names are no guarantee of shared family of origin or marital relationships, particularly with such common names as Cohen and Levy, but other indicators suggest that these individuals may have been related. Eleven pairs of members arrived in the same ship on the same date to Buenos Aires, suggesting they traveled together. The two members of six of these pairs shared the same last name, strongly suggesting a familial relationship. Certain families had more members in the organization, as suggested by the numbers of last names shared by three, four, or five members. President Zacarias Zytnitzky returned to Argentina in 1932, on the same boat as a man five years older who shared his last name and had been a member of the Varsovia Society's board of directors in 1926. Two other pairs of 1926 board members shared last names with one another as well. These familial connections indicate that the Society shared with voluntary associations like family circles and cousin's clubs the function of sustaining kinship relationships in the quest for occupational advancement.[60]

Twenty of the Varsovia Society's members mentioned in the annual report have clearly female names, and the equivalence of their payments to the organization with those of other members suggests that they may have shared relatively equal status. None of these women held any official positions in the organization, but three of them were among the top fifty total contributors. This may suggest that at least certain women had some influence over the organization's decision making, if money had any correlation to power within the association. Five of these women appear to have joined the association within the prior year, making up a significant proportion of the new members paying the group's entrance fee, and indicating an increase over time in women holding official membership, although still excluded from holding office.

In their self-identification of occupation upon arrival or arrest, these female members are more explicitly associated with sex work than male members. Two are listed in arrest records as prostitutes, one as a female owner of a brothel, and one as a brothel doorkeeper. Three self-identify as merchants and two as domestic servants or housewives. Nearly all of those described as property owners or without occupation are women. None of the men, even in their arrest records, are described as pimps or traffickers in women specifically. Most are recorded as merchants or artisans, mirroring the labor patterns of other Jewish immigrants, not the more agricultural orientation of other new arrivals.[61]

Contemporary critics and many later observers have generally framed their criticisms of the Varsovia Society and of prostitution more generally in an assumption of female victims and male exploiters, as seducers, traffickers, pimps, and clients. According to Raquel Liberman's lawyer, no women were allowed to be members of the Society while engaged in prostitution, as all members were involved in "exploiting and obliging" prostitutes.[62] However, the evidence of women members of the Varsovia Society suggests that some women played a role in the upper echelons of sex work, negotiating with other members of the Society in addition to their better-known role as brothel managers or madams. Women thus appeared to at least occasionally have had the opportunity to move up from the practice of prostitution into its management.

### "Impure" Burial, Religiosity, and Respectability

Denied access to the burial grounds of the rest of the Ashkenazi Jewish community, the Varsovia Society emerged from the creation of a cemetery for the tmeim in what was then the Buenos Aires suburb of Avellaneda. The small Moroccan Jewish community lacked the resources to create a Sephardi burial ground on its own and agreed to share a plot of land with the tmeim, with the two properties divided by a wall.[63] Varsovia Society members examined as witnesses in the 1930 court case claimed that they had joined the group only in search of a Jewish burial society and had no idea about any connections to prostitution.[64] Religious burial maintained its attraction even for the largely secular population that settled in Argentina: before 1945, 85 to 95 percent of all local Ashkenazi Jews belonged to the Chevrah Keduscha Ashkenazi, the centralized Ashkenazi burial society, with those who were not members generally barred from membership—primarily the tmeim.[65]

The tmeim claimed religious identity in death despite the efforts of other Jews to exclude them from the collectivity. Period photographs of the Varsovia Society's cemetery show men's and women's elaborate tombstones with traditional Hebrew and Yiddish inscriptions from as early as 1904, including the stone for the organization's founder, later namesake, and first president Luis Migdal, born Lewek Migdal in Warsaw in 1852, who died February 3, 1908.[66] His tombstone describes him as the association's *grinder*, Yiddish for founder or leader. The Hebrew inscriptions on these tombstones and the enormous menorah at the exterior of the entrance to the cemetery, seen from inside the cemetery wall in figure 4.3, provide evidence that members deliberately projected a strong Jewish identity to one another, to other Jews, and to other Argentines.[67]

The Varsovia Society provided burial services both for members and sponsored nonmembers. President Bruskevich testified in 1930 that the price of burial for members was based on their means, and third-class funerals were free of charge.[68] Many services look to have been performed quite lavishly, as nearly 20,000 pesos were spent by the Society on these ceremonies over the sixteen months covered by this report. This record of expenses, along with the Avellaneda burial ground itself (see figure 4.4), corroborates the Society's sepulchral activities as more than just a cover for other functions. Furniture purchased

Figure 4.3. Entrance to the Varsovia Society's cemetery. Source: "En sus indagatorias los tenebrosos niegan la asociación ilícita," *La Última Hora*, May 27, 1930.

Figure 4.4. Plots in the Varsovia Society's cemetery. Source: "En sus indagatorias los tenebrosos niegan la asociación ilícita," *La Última Hora*, May 27, 1930.

for the headquarters included a "black embroidered funereal carpet" and fifty "low stools" for sitting *shiva*, the traditional Jewish mourning ritual.[69] The group's thirty-four newest members made the largest cemetery donations, suggesting that a greater fee for these services was required at initiation. Nearly all other members made ongoing contributions to the burial fund. During the period covered in the 1926 annual report, the Society paid 4,149.92

pesos to expand its cemetery with the purchase of an additional three-thousand-square-yard plot under joint ownership with the Sociedad Israelita de Socorros Mutuos Ashquenasum (Ashkenazim Israelite Mutual Aid Society).[70] There is little nonspeculative information about this related society, but it may have been a splinter group from the Varsovia Society, with its members also involved in sex work.[71]

The Varsovia Society's Cordoba Avenue headquarters highlighted their economic advantage over other voluntary associations. The building housed their administrative offices, meeting rooms, a synagogue space, an elaborate bar, and at least one *salon de fiestas* (party hall), where they hosted lavish parties and wedding receptions. Alsogaray criticizes these celebrations, which he claims included the formal presentation of female arrivals in underworld versions of debutante balls.[72] Newspaper photographs of the interior and exterior of the Cordoba property reveal a luxurious building ornamented with courtyards and gardens (see figures 4.5–4.6 and 4.7–4.9; the structure has since been replaced by apartment buildings).[73] Members' donations of furnishings, detailed in the annual report, give a sense of the interior's luxury.[74] Three members pooled five thousand pesos to purchase two chandeliers for the party hall and the women's "toilette." A stove and several bronze flowerpots featured "oriental" designs, and a donated balcony and theater box enhanced the sumptuous party hall (figure 4.8). More prosaic furnishings included brass lighting fixtures, wardrobes, chairs, mirrors, carpets, small tables and corner stands, and one bed. Costs outlaid also indicate that the group maintained a *casa baña* (bathhouse).[75]

Five individual members purchased the mansion in their names rather than in the name of the Varsovia Society, but paid for it out of funds contributed toward this cause by the broader membership.[76] President Zytnitzky explicitly thanked three of these individuals for becoming legal owners for the sake of the group, without obtaining any personal benefit in exchange for their risk.[77] Real estate was also one of the itemized categories for which members paid the association routinely, and nearly seventy thousand pesos were collected over the period covered by this annual report. These funds may have also been used for the construction and modification of brothels, the costs of which were often shared or loaned between Society members.

The Cordoba Avenue mansion contained a synagogue space that further confirmed members' valuation of Jewish religious life. Journalists' 1930 photographs of the interior of the Varsovia synagogue reveal many elements of a well-appointed, traditional Jewish ritual space (see figure 4.10). Decorative rugs frame a central aisle leading to a lectern draped with fringed coverings, like those commonly used to support the Torah during readings. A curtain decorated with lions, a traditional symbol representing the Jewish people, and a Star of David shield an elaborately carved wooden ark that would conventionally hold a Torah scroll.[78] Carved tables hold piles of books and a seven-branched candelabrum.

Figure 4.5. The Varsovia Society's Cordoba Avenue headquarters. Source: "Police Raids a 'Wash-Out': Only Ten White Slavers Caught," *Buenos Aires Herald*, May 23, 1930.

Figure 4.6. The Varsovia Society's Cordoba Avenue meeting room. Source: "Se hace difícil la búsqueda de los componentes de la 'Zwi Migdal,'" *La Última Hora*, May 23, 1930.

Figure 4.7. Bar in the Varsovia Society's Cordoba Avenue headquarters. Source: "Los tenebrosos de la 'Migdal' gustan del confort," *Crítica*, May 27, 1930.

Another newspaper photograph confirms these traditional elements and shows the larger space to be lined with dark wood pews.[79] Some of these furnishings may have been those detailed in the annual report's list of donations collected for the *Templo* (temple), which included two desks, an engraved silver plaque, a velvet Torah cover with a gold border, a set of Bibles, prayer books, an oak altar, and several hundred pesos' worth of candles.[80]

A list of members' Yom Kippur contributions made on September 17, 1926, further suggests that the Varsovia synagogue space was used for actual religious purposes. According to the Hebrew calendar, this date corresponded with *Kol Nidre*, the eve of Yom Kippur, the Day of Atonement, when tradition encourages charitable contributions to be pledged at the synagogue. The Varsovia Society's report also contains a separate itemized list specifying individuals' Yom Kippur contributions. The individual donations of 187 members made at that time totaled over 30,000 pesos, about a fifth of the year's total contributions. At least 187 members must thus have been involved in the holiday service, if not present. Over half of the total synagogue costs collected over the year was pledged

Figure 4.8. Balcony in the Varsovia Society's Cordoba Avenue ballroom. Source: "Los tenebrosos de la 'Migdal' gustan del confort," *Crítica*, May 27, 1930.

on Yom Kippur (13,985 pesos out of 26,805), and nearly half of the total year's charity collection (7,842 pesos out of 15,855). Charity dispensations included protection of widows and orphans, as the report mentions two financial transactions, loans up to 14,000 pesos, made to one "Widow Corradi and Son."[81] This circulation of information on members' charitable and religious activities accentuates the tmeim's effort to claim respectability on the very terms of the broader society that rejected them.

## ESTHER THE MILLIONAIRE AND OTHER WOMEN OF THE VARSOVIA SOCIETY

The exceptional story of Esther the Millionaire, also known as Emma the Millionairess, captured particular popular attention during the Varsovia court case, for the quantity and source of her wealth as well as her claim to social respectability (see figure 4.11).[82] Legal records and the press suggest that Esther arrived in Argentina from Poland in 1896 at age twenty-six together with her husband, who was also already involved in the underworld. She claimed in court that she

Figure 4.9. Garden of the Varsovia Society's Cordoba Avenue headquarters. Source: "Los tenebrosos de la 'Migdal' gustan del confort," *Crítica*, May 27, 1930.

had joined the Society to bury her husband in its cemetery in 1914, after his death in World War I, though it is doubtful that she transferred his body across the Atlantic. She still appeared on the Society's rolls as an active dues-paying member a dozen years later.[83] As a young prostitute, she added to her income by robbing clients in their sleep. Although arrested for theft seventeen times in these early years, she used lawyers and bribes to remain free and continued to amass assets through this method as well as by living as a mistress with a series of wealthy aristocrats.[84] As she aged and could no longer profit from these endeavors, she further developed her capital through brothel ownership, property management, and money lending, allegedly charging "usurious interest rates" to clients both within and outside of the underworld.[85]

At the time of her arrest, the *Buenos Aires Herald* valued her net worth to be equivalent to over three million dollars in that era's currency, which had enabled her to build and reside in a luxury apartment building in the city's most fashionable neighborhood and to enter the highest social circles without others'

Figure 4.10. The Varsovia Society's synagogue. Source: "El sensacional proceso a la sociedad Migdal," *Caras y Caretas*, June 7, 1930.

knowledge of the source of her wealth.[86] Esther, like the Society's president, became infuriated at the indignity of her arrest in the 1930 sweeps, and her lawyer kept on retainer threatened to sue the police for bothering her.[87] Not only did she leverage sex work into property ownership and wealth, she claimed respectability despite the efforts of many Jews to maintain a hard line excluding the tmeim from that claim. The Varsovia Society supported its members in various religious and relational claims to respectability.

Members of the Varsovia Society differentiated themselves from other groups engaged in prostitution not only by their organization of mutual aid but also by their treatment of women, very often taking as business partners legal or common-law wives. While sex work structures among other national groups in Argentina and in other places range from Rio's greater role for madams to groups of independent women in brothels and streetwalkers attached in groups to a pimp, the particular managerial structure that emerged among organized

Figure 4.11. Esther the Millionaire. Source: "El juez confia limpiar al pais de tenebrosos: La policia no consigue dar con los tratantes de blancas acusados," *Crítica*, May 24, 1930.

Ashkenazi Jews in Buenos Aires in the 1920s was almost always the hetero-sexual couple. The hevra supported these relationships and facilitated "divorces," sometimes at the request of the woman. Couples lived together in large apartments owned by property managers.[88] Jewish interlocutors under-scored their use of romantic and kinship ties rather than forcing individuals to maintain relationships.

Legal and functional marriages served useful purposes for both men and women in organized sex work even beyond a woman's profitable years of directly selling sex. If they lived past age forty, many prostitutes sought to become door-keepers or madams, positions that multiplied as legal changes to the Buenos Aires regulatory system evolved. In Buenos Aires, the demand for older women to act as doorkeepers increased in 1920, with the new municipal ordinance that restricted the legal practice of prostitution to women living individually, shar-ing space with only a housekeeper over age forty-five.[89] This new law also had the result, counter to its intention, of increasing the power of property owners, who used their privileged access to capital to expand their profits, from larger brothels to the smaller single-use dwellings.[90]

Men and women in their forties and older often worked together in their capacities as madams, doorkeepers, brothel owners, and traffickers, dividing up certain tasks along gendered lines and building on the trust within their part-nerships to sustain and expand their business operations. Many older women who surface in these records as madams or doorkeepers were closely tied to men who owned properties and worked together with them on property management. Although it should not be understated that the generally male property owners took at least half of women's earnings in rent, marriage-like partnerships had further benefits for women as well, particularly when they aged out of prostitu-tion. Spouses also shared related business endeavors: according to court records, the Society's last vice president, Harry Benjamin, and his wife worked together in warehousing and selling an "enormous quantity of 'preventatives' [and] . . . some electrical articles."[91]

The Society provided a degree of security not generally afforded to other ex-prostitutes. A female member of the Society who had risen from prostitute to doorkeeper testified in court that she had joined to "help women who in the prac-tice of prostitution were generally . . . abandoned upon becoming useless."[92] While the Society may have provided such long-term support for some women, this also serves as a reminder that most other sex workers would have had to budget and save during their active years to avoid sinking back into poverty, par-ticularly if suffering from long-term effects of sexually transmitted infections.

As the case of Esther the Millionaire demonstrated vividly, brothel land-lord, the most lucrative and powerful position in the hierarchy of Argentine sex work, was sometimes a position held by women. While only several dozen women were listed on the Varsovia Society's membership rolls in the late 1920s, among nearly four hundred men, some women owned multiple properties and others co-owned larger provincial brothels in cooperation with one another.[93] Cases also existed of women jointly and individually owning houses and properties such as restaurants and cafés that were linked to prostitution. Brothel owners were usually men, but they depended on their wives to run their properties. Wives might sign the contracts that owners created for the prostitutes who would work and live in a house for six months. This would comply with the law by giving the prostitute the legal appearance that she owned the property but ensured that she could not seize it from the actual owner.[94]

When managing new property or residents, owners often installed their own wives as doorkeepers to get a clear sense of the location's profitability.[95] Having established standards, the trusted wife would then be replaced with another woman who might be expected to garnish the intake somewhat but would be pressured from leaving with several days' gross profits by having paid a kind of deposit to a commission agent. Generally, these women would be involved with men who were also part of the network of Jewish underworld businessmen, which would also reduce the risk of embezzlement.[96] Documents cited in the 1930 court case suggest that women could have been prevented from working as doorkeepers if not associated with a member of the Society.[97] Kinzie records a conversation in which a pimp recommended a widow as doorkeeper to a major property owner, describing her as "one of unsverlite (our people)."[98] Business standards were thus enforced by the relationships between individuals involved.

Trusted dyadic bonds between men and women were thus supported by managers of sex work to maximize profits, but also as part of broader claims to social respectability. The Varsovia Society began in part as a Jewish burial society and built an enormous menorah on the front gate of its cemetery, proclaiming Jewishness particularly to those coreligionists who had excluded them as "impure" from the Argentine capital's original Jewish burial ground. Claims to Jewish forms of marriage were also made in public and private by these organized members of the underworld. The Spanish term *casado* (married) was interrogated in relation to Jewish tradition during the 1930 court case, as many of those testifying, both as witnesses and as victims, used the term without reference to Argentine civil recognition.[99] Wachman Lusman was interrogated on the question of Jewish marriage tradition. He claimed to be a rabbi, authorized to conduct marriages, and testified that he performed the wedding ceremony between Raquel Liberman and José Solomon Korn. This ceremony had been performed before ten witnesses, and the certifying document was signed by the witnesses rather than participants.[100] The court added that for the marriage to have legal weight, it would have to be registered by the grand rabbi and sent by him to the central government. As this was not done, the value of this ceremony existed only among those involved and of the same religion.[101] However, the chaotic state of religious authority in Argentina at that time and lack of cooperation between the mainstream Jewish community and those they called unclean would have made it impossible for registration to take place. Not only did the underworld have at least one rabbi in its employ, this rabbi was also the only religious authority called into court to testify on Jewish marriage customs—even though the standard for being titled rabbi was flexible, there would have been few other rabbis to call in, as the broader community had been unable to attract or maintain religious leadership. In their association with this religious authority and claim to traditions such as religious marriage and burial, the "impure" of Argentina maintained their claim to Jewish communal identity.

As Rabbi Adler expressed at the 1910 JAPGW conference, something resembling morality could be found in the Varsovia Society's synagogue and burial ritual. The material benefits covering the gap in local services were only a part of what drew Varsovia members, as in other voluntary associations. The collective mutual aid structure allowed personal dignity in the receipt of benefits structured as rights rather than charity. Forbidden from engaging with other Jews, the tmeim focused their quest for respectability on one another. Like other immigrants and sex workers, these marginalized individuals used bourgeois symbols to seek respectability.[102] Just as most voluntary associations had some degree of moral character standard for admission, requiring endorsements of current members, background investigations, and votes on acceptance, the Varsovia Society's founding members established a formal mandate to "accept only those of good reputation."[103] Although "kosher" Jews spearheaded a boycott against the tmeim, ostracism was incomplete, as pimps and prostitutes interacted daily with other members of Argentine society: policemen and judges, politicians and city officials, doctors and health administrators, furniture makers and launderers, and prostitutes' clients. Physical proximity and economic necessity forced other Jews to do business with the tmeim despite condemnation of their activities. Jewish prostitution was integrated into the initial center of Jewish life in Buenos Aires, around Plaza Lavalle.

Pimps have been portrayed as the most extreme examples of capitalist greed, willing to sell human flesh. Yet even among such individuals, the Varsovia reflected an interest in cooperative society. Members engaged in collective activity to protect both themselves as individuals and their peers. Placing this particular and peculiar voluntary association at the center, rather than at the margins of analysis of immigrants' institutions reveals something important about more mainstream groups as well. Like other migrants, Varsovia Society members embraced their ethnic identity and sought social services. In contrast to the Jews who organized against them, who more closely approximated the model of new ethnics trying to assimilate as good Jews and good Argentines, these immigrants crowded the docks to lure new arrivals with furs and jewels. They showed off to one another, tried to top each other's extravagant donations to the group's mansion, and made large cash promises on Yom Kippur. To the shame of other

Jews, they remained within the Jewish idiom, recognizably Jewish to outsiders, to other Jews, and to themselves. As prostitutes, pimps, madams, and fellow travelers of the sex trade, publicly shunned by other Jews, these individuals built an institution to meet their most pressing needs, essentially the same as those of other immigrants: for communal activity, welfare, and social status among peers. This reminds us that more mainstream voluntary associations also served many purposes, furnishing a place for immigrants who suffered indignities at work and in substandard housing to show off to one another, to hold offices and titles, and to be recognized within a small world. Beyond reflecting the values of the world they chose to leave and assuming the dominant values of their new home, new immigrants came together to structure their own universe.

CHAPTER 5

~

# The Impure Shape Jewish Buenos Aires

"Respectable" Jews in Buenos Aires in this period struggled with the difficulty of separating themselves, both figuratively and literally, from the "impure" Jews involved in prostitution. The case of Raquel Liberman vividly illustrates this challenge. Like most other Jewish migrants from Eastern Europe, who arrived in increasing numbers between the 1890s and 1920s, Liberman settled in the city center, where Jewish migrants concentrated, in the area referred to as Once, after the Once de Septiembre train station (literally the Eleventh of September, commemorating the 1852 rebellion of the city against the federal government). In this zone, the homes, businesses, and leisure sites of both "respectable" and "impure" Jews intermixed, producing ongoing conflict over public respectability and Jewish identity. And Liberman herself alternated between the respectable and not so respectable over the course of her career. In court, Liberman claimed that her second husband forced her back into prostitution, but her original complaint, brought to the Varsovia Society, was that he had cheated her financially. It was only after arbitration by the Society failed that she took her complaint, now couched in different terms of victimization, to the civil authorities. Prostitution itself existed in a gray zone—it was legal and regulated and quite profitable for many. It existed in close proximity to other Jewish businesses and residences, and Jews in the Varsovia Society maintained the trappings of Jewish identity with their synagogue and cemetery. As members of the Society branched out into property ownership and other investments, it became even more difficult to see them as outcasts. It was this blurring of the lines that disturbed "respectable" Jews the most. They lived in the same neighborhoods, practiced similar religious ceremonies, and patronized the Yiddish theater—to outsiders, other Jews feared, they all looked the same.

## "Respectable" Jews Unite against the Tmeim

One of the pioneering historians of Argentine Jewry, Robert Weisbrot, characterizes the Varsovia Society as a tragically disruptive element within a larger Jewish community already struggling to establish a sense of unity.[1] Besides the cultural disconnect between Sephardim and Ashkenazim, conflict was particularly high among Ashkenazim around the issues of political ideology, economic class, and, somewhat later, Zionism.[2] A closer examination of this period's battles over Jewish identity suggests the opposite of Weisbrot's claim: the fight against the tmeim brought together otherwise divided local organizations and individuals and contributed to the notable institutional centralization of Argentine Jewry.[3] While not all local Jews officially joined in the boycott of the tmeim, those who drove it often spoke for the entire collectivity's universal opposition to Jewish involvement in sex work. The Jewish display of unity in the face of the Varsovia Society was strongest during its peak of public visibility, during the 1930 police sweeps and court case.

This chapter brings in new sources to assess the decades-long efforts to "boycott" the tmeim.[4] These efforts to keep individuals associated with sex work, and their money, out of other Jewish institutions served as a rallying point for others to define themselves as both "good Jews" and "good Argentines." Struggling against threats from antisemitic, nativist, and xenophobic quarters in their new nation, Jews seeking to define themselves as Argentines made common cause with non-Jewish opponents of visible prostitution and, as part of the broader political upheaval of the late 1920s, pushed back against corruption among police and other political authorities.[5] After joining together with Commissioner Alsogaray and Judge Ocampo, "respectable" Jews claimed victory over the Varsovia Society, strongly articulated social and sexual norms, and despite moving into the darker chapter of the 1930s, could broadcast a greater level of collective unity, legitimacy, and moral strength.

Opponents of Jewish involvement in prostitution locally and internationally articulated their interlocking concerns about antisemitism and Jewish moral purity. British Chief Rabbi Adler opened the JAPGW's 1910 international conference in London with a prayer that framed the event's purpose in this language, asking for God's help in the battle against moral corruption: "Create in us a clean heart so that we may battle against all things evil and impure."[6] In Buenos Aires, the in-group usage of the term "tmeim" constantly invoked the concept of religious and moral purity. Calls to battle against the tmeim exhorted Jews to "purify your homes and streets, spit and point your finger at every vagabond, on the street and in the home, show publicly your attention against those who come into contact with the 'human merchants,' deny their broker, make them claustrophobic on the street and at home, at the salon and at the theater . . . [keep them out of] all the 'pure places.'"[7] With such deployment of language of moral purity, antiprostitution activists sought to define themselves as the only legitimate Jews, defending the collectivity from contamination. This distinction between purity and impurity played out in a dynamic relationship: because "kosher" Jews refused to allow them to contaminate the main Ashkenazi Jewish cemetery, pimps and traffickers built their own in a Buenos Aires suburb, creating a legal institution, the Varsovia Society, that expanded to meet other needs.

A visual analysis of Buenos Aires addresses associated with the tmeim and other Jews between the initial and peak settlement periods clarifies that when the Argentine Jewish population was first becoming established in the late nineteenth century, group members involved in the sex industry were highly visible to other Jews and other immigrant and native Argentines. Jewish antitrafficking organizations responded by becoming very active, trying to shut down the activities of the tmeim and also to publicly separate good from bad Jews, just as some of the evolving municipal prostitution regulations tried to segregate sex workers from the larger population.

## MAPPING THE TMEIM IN THE 1890S

The compilation and spatial representation of local-level data present perhaps a more vivid picture than statistics. Data from the 1895 census and police records of arrested pimps in the mid-1890s allow for the mapping of the locations of registered brothels in the center of Buenos Aires, comparisons of numbers of Jewish and non-Jewish prostitutes, and discussion of the characteristics of Jewish men arrested for pimping in this period of early Jewish urban settlement. The visibility of this element and its concentration in a centralized Jewish district appears to have persisted as the Jewish population grew. While the tmeim stood out as concentrated and wealthy among a small population in the 1890s and some battles against them were won in the following decades, the Varsovia Society still boasted great power and reach in the 1920s. Despite the best efforts of other Jews to drive them out, denying them access to social, cultural, and religious institutions, the tmeim remained in the local area, flaunting their wealth and its source. Evidence from the 1930 court case against the Society, together with press and other records of Jewish brothels and related locations, produces a reconstruction of the urban center that reveals that the physical integration of the homes and businesses of the tmeim into mainstream Jewish life persisted through the 1920s.

Jewish prominence in local prostitution in the 1895 census takes on an even sharper focus when spatially mapped. The 1895 census data on registered brothels, which I have charted in figure 5.1, are within the boundaries of the four police districts in the center of the city.[8] The black circles on the map show

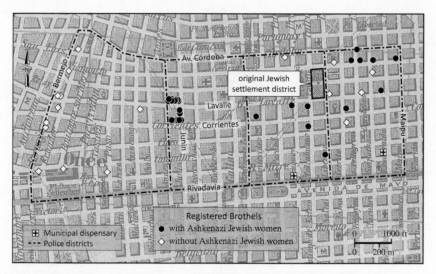

Figure 5.1. Registered brothels in central Buenos Aires, 1895. Source: 1895 Buenos Aires census manuscripts and summary in Marisa Donadío, "La ciudad de las esclavas blancas," *Documentos e investigaciones sobre la historia del tango* 3, no. 3 (1996): 140–176.

brothels that include registered prostitutes who appear to have been Ashkenazi Jews—all the women in each brothel had apparently Jewish names, in some cases with one or two exceptions, usually French or Spanish names—while the white diamonds show brothels without any Jewish women.[9] While brothels housing both Jewish and non-Jewish prostitutes were dispersed throughout the urban area near the Plaza, the densest concentration of prostitution fit into a one-block area in what was just beginning to emerge as the primary Jewish neighborhood.

The most concentrated zone of prostitution according to these data was the Seventh Police District, later under Alsogaray's jurisdiction, which largely overlapped with the heart of the Jewish center, Once, which would in the early twentieth century become the city's most visible Jewish neighborhood, with institutions, businesses, and residences centralizing there through the 1920s.[10] As shown in figure 5.1, all of the twenty registered brothels in the Seventh Police District recorded in the 1895 census were located on three sides of one square block. One block of Lavalle Street, between Junin and De los Andes (today José Evaristo Uriburu), had fifteen registered brothels, occupying nearly every address on the street.[11] This was before Once was consolidated as the central residential and business district it would become by the First World War, when this block became the symbolic heart of the district.[12] Although clandestine brothels may have existed elsewhere in the zone, this concentration of all registered addresses in one block is notable. Of the 191 prostitutes registered at these addresses, 147 had Jewish names and nationalities. None of the other census districts had a similar exclusive one-block cluster of brothels, this many prostitutes, or this many Jewish women.

The center of Once thus appears to have already been in 1895 one of the city's two main centers of registered prostitution and certainly of Jewish women. Many of the brothels in this neighborhood were arranged in a de facto red-light district, while other registered brothels were more dispersed. Other parts of the city had both fewer registered sex workers and fewer Jewish women among them. Of the city's twenty-eight total census zones, fourteen had only one or zero registered prostitutes, and the remaining half had between four and fifty-nine each, including both Jews and non-Jews.[13] The infamous port zone of La Boca had the next largest concentration of registered prostitution after Once, among whom 13 percent of the women were Jewish.[14] The ninth zone, which bordered Once to the west and contained the syphilis hospital, had no Jews in any of its fourteen brothels.[15] The physical concentration of Jewish sex workers thus corresponds more highly to the presence of other Jews than other sex workers; La Boca's registered prostitutes were over a third Argentine-born and less than 10 percent Jewish.

Census data for many of the brothels in the most concentrated prostitution districts of Once and La Boca include managers and pimps with Jewish names, though men from Western Europe and Argentina also appear as both bosses and servants. Ashkenazi Jews figured in these data more prominently as prostitutes than as pimps or brothel managers, though the latter categories of men would have generally been off-site and thus invisible. Servants in these brothels were rarely Jews. Clients appear to have been caught up in census data collection on more than one occasion; several young Spanish and Italian men working as day laborers are counted in some of these brothels. Clients are the most difficult underworld participants to locate in the historical record.

In the mid-1890s, the Buenos Aires Police created bound volumes with the mug shots and physical descriptions of 164 suspects, all listed as *rufián* or *alcahuete*, both meaning "pimp," nearly all of whom appear to be Ashkenazi Jewish men.[16] At least ten of these individuals appeared on the Society's rolls or the court's warrant list thirty years later, including founder and namesake Luis Migdal. Each of these records includes front and side facial photographs and personal data ranging from parents' names and length of residence in Argentina to detailed physical characteristics such as arm, ear, and finger lengths and scars, tattoos, and birthmarks, probably for both identification and criminological analyses.[17] The geographic origins listed suggest the transnational perambulations of these men, discussed in chapter 2. These men thus tied the burgeoning Argentine port to existing international trafficking networks between Eastern and Western Europe and the Ottoman and Austro-Hungarian empires.

These data suggest not only far-flung transnational mobility but also that the men were among the first Jews to settle in Argentina in the late nineteenth century. An analysis of the length of time those arrested in the early 1890s had been in the country reveals that many were not new arrivals. Over half had come before 1890, with a quarter there for longer than five years. Sixteen arrested as pimps first arrived in the 1860s and 1870s, which makes them pioneering Jewish migrants to Argentina. At least a core group of Ashkenazi men involved in the sex trade were already established in the Argentine capital before major immigration from Eastern Europe began. Even if they were not working in the field before the 1890s, their early immigration relative to other Jews stands out and would have made them particularly visible at the time. If police accusations reflected in these arrests were even partially correct, rufián and alcahuete would have made up a notable percentage of the professions of some of the earliest Jewish immigrants to Argentina in this period.[18]

Prostitution was thus tremendously visible during this initial period of urban Jewish settlement in the Argentine capital. Spatial concentration of Jewish women in brothels in the heart of the emergent Jewish zone would mark that area indelibly. Jewish men arrested for pimping and Jewish women registered as prostitutes made up large fractions of the total Jewish population of the city. The existence of a red-light block in the symbolic heart of the community would also have been well known, and as increasing numbers of migrants arrived each year, this would shape their perceptions as well as the opinions of other Argentines about Jews.

## PINK CURTAINS AND URBAN INTEGRATION IN THE 1920S

Sex work continued to thrive in highly organized ways in Buenos Aires in the 1920s, though the visibility of brothels was reduced. Changes to municipal regulation of prostitution over this period attempted to reduce the power of pimps and managers. The Buenos Aires municipal council began 1920 with a new ordinance that closed all licensed houses and was pushed through by socialist deputies who hoped that abolishing licensed brothels would end white slavery. Women could still legally practice prostitution only if they lived alone, on a street where no other prostitute worked. A female maid or housekeeper was the only other person allowed to live with her, and that woman must have been over the age of forty-five.[19] This law meant that the *apparent* number of licensed brothels increased in the capital, as each prostitute was now counted as one brothel.[20] Because sex workers could not afford to rent or renovate properties on their own in accordance with these regulations, the power of property owners increased.[21]

Goldberg explained this paradox to Kinzie: while this regulatory system was meant to do away with pimps and madams, it actually made prostitutes more dependent on them because for houses to comply with the regulation, they need to be remodeled. Once owners have suitable houses, they

> require long leases and exorbitant rentals, all of which the prostitute ordinar-
> ily cannot afford. Therefore, each house of prostitution is owned and operated
> by madams or pimps or both, who make a specialty of providing such houses
> for the prostitutes. Inasmuch as the Rules and Regulations require the pros-
> titute personally to own or lease the houses, the pimps, and also the madams,
> when turning a house over to a prostitute, require her either to put up any sum
> of money varying from $500 to $1,000, or to sign a blank agreement where-
> with . . . [thus] disorderly-house keepers have been able to control a majority
> of the houses of prostitution now operating in Buenos Aires.[22]

This response reflects another aspect of the dialectical relationship between the tmeim and the mainstream—efforts to minimize their power often strengthened it. The Varsovia Society appears to have swelled in wealth and influence in this period because of the system of circulating loans and joint property ownership, which they consolidated in response to these restrictions.[23]

A striking visual marker denoted which residential properties were used for sex work: "The glass in the doors must be covered with a translucent curtain, usually pink or white. This curtain serves as a 'mark of identification' for houses of prostitution, inasmuch as the curtains on the doors of respectable houses in Buenos [Aires] are usually of lace."[24] These served as subtle signals to potential clients: "Everybody knows these curtains, and you don't need steerers or any-thing else. The johns (customers) just come in. The window curtains must always be drawn, the shutters closed, and the girl can't hustle (invite-accost) them in from the window or doorway."[25] This system marked and separated addresses linked to prostitution. Ideally, those who didn't know the code wouldn't know what was happening and be thus undisturbed—though high numbers of clients in dense residential areas would have made this outcome unlikely. Brothels con-tinued to be concentrated outside of the city's wealthiest zones. While the limi-tation of one house per block was supposed to disperse concentrated vice zones, houses could still be clustered by strategic uses of corner lots.[26] While nothing in the regulations specified which neighborhoods a house could or could not be located in, the League investigator verified that "very often, in the better sections of the city, neighbors are apt to complain; therefore, the prostitutes are usually found in the localities where the poorer element resides."[27] Mapping addresses of homes and workplaces tied to the tmeim in legal records and the press con-firms that they were more dispersed in the 1920s than in the 1890s but still remained legibly connected to the central Jewish district.

In the 1920s, both legal and clandestine brothels were spread throughout the heavily Jewish area of Once. While certainly not a walled-in ghetto, the area outlined in figure 5.2 between the port and Pueyrredon, bordered on the north and south by Cordoba and Rivadavia, contained sections densely populated with enough Jews for Eugene Sofer to argue they "comprised a ghetto."[28] As can be seen in figures 5.1 and 5.2, throughout these initial decades of Jewish settlement, Jewish-run brothels and related dwellings were most densely clustered in the zone of greatest Jewish residential concentration.[29] Traces of the first Jewish settlement district near Plaza Lavalle, marked in figure 5.2 with a small vertical rectangle, remained in 1930, even as expanding Jewish settlement shifted westward. The greatest concentration of Jewish brothels and related domiciles can be seen still in the Jewish center of Once and the Seventh Police District headed by Alsogaray, marked in the larger vertical rectangle. The large vertical polygon outlines the main Jewish settlement district described by Sofer.

Figure 5.2 shows the same urban area as the 1895 map, highlighting the interactions between spaces of the tmeim and mainstream Jewish community institutions. The first Jewish settlement area, near Plaza Lavalle, where the majority of city's Ashkenazi Jews lived in 1895, has been marked to further highlight the continuity of concentration in the historically Jewish district.[30] Black symbols mark locations used as headquarters and meeting places by members of the Varsovia Society, with the mansion headquarters described in detail in chapter 4 visible on Avenue Córdoba on the far left of this map. Black circles show brothels run by Varsovia Society members and other Jews, and black diamonds mark associated residences, cafés, and cabarets, some of which may also have been used informally as brothels.[31]

Society members ran other businesses that may or may not have been connected to the sex industry. Roberto Arlt, literary chronicler of the Buenos Aires underworld, wrote in his column in *El Mundo* several weeks before the Varsovia Society arrests that he was once told by a pimp while walking down Once's main artery Avenue Corrientes that a shop selling fabrics and leather was simply a front for a more nefarious trade.[32] Society members Felipe Schon and Mauricio Caro ran a restaurant and, in union with other members, three cafés, a bar, and an inn.[33] Member Mauricio Lachman had cards and envelopes printed with the address of his women's handbag factory on upscale Santa Fe Avenue.[34] Cabaret Montmartre, discussed in Ezres Noshim records as a hangout for prostitutes, can be found just off of Avenue Corrientes near the port.[35]

The white star in figure 5.2 marks the symbolic center of Once, at Lavalle and Junin, which had been the location of the twenty registered brothels in 1895 with the largest concentration of registered prostitutes in the city, predominantly Jewish women. Other white markers locate important mainstream Jewish institutions, including Congregación Israelita, Temple Max Nordau, the Orthodox Polish Temple, the mikvah or ritual bath, the social center of the Union Israelita Argentina, and the headquarters of daily Yiddish newspapers *Di Prese* and *Di Yidishe Tsaytung*, as well as the Yiddish edition of socialist newspaper *La*

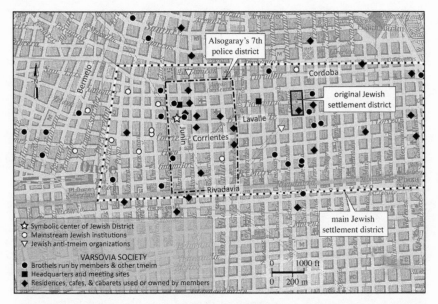

Figure 5.2. Brothels and tmeim residences in central Buenos Aires, late 1920s. Sources: "Juzgados de Instrucción: Número 3—Asociación Ilícita," *Gaceta del Foro* 15, no. 4729 (November 1, 1930): 1, 5–18, with others mentioned in Alsogaray, *Trilogía de la trata de blancas*, 46, 50; "Un tenebroso indagado hoy compro una casa al contado en novecientos mil pesos," *Crítica*, June 3, 1930, 8; "El gobierno debe limpiar al país de la verguenza de la trata de blancas," *Crítica*, September 17, 1930, 1; EN Letter Report 99, May 19, 1924, 454–472, EN box 2, IWO; EN Letter Report 140, p. 2, December 10, 1928, EN box 1, IWO; Letter Report 144, 45, February 5, 1929, EN box 1, IWO; Letter Report 144, 45, February 5, 1929, EN box 1, IWO; Letter Report 148, 84, 87, 97, 99, July 10, 1929, EN box 1, IWO; Letter Report 149, 127, 131–132, 137–138, September 4, 1929, EN box 1, IWO; *Memorias de la "Ezras Noschim" de Buenos Aires* (1936), 5, EN box 3, IWO, 17–21; "Codebook [to code used in Field Reports]," Field Reports on Investigation of International Traffic in Women and Children Made for the Special Body of Experts to Study the International Traffic in Women and Children, S171, League of Nations Archive, Geneva.

*Vanguardia* and Zionist organizations Poale Sion and the Argentine Zionist Federation.[36] White triangles denote the headquarters of Ezres Noshim and the homes of several individuals who worked closely with that organization.[37]

By comparing sets of black and white markers, the physical integration of the homes and brothels of the tmeim with the homes and businesses of those who attempted to ostracize them can be clearly seen through the late 1920s. A shift was under way in this period, though, as the center of gravity of Jewish settlement moved westward and became increasingly residential, while the concentration of brothels run by Jews and associated residences remained in the older areas of the city, as demonstrated in figure 5.3. Although some brothels can be

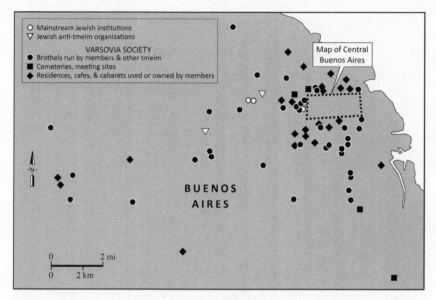

Figure 5.3. Jewish brothels and tmeim residences in Buenos Aires province, late 1920s.
Sources: Same as figure 5.2 and Eugene F. Sofer, *From Pale to Pampa: A Social History
of the Jews of Buenos Aires* (New York: Holmes and Meier, 1982), 73; Ricardo Feierstein,
*Historia de los judíos argentinos*, 3rd ed. (Buenos Aires: Galerna, 2006), 150. Address
for the National Association from a report related to a League of Nations investigation
by "the Committee on Trata de Mujeres y Ninas, July 1934 to Dec 1934," 7, 9, EN box 2,
IWO; "El gobierno debe limpiar al pais de la verguenza de la trata de blancas," *Crítica*,
September 17, 1930, 1.

seen along the main corridor of Corrientes moving to the west, the tmeim did
not appear to follow the westward shift toward Villa Crespo, where a quarter of
the city's Jews lived by 1936.[38] Almost half the members of the mainstream Ashkenazi burial society lived in Once in 1920 but only a third lived there in 1936, as
many upwardly mobile Jews moved away from the crowded downtown zone.[39]
Jewish residence patterns became increasingly suburban, but brothels and residences of the tmeim remained concentrated in more urban areas.

Figure 5.3 shows the entire city of Buenos Aires in this era, with the same black
and white markers as those listed for figure 5.2. The concentration of Jewish-run
brothels and associated residences in the central region of the city can be clearly
seen here, with a few in Flores and scattered along the outskirts of the city along
the boundary today marked by Avenue General Paz, as well as in the greater area
of Buenos Aires Province. The infamous cemetery of the Varsovia Society is
marked with a black square at the lower right corner of the map, with another
black square closer to the city's southern water boundary marking a 1921 address
for a Varsovia Society meeting place.[40] While several brothels remain in the

neighboring area of Barracas, which had been a previous center of prostitution, the only addresses in these data in La Boca itself are those of café Boston Bar and Cabaret Charleston, owned by Society members. When compared with the 1895 data on prostitution in La Boca, the conclusion can be drawn that Jewish prostitutes and brothel managers were less involved in La Boca throughout this period than in the central region of the city. La Boca and Barracas did have a sizeable Jewish population in the early migration period, particularly of Sephardi Jews, many of whom moved their homes to the suburb of Flores in the 1910s and 1920s. A few brothels can be found in Flores by 1930, close to the office of the Argentine National Association against the White Slave Trade.[41] Traces of both these settlements can be seen on this map, and some brothels were established in Flores and Barracas—a number of the latter were run by the last president of the Society, Simon Bruskevich or Zisman Zusman.[42] In general, the evolution of the geography of the Jewish sex industry followed both shifting municipal regulations and ethnic settlement patterns.

Overall, the 1895 and 1920s maps underscore the ongoing integration of the tmeim into the physical and symbolic heart of Jewish Buenos Aires, despite the efforts of certain community institutions to blot out this unwanted blemish. While loud claims of disavowal frequently roiled the Yiddish press and other community spaces, the continued power and visible presence of the tmeim also underscore the failure of moralizing community efforts to fully define acceptable community behavior.

## Separating the Impure

By the 1910 JAPGW international conference in London, not only were the Argentine tmeim a particular source of concern, but the British chief rabbi mentioned that Argentine "orthodox congregations boycott these people."[43] While this reference was slightly inaccurate, as there were not multiple Orthodox Jewish congregations in Argentina or even an ordained rabbi, leaders and members of both secular and religious budding Jewish institutions had loudly proclaimed their exclusion of the tmeim, from the foundation of the earliest organizations. One of the founders of an early community organization, the Society Obrera Israelita (Jewish Workers' Society), later reported that the term "worker" was used to distinguish its members from the tmeim.[44] When the main Ashkenazi Jewish burial society, the Chevrah Keduscha Ashkenazi, was founded, its statutes forbid the entry of the tmeim and their relatives, not only from becoming members but also from being buried in the cemetery, entering synagogues, and being treated in its clinics.[45] Denied access to other community institutions, the tmeim created their own but also held their ground in collective spaces such as the Yiddish theater. The insistence of the tmeim on Jewish identity fueled the self-defensive rage of their coreligionists. They needed other Jews around them, involved in communal life, in order to act as Jews. The central question of who got to claim Jewish identity in public space thus became a crucial point of contestation in the first decades of the twentieth century.

Burial as Jews was the biggest collective project after the establishment of the first synagogue, and the inclusion of the tmeim and their financial resources was a central point of debate. Before 1892 Jews could be buried only in the Dissidents' Cemetery, and after that time in the British section at the growing Chacarita cemetery.[46] Sephardi and Ashkenazi groups could not mutually agree on the terms of creating a private burial ground and they split into two camps, both of which were courted by the tmeim, who offered large sums of money, then in short supply.[47] The Ashkenazim had more numbers and financial resources and were able to refuse the tmeim's financial offers, but the Moroccan Jews decided to cooperate with the tmeim, and they together established the cemetery in Barracas al Sur, later the Buenos Aires suburb of Avellaneda, with a wall separating the tmeim from the Sephardi group.[48] This became the cornerstone of the 1906 legal formal foundation of the Varsovia Society as a Mutual Aid and Burial Society. One scholar attributes the location of the primary mainstream Ashkenazi Jewish burial ground far out in Liniers, at the southwestern edge of Buenos Aires Province, as due to the desire to maintain a clear distinction from the cemetery of the tmeim.[49] The effort to exclude prompted a counterforce: denied burial with the larger Jewish population, the tmeim made common cause with other marginalized Jews to build their own cemetery.

The boycott tactic extended beyond the capital city. In the same era, in the northern Argentine province of Tucuman, the local Jewish community punished a former sex worker who had come there from the capital. Although Malka Abraham had left prostitution and become a moneylender, struggling valiantly to be accepted by other Jews in her new home, they considered her money to be forever tainted, excluded her from collective events and spaces, or charged her three times what they charged others for participation in community activities. Finally, after death, she was buried in the cemetery's section for outcasts and suicides.[50] Her segregation in death symbolized the separation forced upon her in life. Despite her effort to leave her past behind, the rest of the community used her as a scapegoat, warning, and symbol of the "impure."

The tmeim's early visibility and central location in the Jewish street as well as relative wealth and power terrified other Jews who hoped to be clearly distinguished from this "shameful blemish."[51] The intensity of the need to powerfully separate drew on fears of migration restriction and antisemitism should all Jews be seen as involved or in collusion.[52] From the establishment of the Varsovia Society's cemetery, critics complained in Yiddish that it was a "plague" that would shape the opinions of non-Jews about Jews and damage future generations.[53] During the frenzy of press coverage during the 1930 trial, Yiddish newspaper *Di*

*Prese* complained that national Spanish-language daily *La Prensa* effectively blamed all prostitution on foreigners: "True, the suggestion could have been even worse, they could have suggested, and others have already done so, that all the arrested members of Migdal who are standing trial are Jews, even religious Jews with a synagogue and a charity and good deeds, and that would not be false, because they are indeed Jews and it couldn't be otherwise, because a Jewish association, and a religious one at that, cannot consist of non-Jews."[54] The question of the religious and national affiliations of the tmeim, particularly as the Varsovia Society, garnered additional attention, prompted complaints at local and international levels that members not be labeled as Jews, for fear that all Jews would be labeled as members.

In the months surrounding the 1930 court case, the local and international Jewish and non-Jewish press published hundreds of articles on the subject, which allow for a comparison of perspectives from inside and outside the local Jewish community.[55] Jewish community publications were far more likely to address this as a Jewish problem, though national papers often implied that traffickers were Jewish through foreign descriptors and use of names and clearly assumed readers knew the group identity of the Society's membership. Spanish-language Jewish newspapers touched on prostitution circumspectly if at all, as the reading audience could have been broader and the more assimilated, often higher-class earlier arrivals who read Spanish had different reputation concerns than later immigrants.[56] The two principal Yiddish daily newspapers took on an active role for years in the fight against the tmeim, with extensive editorials, publication of lists of names of suspected traffickers and pimps, meeting announcements, and criticism of Jewish outlets that did not take the same position, for example by advertising the legitimate side businesses of the tmeim.[57] These publications often presented Jewish women's vulnerability to trafficking as a metaphor for the vulnerability of the Jewish community at large to antisemitism, not far removed from European pogroms and the building xenophobia of the local nationalist movement. In positing the mainstream Jewish community as victimized by the Society, community organs tried to displace blame from Jews in general to Jews who were marginal to the collectivity. Thus they defended Jewish membership in the nation and made common cause with authorities who aided in the court case.

Like other mainstream Argentine Jewish organizations, Jewish newspapers played to a broader audience as they fought the association of Jews with immorality, pushed back against antisemitic generalizations, highlighted the role of other national groups in prostitution, and promoted images of productive, upstanding Jewish community members and institutions. Non-Jewish Argentine national and regional newspapers, on the other hand, while rarely veering into overt antisemitism, focused their coverage on the Society with such exclusivity and sensationalism that the Jewish foreigner became the sole apparent cause of immorality. The Jewish scapegoat could siphon off public outrage at the current economic and political crises and publicity promoting the police and official response could offset widespread accusations of corruption. Even as mainstream Jewish community institutions tried to leverage their decades-long opposition to the tmeim into broader acceptance, their very opposition increased the visibility of the tmeim as Jews, providing further fodder for the nativist movement. This story thus reflects continuity with long-standing nativist tensions and Jewish self-policing efforts as well as the moment's rise of xenophobic nationalism.

The Yiddish press joined other local Jewish community institutions in ostracizing the tmeim. The editor of the Yiddish-language daily *Di Yidishe Tsaytung*, who had published articles against the tmeim for over sixteen years, testified in the 1930 court case that "organizations dedicated to the protection of women . . . had always resisted undesirable contact with the Varsovia, either direct or indirect. . . . None were invited from the Varsovia by any of the Jewish institutions to participate in any action whatsoever; they were systematically excluded; moreover, all the institutions would safeguard themselves that members of the Varsovia should not even surreptitiously enter their places."[58] The Association Talmud Torah Max Nordau had a clause in its membership statues that potential members could not provoke the slightest suspicion regarding their moral conduct.[59] The Poilisher Farband shared this membership policy and claimed to return any donations sent by members of the infamous society.[60]

In the back-and-forth of this battle, "respectable" Jews claimed to score a victory against the tmeim over the name of their infamous Society. In 1927, Ezres Noshim's principal paid employee Selig Ganopol complained to the Polish government's representative in Buenos Aires that the society that bore the name of the Polish capital city constituted an insult to respectable immigrants. The ambassador from Poland launched a formal protest, arguing that the notoriety of the Varsovia Society was causing "offense to Polish national honor."[61] Ezres Noshim also lodged a protest in 1928 with the inspector responsible for legal societies, requesting that the organization's legal status be withdrawn as it was "a band of undesirables (pimps)."[62] The Varsovia Society was then legally dissolved, technically ceasing to exist. It did continue to run, however, under the new name Sociedad de Socorros Mutuos Sinagoga y Cementerio Zwi Migdal, the Zwi Migdal Mutual Aid, Synagogue, and Cemetery Society, and was from then on generally called the Zwi Migdal, though the name Varsovia also persisted.[63] Responsibility for dissolving the Varsovia Society was proudly advertised by the international JAPGW in its February 1928 report to the League of Nations' newly formed Traffic in Women and Children Committee: "A society of persons calling themselves the Jewish Warsaw Society, and alleged to be largely composed of traffickers, has been deprived of its rights of recognition on the

intervention of our Committee with the Polish Consul and the Argentine Government."[64] Although the Varsovia members continued their activity as a legal
association under a new name, the JAPGW's celebration of this symbolic dis-
sociation from the Ashkenazi Jewish community's homeland echoed the logic
of the boycott: if organized Jewish prostitution could not be stopped, at least its
perpetrators could be publicly separated.

Concern with the link between the Varsovia Society's name and the city of
Warsaw re-emerged with the 1930 court case and reached beyond the Jewish
community. On May 24, 1930, *Crítica* published an exclusive interview with
Polish ambassador Ladislao Mazurkievicz and visiting diplomat Michael Pankiewicz, who had arrived several days earlier to study Polish-Argentine immigration. This piece interweaves discussion of the Varsovia Society with a broader
conversation about migration from Poland to Argentina. While probably not
specifically sent by the Polish government to address the nation's connection to
prostitution, as the timing of his arrival was too close to the beginning of the
arrests, the two diplomats took advantage of the opportunity to argue in the
popular press for Poland's innocence in the white slave trade and to lobby for
an increase in the Polish immigration quota. Mazurkievicz begins the interview
by attempting to deflect focus from both Argentina and Poland, pointing out
that all counties suffer from the scourge of white slavery at one time or another.
The two men both compliment Argentina's greatness, beauty, and progressiveness,
and Pankiewicz couches his criticism of the current cap on Polish immigrants
at three hundred per month in a larger paean to the possibilities of continuing
economic growth through rural colonization, a project for which the Polish
migrant, "made for rural labor," is a perfect candidate.[65]

This lobbying project takes on particular urgency in response to the possible
contamination of the Polish reputation by association with the Varsovia Society. Mazurkievicz points out that Argentine authorities have long received his
denunciations and those of local Polish national societies and organs pointing
out that the Varsovia was not truly a mutual aid society but a center of delin-
quents. He also underscores the jubilation of the entire Polish community in
Argentina at the action begun by Judge Ocampo and promotes the national
engagement of the Polish collectivity, which is ready to collaborate with "enthusiasm and patriotism."[66] Like the "respectable" Jewish organizations and Yiddish
press, these Polish authorities argued for their integration into and attachment
to Argentina and differentiated themselves from the undesirables as deserving
ongoing or expanded immigration into the country. Many interested parties
thus worried about the pervasive identification of the polaca as a prostitute and
worked to publicly distinguish themselves from the tmeim.

Within Jewish community institutions, the battle against the tmeim was
exploited by leaders who hoped to increase the centralization of the Argentine
Jewish community.[67] Ezres Noshim tried to take on a leadership role in the entire

collectivity during and after the court case, reaching out through the Yiddish press and other avenues to all of the other organizations for joint meetings as the arrests of Society members escalated.[68] Acting vice-president Elena R. de Aslan testified in the 1930 court case that fifty-two local cultural and benevolent societies supported its work, "which comprise as members nearly all the honest and industrious Jews of Buenos Aires," and had jointly thanked Ezres Noshim on May 25, 1930, for the organization's leadership in bringing the Society to justice.[69] Ezres Noshim worked particularly closely with Soprotimis, the Society for the Protection of Jewish Immigrants, and often cooperated on requests from Eastern Europe to find missing relatives and shared information on the morality of suspicious new arrivals.[70] Soprotimis also often contributed to Ezres Noshim's coffers and was listed on Ezres Noshim's letterhead.[71] In April 1930, before the Varsovia court case generated widespread publicity for Ezres Noshim, the other organizations listed as close local collaborators on Ezres Noshim's letterhead were Congregación Israelita de la República Argentina; Chevrah Keduscha Ashkenazi, the main Ashkenazi burial society; Sociedad de Beneficencia de Damas Israelitas, the Jewish women's charity organization; and Sociedad de Beneficencia Ezrah, the "Ezrah" charity society.

As these organizations evolved over time, so too did their connection with Ezres Noshim. In 1944, Ezres Noshim continued to receive donations from Ezrah, the Sociedad de Beneficencia, and the Chevrah Keduscha, whose restructuring had resulted in a name change to Asociación Mutual Israelita Argentina (AMIA). AMIA by this time had become Ezres Noshim's major local donor, contributing nearly half of its 1944 income.[72] New contributors included the Jewish Union from Galitzia and three charity organizations predominantly geared toward children. Both the Israelite Congregation and the Paso Temple collected donations for Ezres Noshim at their 1944 High Holiday services, as did several Jewish neighborhood associations.[73] This network of connections suggests that Ezres Noshim could draw on relationships with many institutions in the Buenos Aires Jewish community. But common cause against the tmeim could not totally erase differences among Jewish organizations. Although multiple Jewish institutions got involved in the boycott against the tmeim over the decades, they appear to have resisted the leadership efforts of Ezres Noshim, never completely centralizing around this issue. The entire community did not support Ezres Noshim's particular moralizing vision and tactics.

## Preserving the Jewish Future from Degeneration

Ezres Noshim's day-to-day gatekeeping work took place in the busy Buenos Aires port. As passenger ships arrived at the dock, the organization's inspector intercepted young women, particularly minors, who appeared to be traveling alone or in suspicious company.[74] If arriving women had friends or relatives to meet, the inspector tried to ensure that these individuals were indeed who they claimed to be and not madams or pimps engaged in subterfuge. Depending on current immigration laws and the agency's shifting relationship with Argentine authorities, the inspector was in some periods allowed to go on board steamships before the passengers disembarked. Ezres Noshim reported interactions with hundreds of women each year, who were then escorted to meetings with friends or relatives or to the Immigrants' Hotel, where aid in securing employment and lodgings was provided.[75] Dock work was central to the Gentlemen's Committee's original vision of the agency's undertakings in Buenos Aires, which imagined in 1900 that "traffickers would be arrested in the docks and houses of ill-fame entered by the Police, accompanied by [our inspector]."[76] In reality, successful interventions in actual trafficking occurred in relatively few cases: in 1925, out of 450 interactions with women at the docks, the JAPGW inspector intercepted only four women headed into "the hands of people known to be undesirable, who had gained their confidence."[77] Dock inspectors demonstrated to new arrivals the community's concern with protecting young women and intervened in the meetings of migrants with other Jews, attempting to ensure that they did not interact with the undesirables and thus join their ranks.

Ezres Noshim's monitoring of community morality centered on physical mobility and marriage. The organization mediated between prospective husbands and newly arriving immigrant brides. These women would generally be housed in the Immigrants' Hotel until the moment of marriage. Eager prospective husbands would often go to the Ezres Noshim office in hopes of preventing their fiancées from staying in the Immigrants' Hotel longer than strictly necessary. Ezres Noshim also answered requests from various parties, including the Polish Consulate and the Montevideo branch of the JAPGW, about the moral antecedents of individuals wishing to travel, which they would investigate to determine if those named were of satisfactory morality.[78]

Jurisdictional tensions appear to have existed between Ezres Noshim and the National Vigilance Association (NVA), a British antitrafficking organization tied to the IBSTW—the NVA was basically the British national counterpart of the international organization, but the two could be conflated, as in sources that referred to employees posted internationally as belonging to the NVA. The organization's local secretary and dock worker Rosalie Lighton Robinson first arrived in Buenos Aires from England in October 1913 after a visit from NVA's founder William Alexander Coote and arranged with immigration authorities to board arriving steamships and intervene with women traveling alone.[79] In a letter to NVA secretary Frederick Sempkins sixteen years later, Robinson claimed that while the Jewish Society, meaning Ezres Noshim, was established in the area much earlier, the IBSTW was responsible for initiating work at the port, one of several areas of dispute between the two organizations. In 1925, changes in customs regulations caused the termination of all such onboard inspections, and while Ezres Noshim's onboard inspections were restored the following year, the inspectors of non-Jewish societies were not allowed to resume these operations.[80] Dr. Samuel Halphon, the Argentine Chief Rabbi, served as president of Ezres Noshim in the 1920s, and his personal interventions with Argentine authorities were credited with the restoration of Ezres Noshim's onboard inspections.[81] These interactions with the state suggest that Argentine authorities viewed the entry of new prostitutes as a particularly Jewish problem and also underscore the popular disagreement around the work done by these rescue organizations.

Ezres Noshim made implicit moral judgments of the women it worked to save, which can be read as evidence for a particular vision of ideal family structure and sexual behavior. The organization's responses often reflected the language and assumptions of the evolving field of criminology as it influenced Argentine legal and penal thought and seeped into popular culture.[82] One strand of this thought, inspired by the extreme hereditarianism of late nineteenth-century Italian criminologists Cesare Lombroso and William Ferrero, who were particularly influential in Argentina, argued that the physical characteristics of criminals could be passed along with their antisocial behaviors from one generation to the next.[83] Acquired characteristics could be inherited, creating new generations "born to crime." In language popularized on both sides of the Atlantic by Max Nordau, the "degeneration" of subsequent generations thus caused increasing criminal behavior. The purpose of reform and punishment became the protection of society at large rather than punishment of guilty individuals.[84] Boycott tactics against the tmeim echoed the effort to segregate social contagion and the language of degeneration entered Ezres Noshim's assessments of particular women involved in sex work. Although much of the broader field of eugenic thought emerged from racist and antisemitic principles, eugenic ideas could be found across the political spectrum, harnessed to a broad range of causes.[85]

Analyses of female criminality centered on the prostitute as archetype of the moral degeneration of the female. According to these theories, women were responsible for both the biological and moral propagation of the species, shaping the nation's future citizens.[86] Because maternity represented the apogee of female function, the very existence of the prostitute mother became something of a worst case in this intellectual schema. Lombroso and Ferrero wrote in *The Female Offender* that the exaggerated sensuality of prostitutes destroyed the "spirit of self-abnegation inseparable from the maternal function."[87] Prostitutes' embodiment of women's degeneration clashed with the idealization of motherhood as its opposite. Prostitute mothers would threaten future generations with their degenerative influence.[88]

Concern with the moral purity of future generations of Argentine Jews motivated Ezres Noshim's response to prostitute mothers. While some of the cases in their records describe fallen but salvageable women, most prostitute mothers emerge as beyond reform, dangerous to their children and the broader community and its future: "Fortunately, the number of prostituted mothers is very small compared to those who have not established homes. The fall of the former is much deeper and is the prototype of a complete degeneration. The responsibility assumed by a prostitute mother is much more serious than that of a single woman, because with the desecration of her own home, she violates the sacred principles of family, sowing the seed of evil in the breasts of her relatives."[89] Ezres Noshim thus distinguished between prostitutes with and without children, placing blame for the degeneration of future generations on these unfit mothers.

Although Lombrosian criminology emphasized the influence of heredity, other lines of thought supported environmental change as a remedy. The only hope of preventing the seeds of evil sown by prostitute mothers from being reaped by their deviant offspring was to remove the source of contagion, taking children away from unfit mothers. Frustrated with its lack of legal leverage, Ezres Noshim employed tactics that often included Jewish community pressure and bringing in family members whom the group "believed [it] could use as effective auxiliaries."[90] In one case, Ezres Noshim asked relatives to pressure a mother whose hairdresser husband, it was noted, was not the cause of her descent into prostitution; instead, she drew him into becoming her pimp. This placed her outside of the standard narrative of male seduction and exploitation and gave her the responsibility for endangering their children. Ezres Noshim threatened the couple with removing their legal custody over their children and the husband with expulsion from the country. In another case, Ezres Noshim wrote a letter in support of a man's 1931 petition to the Defender of Minors to take custody of a fourteen-year-old girl whose mother was reportedly a procuress.[91]

The distinction between prostitution and any female sexual activity outside of marriage was often blurred, and women who pursued extramarital sexual activities were pathologized and deemed beyond hope of rehabilitation. Ezres Noshim describes one such case as an example of "sexual pathology, as one of the causes in which prostitution originates."[92] This wayward young woman lost her mother in Krakow at an early age, by which time her father had already immigrated to Buenos Aires, and she was left in the care of other relatives. When she turned eighteen, her father brought her to Buenos Aires, at which point Ezres Noshim became involved as it had to give permission for the minor to disembark.[93] Father and daughter soon came into conflict around her choice of friends, and he turned to Ezres Noshim for help. Despite initial skepticism, the Ezres Noshim office verified that "the young woman was currently living a disorderly or wild life, maintaining relations with various men."[94] She was summoned to the office and told in no uncertain terms that "because she was still a minor, this was sufficient to deprive her of her liberty, imprisoning her in some establishment," although Ezres Noshim privately admitted this threat to be empty due to lack of actual legal leverage.[95] The association's prognosis for her future was poor: she continued to hold down a factory job, which suggested that her sexual licentiousness was driven by sensual rather than material need—although critics often linked women's factory labor to sexual promiscuity and other negative social outcomes.[96] Ezres Noshim placed her under the charge of a family who controlled her activities, but noted that "given her morbid character there is not much hope that she can be regenerated [*regenerarse*: the opposite of degeneration], as it is possible that in the face of such restriction on her movements she could disappear entirely into a life of shame."[97] A similar young woman rebelling against a strict aunt began to spend time "in certain circles of friends with depraved morals, in which sensuality dominated. . . . [She soon] initiated her sexual life and within a year she changed lovers twice."[98] She was also diagnosed as beyond hope of redemption.

Some women who themselves sought protection at Ezres Noshim's office were denied it on the basis of a judgment of sexual pathology. In 1936, several women came to the organization claiming persecution by individuals coercing them into prostitution. Ezres Noshim staff interpreted them as "sick women, generally young girls, [with] complaints against imaginary enemies, soliciting our protection . . . who suffered from persecution mania, particularly concentrated all their fears around the existence of evil-minded individuals who sought to seize them and deliver them by violent means to a dissolute life. According to medical opinion, these failures of their mental functions had a probable sexual cause."[99] Ironically, "evil-minded individuals who sought to . . . deliver [women] by violent means to a dissolute life" was the basic definition of white slavery, which had preoccupied the organization for decades. But after the 1930 court case, Ezres Noshim assumed that the existence of these individuals was evidence of a delusion and that white slavery would no longer be a substantial threat to Jewish women. A certain distrust of women's evidence comes through in these cases, connected to the stigmatization of women's sexuality.

Although motherhood could not provide a sure exit route from the moral degradation of prostitution, maternity could sometimes be a way out, if connected to desirable behavior and salvaged by marriage. In some cases, prostitute mothers' maternal feelings could signal the probability of rehabilitation. One young single mother, who had been seduced and abandoned when pregnant, was judged redeemable even though she had begun "relating freely with men, without considering the consequences, until her degradation was complete."[100] In this situation, however, perhaps because she had been the victim of a predatory man, Ezres Noshim assessed that she might be saved if "she met a man who would take an interest in pulling her out of the mud, in order to make her his wife."[101] Sometimes, although under unpredictable logic, a male savior and the legitimacy of marriage could rehabilitate certain fallen women. The variability in Ezres Noshim's responses suggests the improvised nature of the line between purity and impurity.

## Marriage and Morality Certificates

In 1931, in the wake of its successful campaign against the Varsovia Society, Ezres Noshim harnessed its community influence to promote the creation of new Jewish family units: in order to conduct a Jewish marriage, many local officiants would require an Ezres Noshim–authorized certificate of morality for both bride and groom.[102] Concerned with its reputation, much of the mainstream Jewish community granted the organization jurisdiction to investigate and certify individuals' moral character and to block certain undesirable unions from taking place. Ezres Noshim's 1936 revision of its regulations on religious weddings called for the following: no religious weddings could take place without permission granted by Ezres Noshim; both bride and groom must report to the Ezres Noshim office for investigation twenty days before the wedding, or two months if minors or lacking close relatives in Argentina and there for less than six years; names of bride and groom would be published in the newspaper ten days before the wedding; and all officiants must be specifically examined and licensed by Ezres Noshim and have a permit from the organization for that particular wedding.[103] Newly arriving women were marked as still under particular risk. Investigations became required for brides being newly called from Eastern Europe, who would be married under observation before leaving the port. Documents sent to Eastern Europe to be filled out by the prospective bride and her family included a warning letter from Ezres Noshim in Yiddish urging that caution be exercised in responding to overseas suitors, as young women could easily be entrapped by men of dubious character.[104] The morality certificate also became necessary for relatives to bring minor children to the country. Ezres Noshim thus broadened its function beyond antiprostitution work to become gatekeeper of the family structure of the Buenos Aires Jewish community, to guarantee a pure future generation, free of the lingering taint of the tmeim.

The requirements for issuance of the morality certificates indicated that Ezres Noshim's primary concern was severing any possible connections to the tmeim. The data requested for the groom's application implied an investigation of social stability. Connection to business was emphasized, through both his employment history and references from respectable businessmen. Some requests were rejected despite references.[105] Questions about Argentine residence, references from other local Jews, and membership in associations underscored the importance of connection to the proper elements of the mainstream Jewish community. Prospective brides had less to prove beyond the relationship to the prospective groom and names of other relatives in Argentina. The primary concern thus seemed to be whether the groom was a known pimp or trafficker.

By the 1930s, oversight of Jewish marriage replaced the fight against prostitution as the predominant concern of Ezres Noshim. In 1932, out of the 1,209 total cases that Ezres Noshim reported to the JAPGW London office, over half related directly to the regulation of Jewish marriage. By far the largest single category was 343 cases of questionable religious marriage, in which Ezres Noshim urged civil as well as religious commitment. Other categories of Ezres Noshim's work included policing disembarkation of minors and prospective brides, prevention of illegal marriage, reconciliation of married couples, religious divorce, and bigamy. The organization often made determinations that would have been handed down by religious authorities in Eastern Europe. Only 89 cases were identified as specifically dealing with prostitution or white slavery.[106] Similar numbers were reported in 1935, with over half of the specified cases connected to marriage or divorce. Out of 1,372 total cases, only 46 port inspections were reported and no cases of white slavery or prostitution were specified, a major shift from the organization's emphasis in earlier decades.[107] For comparison, in 1926, at the peak of the Varsovia Society's strength, Ezres Noshim reported that its inspector met and interrogated 774 young women at the docks who were "either unaccompanied or in doubtful company."[108]

This shift in focus also reflected decreasing migratory flow. Increasing immigration restrictions during the Argentine military dictatorship of the 1930s sharply curtailed the entry of single women claiming to be heading for marriage. Under these regulations, the contractual legal commitment would have to be carried out as soon as the immigrant arrived, with the marriage often taking place at the dock.[109] In 1936, Ezres Noshim verified that the Directorate of Immigration was under orders to strictly enforce this requirement and "make any immigrant return to their native country whose legal commitment [marriage] cannot be immediately realized; in anticipation of which the authorities require the bride to deposit a return ticket at the Argentine Consulate."[110] Ezres Noshim implicitly criticized this policy, noting the ease with such an engagement might be broken or how the bride might be forced to comply with an undesired marriage contract.[111] Ezres Noshim complained that this problem was compounded by Argentina's lack of a civil divorce law: "The amoral situation in which these young women fall into, due to the duplication of their single and married status, can only be resolved through their religious union with another man, which would be equivalent from a legal perspective to concubinage, as no civil divorce law exists in the country."[112] Ezres Noshim, therefore, began to work together with the Polish Consulate and Soprotimis to verify the morality of the groom and the form in which the engagement was contracted.[113]

As in Ezres Noshim's earlier years, bigamy was a major concern, and the organization worked to bring preexisting spouses and families from Europe to discourage men from making illegal second marriages in Argentina. In 1934, Ezres Noshim identified four cases of bigamy and attempted "to normalize the material and legal situation of the original families."[114] The organization often facilitated financial support of spouses still in Eastern Europe and routinely ran announcements in the Argentine Jewish press searching for individuals declared missing by relatives in Eastern Europe.[115] By the mid-1940s, much of its work involved mediating alimony payments to support the children of separated immigrant parents, sometimes justifying the use of coercive techniques to ensure payment by arguing that the local legal system failed to address such situations.[116]

Ezres Noshim granted morality certificates to the majority of couples who requested them. The group's report to London headquarters for the first half of 1934 stated that out of 119 requests, 27 morality certificates were denied based on "lack of sufficient data, verification of [preexisting] married civil status, doubtful morality, or for the couple's resistance to obtaining the obligatory Civil Registry identification card."[117] In 1935 Ezres Noshim rejected one out of 49 applicants.[118] In 1936 the organization gave out 211 morality certificates, many for husbands attempting to bring already established families to join them, to whom Ezres Noshim gave "for obvious reasons . . . preferential attention," and rejected six applications based on "the applicants' lack of moral responsibility."[119] These data show the organization's preference for marriages already established in Eastern Europe, granting precedence to existing formal relationships over newer ones.

Ezres Noshim was not the only Argentine Jewish community organization to issue morality certificates, although it alone focused on marriage. The large and powerful Poilisher Farband cooperated with the Polish ambassador Mazurkievicz "to show that no person had been given consideration at the Consulate unless he presented a card signed by the Union of Polish Jews [Poilisher Farband], testifying to the perfect morality of the bearer."[120] Ezres Noshim seems to have engaged in something of a territorial dispute with the larger Farband, which also claimed to have been founded at least in part to combat the tmeim, and open conflict developed between late 1931 and late 1933, when Ezres Noshim's power had increased.[121] The Farband accused Ezres Noshim's employee Ganopol of condescending to clients, being physically violent, taking actions in secret, and generally acting "as if someone had appointed him guardian of our morality."[122] This conflict reflects broader tensions around community leadership and representation. Various parties thus competed to articulate the local Jewish community's values and community boundaries: who would be included and excluded, elevated and punished.

## BATTLE FOR THE YIDDISH THEATER

The Yiddish theater was the site of particularly open conflict on the issue of visibility throughout this period. Pimps provided financial backing and enthusiastic audiences for Yiddish theatrical productions.[123] Boxes and balconies in Buenos Aires theaters served as sites of solicitation and assignation. Manuel

Galvez's memoirs discussed the 1908 Buenos Aires street protests that erupted after Jews threw some recognized tmeim out of the Yiddish theater during a production that showed a woman seduced by a Jewish trafficker.[124] Also in 1908, Gerardo Bra reports that in the middle of Yiddish theatrical performances the audience might loudly turn on the "unclean" element, yelling "Out with the pimps!"[125] This increase in popular dissatisfaction seems to have been inspired by that year's changes in Buenos Aires municipal regulations, which briefly increased the power of pimps and madams, who could locate brothels anywhere in the city and on side streets in the downtown center, without restrictions on the number of sex workers.[126]

According to later references, "decent families" won the 1908 round, but by the 1920s the Argentine Yiddish press complained that the tmeim had taken over the theaters once again.[127] A group of Jewish workers complained that the "cast-outs disguised as people" had retaken the "temple of art," tricking honest workers into seeing "supposedly progressive plays" performed in ways that would have caused great playwrights to rise from the grave and fight back.[128] The Buenos Aires Yiddish theater Noah's Ark was critiqued as "a nest for all sorts of animals ... where prostitution and debauchery occupy the place of honor," where "honest Jewish women and girls sit side by side with white flesh traders, with street walkers in furs and made-up beauties."[129] Again, "respectable" Jews worried about being confused by non-Jews with the tmeim: that "on going in and out of the theater all Jews must be taken for woman traffickers, all Jewish women as sellers of honor, by the Christian neighbors standing nearby."[130] Another long-held fear was that young Jewish women and men would be tempted into either providing or purchasing sex. Women's poverty would become even less bearable, as "the awful question must nag at every innocent Jewish girl: why? Why do they sit in gold and diamonds, happy and cute, winking and batting, and I must go in a plain dress?" Two temptations threatened young men: "the test to see if a lady of the night won't lead him into filth, and if a pimp won't tempt him with his easy life."[131] These fears, of internal temptation and external reputation, echoed throughout the decades of community boycott. The suggested response was the boycott of these similar theaters, until owners threw out the tmeim.

Like New York concert saloons, these sites were not solely of the underworld; working-class families with children came for low-cost entertainment and might or might not have resented the mixed clientele.[132] Protection of children and families and the defense of clean leisure opportunities for "respectable" Jews thus justified boycott strategies. In the 1920s, the Excelsior Theater, the most prominent Yiddish theater in Buenos Aires, issued multicolored advertising posters that warned in Spanish, "Highly moral shows for families. The establishment reserves the right [to refuse] admission," and in Yiddish, "Tmeim are forbidden to enter."[133] The difference in the text printed in Spanish and Yiddish highlights the way in which the term "tmeim" served as an in-group code, while the Spanish that could be read by outsiders was more ambiguous. The president of the Chevra Keduscha described this tactic during the 1930 court case as blocking the tmeim from accessing "the rooms of theaters so that their children should not see them."[134]

The tmeim fought back: the intensity of the tmeim's protest against the 1927 production of Leib Malach's *Ibergus* (Regeneration), which criticized the local traffic in Jewish women, drove the author out of Buenos Aires to Paris, where he soon died.[135] And some Jews involved in creating these theatrical productions complained about the boycott. One group reacted to the defense of *Ibergus*, boycott of theaters, and campaign of *Di Prese* by accusing the tmeim's opponents of old-fashioned superstition and hypocritical morality.[136] Such resistance to the boycott was overcome by the dissolution of the Varsovia Society. After the court case, productions such as Isadore Solotarevsky's antitrafficking melodrama *Di vayse shklavin* (The white slaves), featuring international Yiddish theatrical stars Stella Adler and Samuel Goldenberg, could run without protest.[137] However, although "respectable" Jews won back the Yiddish theater, by this time its peak as a form of entertainment had passed.[138] Memory of the tmeim's presence in the theater persisted in the Jewish world for decades: in Isaac Bashevis Singer's 1968 short story "The Colony," published in *Commentary*, characters discuss the conflict between Argentine Jewish leaders and the tmeim, and the leverage that the "impure" had in the Yiddish theater to halt the production of plays they didn't like.[139]

Onstage and off, in Yiddish theaters and newspapers, at the doors of Jewish community institutions and in the streets, sex workers and managers flaunted their wealth, sexuality, and identity as Jews, while evolving boycott tactics tried to reduce their visibility and possible conflation with all Jews. Jewish community leaders often responded with anxiety to modern developments, as Ashkenazim lived increasingly urban and secular lives on both sides of the Atlantic. While the new immigrant population in Buenos Aires grew large enough to create institutions, many of its leaders sought to draw bright lines between respectable and disreputable Jews. Policing women's morals, in particular, became a priority. The reputational attack on Jewish honor was made even more extreme by the traditional ascription of women as the repositories of communal honor.[140] Ezres Noshim's engagement with prostitutes who were also mothers highlighted the moral policing intrinsic to its work, as some women could be rehabilitated, while others judged irredeemable threatened future Jewish generations with hereditary degeneration. The community was not entirely united, however, in its moral concerns. While some loudly proclaimed themselves to speak for all other "pure" Jews in holding a bright line against the "impure," others resented these efforts. Yiddish newspapers and other organizations pushed back against the tmeim in various ways, but did not appear to accede to the leadership efforts of Ezres Noshim until after the legal defeat of the Varsovia Society, if then.

Even after Jewish involvement in prostitution waned, Ezres Noshim continued to work against possible immorality in the Jewish community, trying to
protect future generations from stigma through the regulation of marriage.
Contaminated future generations would be beyond redemption and could, like
the tmeim, clamor for inclusion in the Jewish community. Therefore, morality
certificates issued to prospective Jewish immigrants and spouses beginning in
1931 reflected an effort to consolidate religious authority over sexual morality.
Although Ezres Noshim moved away from antiprostitution work in the 1930s,
its concerns continued to center on women's appropriate sexuality and on the
policing of the community's moral boundaries, defending the Jewish community's future by monitoring how it would grow through immigration and procreation. While many Jewish neighbors fought and boycotted the tmeim, sometimes
through cooperating in community institutions, others resented the control-
ling moral efforts of self-styled leaders. After the flare-up of Jewish prostitution's increased visibility with the 1930 court case, nativist military rule of the
1930s suppressed public conversations in Yiddish and prostitution was driven
further underground and no longer disproportionally involved Jews. Even as big-
ger concerns came to dominate Argentine Jewry in the 1930s, the community's
formation, like that of the tango, had been fundamentally shaped by the brothels of Buenos Aires.

# Conclusion

## AFTER THE VARSOVIA SOCIETY

Raquel Liberman and Julio Alsogaray faced 120 Varsovia Society members in Judge Ocampo's courtroom two years after her denunciation. The rehabilitated prostitute and principled police commissioner presented stories of multiple exploited women, and with the help of the two Buenos Aires Yiddish daily newspapers and dozens of Jewish community groups, thousands of pages of supporting evidence were presented against the tmeim. The trial was widely reported to be the end of organized prostitution in Buenos Aires. Three months after this trial, on September 6, 1930, a military coup launched the "Infamous Decade" of military rule, which would continue in various forms for the next half century. Prostitution was discouraged along with other forms of social disorder and immorality, and brothels were outlawed in 1936. Although the arrested members of the Varsovia Society were released after only eight months, many left the country, with their right of re-entry canceled, and the Society ceased to exist.[1] The "respectable" Jews of Buenos Aires built on their victory to preserve their good reputation for future generations.

Most historians of Argentine Jewry and sex work describe Alsogaray as he presented himself in his 1933 memoir that narrated his battle against the Varsovia Society, as a dedicated and incorruptible police officer devoted to a lifelong battle against both the internal enemy of corruption and the external enemy, best represented by the Jewish trafficker in women.[2] Both older and more recent works have described him as "a man of courage and integrity" and "a sober, conservative professional . . . careful, but he was also passionate, a man obsessed with cleaning up the crime and corruption that dominated his beloved country."[3] A more critical response associates him with a xenophobic social tendency in Argentina that preferred to hold immigrant Jews responsible for the high levels of prostitution rather than blame corrupt officials.[4] This criticism could be pushed even further, given that Alsogaray ignored the involvement of other ethnic groups in Argentine prostitution. He associated Jews with trafficking to such an extent that if a reader consulted only his account, it would appear Jews were solely responsible for the trade. Although the organization cooperated with him during the court case, Ezres Noshim responded defensively to his memoir's characterization of Argentine prostitution as predominantly run by Jews and refuted his claims with its own statistics.[5]

Alsogaray frequently nodded toward this cooperative relationship during his court testimony and memoir, by distinguishing "good sons of Israel" from those involved in prostitution.[6] However, Alsogaray blamed all of the Buenos Aires central zone's prostitution on the Varsovia Society and described its members in inherently antisemitic language.[7] Unlike pimps of other nationalities, whom he characterized as extravagant and generous, the Varsovia's members in his account were "consumed with the fever to possess more and more money, which they give away only in order to gain the complicity of a third party."[8] He introduced the entire saga of his fight against the Varsovia with a chapter called "The Hebrew People," grounding his analysis of the pimps' society in their Jewish background and noting "essential characteristics" that continued to mark even assimilated Jews.[9] Alsogaray's "essential characteristics" map onto common antisemitic tropes: the pimp is the most cowardly of all criminals, avoiding action that might compromise his physical safety; he is driven only by obsession with money, for which he doesn't work, but feeds off of the women he exploits; he lacks firmness and masculinity.[10] No rehabilitation is possible—the pimp's psychic makeup makes deportation the only solution to this social problem.[11] This call for deportation might have terrified "respectable" Jews earlier, but by then the Varsovia Society had been vanquished and the project of distancing the "good sons of Israel" from the "impure" was well under way.

Alsogaray's leadership role against Jewish immorality served him well in this moment of nationalist and xenophobic consolidation. The day after the military coup, the front page of the Buenos Aires Yiddish press broadcast Alsogaray's promotion to commissioner of order, second in command of the entire capital police force.[12] His central role in dismantling the Varsovia Society was heavily broadcast, as were his related efforts to uproot corruption among the police and in the legal system.[13] In presenting a long report on the Varsovia Society case to his new boss a few days later, Alsogaray made the connection between the Society's power and rampant bribery among local police, corrupt lawyers, and other systemic failures, which presumably the new government could uproot.[14] It would not have damaged Alsogaray's career that the corruption he uncovered could be blamed on the Jews. A month after his promotion, he was honored with an event in the Plaza Hotel, attended by police and political luminaries, where he was credited with cleaning up the rabble-rousing leftist elements in his predominantly Jewish district.[15] Alsogaray's ascension was short-lived, however, and he resigned from his new post on December 4, 1930, allegedly in protest of the new government's failures to seriously attack corruption.[16] His rapid promotion and fall could also be understood as part of what Lila Caimari has dubbed an "internal purge" of anyone possibly disloyal to the new government.[17]

Before the coup, political and economic unrest provoked new strategies of order, culminating in the military takeover. The particular timing of Raquel Liberman's denunciation of the Varsovia Society may have contributed to its eventual success at bringing legal proceedings—nearly two years passed between Liberman's appearance in Alsogaray's office and the arrests targeting Society members, perhaps awaiting a more opportune moment as well as additional evidence. In the wake of the worldwide economic collapse, Argentine political authorities struggled to maintain popular legitimacy. Taking down the Varsovia Society in 1930 served multiple interests. Police and other officials had a reputation for bribery, corruption, and inefficacy, which the public success and power of the Society had highlighted. The Buenos Aires police force responded in the 1920s and 1930s to public complaints about police inefficacy with efforts to professionalize.[18] The police raids against the Varsovia Society may have been part of this trend, responding to the blame antiprostitution critics levied at corrupt police. Newspapers broadcasted the cooperation of capital and provincial police with Ocampo's court, suggesting that the system might still be redeemable.

"The good sons of Israel" did get some credit for the dissolution of the Varsovia Society. As international publicity sensationalized the late-night arrest sweeps, the *New York Times* credited Ezres Noshim and specifically Argentine chief rabbi Dr. Samuel Halphon: "It was largely due to his untiring efforts over a long period that an international white slave organization was broken up, at least as far as its Argentine operations are concerned."[19] However, despite the cooperation of "respectable" Jews in the court case and decades of efforts to distinguish themselves from the tmeim, press coverage of the court case often underscored the Society's Jewishness. The Buenos Aires English-language newspaper, oriented toward the business community, reported in its story on members' acquittal that "the records of the society show that it devoted a good deal of attention to the maintenance of the Jewish faith, to the assistance of poor Jews, and to the administration of a burial ground."[20]

It was an ambiguous victory. While the court found that some individual members may indeed have been white slave traffickers, no victims had come forward to substantiate the original charges and no evidence proved that the Society itself operated in the white slave market or that all its members were thus involved. Despite the coordinated arrest efforts, which targeted addresses in multiple districts simultaneously, most of the 424 Society members sought by police had escaped before arrest, many disappearing shortly before police knocked on their doors. Frustrated IBSTW employee Rosalie Lighton Robinson expressed her bitterness about the lack of resolution to the case, writing in an attempt to resign her post in January 1931, "You see the whole affair has fizzled out, and nothing at all has been done!"[21] She was convinced to carry on her work, and "respectable" Jews kept up the fight against the attachment of immorality to Jewishness.[22]

Despite Alsogaray's reflexive antisemitism, at least some members of the "respectable" Argentine Jewish community had already established a strategic cooperative relationship with him by the time of the 1930 court case. In early 1927, a year after Alsogaray's appointment to head the Seventh Police District, the zone's Jewish residents celebrated his work cleaning up prostitution with a champagne lunch and presented him with an album emblazoned with his face in gold.[23] While the police often reflected antisemitic and nationalist tendencies, sometimes their agendas intersected with those of marginal groups. Jews not connected to prostitution encouraged efforts to improve the reputation of the local system of law and order.[24] The trial was a boon for Jewish organizations seeking to publicize their opposition to and distance from the tmeim. Local Jewish reform organizations had spent decades lobbying officials to take action, promoting among their few successes the cooperation of the Polish ambassador in pressuring the Varsovia Society to change its name from that of the Polish city. Throughout the decade following the case, certain Jewish community organizations built on this success to enforce the separation between "respectable" Jews and any vestige of the tmeim, helping authorities to monitor migration and themselves monitoring marriage efforts. The breakup of the Society thus enabled Argentine police and other authorities to improve their public image, strengthen mainstream Jewish institutions, and, along the way, sell many newspapers.

## REREADING RAQUEL LIBERMAN AND ESTHER THE MILLIONAIRE

As Alsogaray's story thus becomes more complex than that of a principled policeman working against corruption, Raquel Liberman's life story can also be interpreted as more complicated than the version of an entrapped victim turned heroine. The research of Nora Glickman, who interviewed Liberman's grandchildren and translated her Yiddish correspondence with her husband from Poland, unveils another dimension of her story.[25] This first husband's death shortly after Liberman arrived with their two children to meet him in Buenos Aires prompted her initial entry into prostitution, during which time she operated without a manager. Details about this period of sex work do not appear in the trial summaries or popular discourse around her. While Glickman speculates that Liberman remained silent about this in order to keep her happiest personal memories private in the wake of her subsequent traumas, it is also possible that Liberman deliberately structured her own story in order to better fit with the victim narrative promoted by antiprostitution activists.[26] The aspects of Liberman's story in which she elected to enter sex work to support her children in the wake of her first husband's death and made enough money to open her own business would not have been sufficiently inspirational to Argentine authorities or the Jewish reformers eager to take down the infamous Society. In a more palatable version, her story echoed white slave tropes: seduction and trickery, often into marriage, and prostitution as necessarily coercive.

The conventional narrative says that despite marrying her second husband in a Jewish ceremony at the synagogue in the Society's lavish Cordoba Avenue headquarters, Liberman did not know that this location housed the central office of the Varsovia Society, nor that her husband was a member. Sections of legal testimony in the 1930 court case, however, imply that she not only knew of his membership but tried to use the organization's own mechanisms to resolve their conflict before she eventually went to the Argentine authorities.[27] Angry that her husband Korn had taken tens of thousands of pesos from her in addition to valuable clothing and jewelry, she lobbied several other Society members to help retrieve her property.[28] Unhappy with the lack of resolution to her claim, she visited the Society's president at his home, but after an hour's negotiation and several further appeals, she was not satisfied.[29] Only at that point did she go to the police. This timeline of Liberman's actions positions her as a rational actor demanding justice from a Society that offered conflict resolution to its members. She went to at least five members of the Society and its president before turning outward. She used its structure to seek satisfaction and, when denied it, turned to state authorities. Her alliance with Alsogaray and Judge Ocampo was calculated, perhaps as an act of revenge for this frustration. Liberman's denunciation was probably not motivated by opposition to the broader exploitation of prostituted women or the power of the Society itself.

In support of this theory, Liberman demonstrated no ongoing interest in cooperating with "respectable" Jewish organizations, which in turn appeared to trust her as little as their other fallen subjects. Ezres Noshim entertained at least one allegation of Liberman's ongoing bad character: in 1932 it received a letter from one Maria Vainstok complaining that her husband Natalio had abandoned his parental responsibilities and taken up with "the Liberman woman, famously célèbre in the 'Migdal' case." Rather than defending Liberman, Ezres Noshim worked with Vainstok to facilitate a divorce and alimony settlement.[30] In 1934, Ezres Noshim responded to an official request and paid a surprise visit to Liberman's house to check on her moral condition, to which she responded with unveiled hostility. Liberman had applied for a visa to visit family in Poland, and Argentine officials asked Ezres Noshim to verify that she no longer practiced prostitution. The request and the surprise nature of the visit suggest both Ezres Noshim's cooperative relationship with Argentine authorities and a mutual lack of interest between Ezres Noshim and Liberman in continuing to work together.[31] Two larger dynamics also appear: the mainstream Jewish community's ongoing mutually beneficial relationship with Argentine authorities around the issue of sex work management and the minimal amount of actual rescue from coerced traffic achieved by local and international organizations.

Although exceptional, Liberman was not the only woman associated with the Varsovia society whose story complicates the victim narrative favored by anti-prostitution activists. Like Liberman, Esther the Millionaire gathered enough capital as a prostitute (by emptying sleeping clients' pockets) to purchase her own property, and the two women both moved in and out of prostitution over the course of their lives, disrupting the usual story of prostitution as a terminal fate. Esther's membership in the Society and role in brothel ownership reflected the complex gendered hierarchy of sex work management, more elaborate than the female victim–male exploiter dichotomy. Esther epitomized what "respectable" Jews most feared: rather than an innocent victim, since the 1890s she had been notorious for theft as well as prostitution. She was able to buy her way out of all legal trouble, even as the incipient urban Jewish population generally struggled in poverty. Esther reflected antisemitic stereotypes as a moneylender and landlord. But perhaps worst of all, she integrated with the city's non-Jewish elites first as a mistress, then as a property owner, and publicly demonstrated her wealth, with furs, jewels, luxury property, and lawyers on retainer. She and others like her undermined the efforts of "respectable" Jews to prove themselves good citizens.

Raquel Liberman and Esther the Millionaire traveled a well-worn road from the Eastern European Jewish Pale of Settlement to the brothels of Argentina. But the usual white slave narrative did not fit the lives of either. Both journeyed across the Atlantic as married women with children, either with or in order to meet husbands who did not exploit them. Both moved in and out of prostitution over the course of their lives, and neither was necessarily forced into the work. Both made their own fortunes. Esther escaped jail for robbing her clients seventeen times, while Liberman first managed her own career as a prostitute, then brought charges against a would-be exploiter, denouncing the infamous Society to officials who would help bring the entire structure down. Both women tried to work outside the circles of the tmeim—Liberman's antique store, Esther's luxury apartment building—yet were propelled back into association with prostitution not only by the Society itself but by the organized Jewish effort to maintain and publicize the distinction between honest Jews and the "impure." The power of the white slave victim story, however, has been strong enough to gain Liberman posthumous fame as an antitrafficking role model, while Esther the Millionaire has faded from historical memory.

### TRAFFICKING VICTIMS, SEX WORKERS, AND MODIFIED CHOICES

The victim narrative of the anti–white slavery movements of the late nineteenth and early twentieth centuries, in which prostituted women are viewed as trapped and taken advantage of by unscrupulous and violent men, corresponds today to antitrafficking rhetoric. Despite admirable intentions of activists, viewing prostitutes fundamentally as victims has been criticized not only by some scholars but by a number of sex workers themselves. Women's rights, coercion, and consent have been central to debates over prostitution for over a century and currently inform global governmental decision making. Today, the two principal positions on sex trafficking echo the two predominant arguments made by antiprostitution activists and some feminists over the past century and a half.

The first position, that all prostitution inherently exploits women and should be abolished, first became globally influential through Josephine Butler's leadership of the opposition to the British Empire's Contagious Diseases Acts from the 1860s to the 1880s, which regulated prostitution in the British Empire.[32] Abolitionism motivated many of the leading international antitrafficking reformers from the Victorian era through the mid-twentieth century.[33] Beginning in the 1970s, feminists such as Kathleen Barry, Sheila Jeffries, and Catharine MacKinnon and groups like the Coalition Against Trafficking in Women updated this position with a new energy and an ideological framework that equated all prostitution and pornography with women's systematic exploitation—they were dubbed antipornography feminists by their opponents.[34] More recent global antitrafficking or sexual slavery campaigns generally share this orientation on the fundamental victimization of prostitutes with critics of several decades and over a century ago.[35] Not all feminists agree with this perspective, but it is often interpreted as the only pro-woman, feminist position on prostitution.

In the second position, usually held by "pro-sex" or "sex-positive" feminist opponents of those in the prior camp, whom they dubbed "anti-sex" or "dominance" feminists, and organized groups of sex workers themselves, the risks of prostitution emerge from its being a form of labor, with suggested responses ranging from state regulation to unionization.[36] Public health advocates in late nineteenth-century modernizing regimes proposed that the problems linked to prostitution, such as sexually transmitted infections, could be best managed through legal regulation and medical oversight. The Argentine system during this period, along with those in many other societies following the French example, fell in this category. Feminist abolitionists from Josephine Butler onward worried that regulatory regimes fundamentally restricted prostitutes' agency by forcing them to submit to invasive medical inspections and to stop working if diagnosed with syphilis—and perhaps be confined inside a "lock" hospital.

An alternative argument for decriminalization, based on the idea that prostitution is a form of labor made exploitative by its conditions, was initially voiced by Emma Goldman, who compared it to women's oppression in marriage and under capitalism more generally.[37] Parallel to this defense of legalization, some prostitutes began to organize collectively in the 1960s and 1970s as sex workers, demanding respect as free agents rather than pity as victims. The term "sex work" originated with the political liberation and feminist movements of this era and spread with public health campaigns related to HIV and AIDS. These activists and their academic supporters argue that abolitionists deny prostitutes agency in their own lives.[38] Some have gone even further than promoting decriminalization, arguing that sex work can be a liberatory practice, enabling a broader range of life, love, and leisure choices than otherwise available.[39]

Scholars influenced by the latter perspective have recently tried to move beyond a dichotomy of internationally mobile prostitutes as tragic victims or powerful agents by complicating the idea of consent and putting international trafficking in the context of migration.[40] This framework extends the "modified choice" model, the idea that sex workers make difficult choices out of a limited, less-than-ideal range. This view tries to balance structure and agency and cautions against the romanticization of sex workers' decisions: women's lives must be understood as never permitting total freedom of choice, due to hierarchies of race, sex, and class.[41] Argentine novelist Mario Szichman imagines a Jewish prostitute's decision making in this model, as his recurrent character Dora chooses prostitution as an alternative to hunger: "I discovered that the world belonged to men, and since I could not conquer it with my head, I used my tukhes."[42]

Whether viewing prostitution as sex work or as modified choice, these can be difficult conversations for historians and other scholars to have with current antitrafficking activists and policy makers, who worry that regulationist and modified choice perspectives sidestep the very real exploitation of women. Prostitutes routinely face violence at the hands of pimps, clients, police, and the criminal justice system and have throughout the modern era. Regulationists hope that their proposals can reduce certain aspects of this violence, and advocates of total legalization call for legal and health protection for all workers, while both camps point out that abolitionists have never been successful in enlisting their targets of rescue themselves to their cause. The language of victim and exploiter does reflect horrifying realities, but as terms of historical analysis, this dichotomy simplifies a complex range of lived experience and erases the agency of people who trade sex for something they need.

Like her predecessor the white slave, the trafficking victim fits into broader projects and policies more easily than the sex worker, but her long-term rescue rarely succeeds. Sex workers' recidivism past and present can be reframed if they are viewed as agents responding to opportunities for social and material improvement. Today's antitrafficking organizations might improve outcomes for clients by promoting alternative social networks as well as job skills.[43] Historically and today, restrictive regulatory systems to prevent undesirable migration have inspired new tactics that often increase danger for the most vulnerable. Indeed, sex workers and other working-class women have generally viewed regulation as behavior control rather than as offering protection from disease or exploitation.[44] As well-intentioned listeners, we must seek to hear the voices of our subjects within their own paradigms.

## WHITE SLAVERY AS IMPURE MIGRATION

There is considerable evidence that claims of the epidemic proportion of white slavery were dramatically overstated in the period of the late nineteenth century through the mid-twentieth. The image of the swarthy Semitic seducer haunted social reformers and parents of young white women around the world at the fin de siècle. Voyeuristic publications exaggerated the numbers of innocent victims drugged and shipped through steerage to the underworld of Buenos Aires. The rapidly growing port capital became a metonym for unrestricted vice and shorthand in lurid international tales of white slavery for sexual exploitation and racial mixing. As a powerful and threatening story, the idea of white slavery had remarkable staying power. Its stubborn persistence rested on a combination of factors: its resonance with chattel slavery, the visibility of legalized prostitution in this era of mass migration, and the nationalist anxieties roused by the symbol of threatened white womanhood. The association of white slavery with both the Jews and the city of Buenos Aires resonated with other concerns that exacerbated the outrage around these connections, as illuminated by the genealogy of the term "white slave," which was intrinsically tied to race and labor.

This was a time of racial and national boundary definition, as post–chattel slavery social reorganization in the Americas and mass migration provoked elite fears of displacement. Population shifts threw new neighbors into close contact in burgeoning cities. The language of white slavery reified the whiteness of European women, sharpening a dichotomy between ambiguous races as white slave masters became coded as nonwhite. The white slave's whiteness set off the darkness of her exploiter. Narratives of the white slave united the shadowy Others of the United States and Europe—black and Jew—in transatlantic debates over immigration, miscegenation, urbanization, marriage, suffrage, and the end of empire. Along with other racialized threats, the dark master propelled popular hysteria and public policy. As North Atlantic reformers blamed social problems on undesirable mobile foreigners, they helped reconstruct shifting boundaries of race and civilization.

Sensationalist international impressions of Argentine prostitution and Jewish white slave traffickers were not completely uncoupled from reality. From the beginning of the late nineteenth-century migration, as most Eastern European Jewish immigrants to Argentina sought to make a living off the land in the JCA's rural agricultural colonies or in traditional urban occupations, a substantial number of these earliest arrivals were involved in prostitution. Although perhaps exotic to the modern reader in the United States, Jewish pimps, prostitutes, and brothel owners were familiar neighborhood fixtures in the early urban settlement of Buenos Aires. Despite the efforts of respectability seekers at the time and later, traces remain in popular memory and language. Denial of this phenomenon's significance and self-defensive emphasis on opposition minimize the contemporary visibility of Jewish participation in the port capital's enormous underworld, which was interwoven with the geography of the city's first Jewish neighborhoods. Pimps and prostitutes, madams and brothel owners flaunted their wealth and explicitly articulated their identity as Jews in the balconies of the Yiddish theater and on the streets of the Jewish town center. In the 1890s, as the Jewish center of Buenos Aires began to flourish, Jewish women made up a disproportionate amount of registered prostitutes and Jewish men played a conspicuous role in managing sex work. In the 1920s, the peak period of Jewish immigration, Jewish sex workers continued to be highly visible and organized Jewish management further consolidated, just as local tolerance for prostitution declined. The density of residences and businesses of Jewish pimps and prostitutes in the city's original Jewish residential and business districts as well as the large numbers of Jewish prostitutes and managers across this era help to account for the intensity of the rest of the Jewish community's reaction to the tmeim.

The community institutions given most attention by historians—AMIA, the rural colonies, schools, and synagogues—did not reflect the full range of Jewish concerns in the first decades of the century. Prostitution and the fight against it reflected a wider spectrum of interests, fears, and priorities. "Respectable" Jews sought to protect themselves from the reinforcement of antisemitic stereotypes and other backlash that the widespread visibility of underworld Jews might inspire. Their boycott, like transnational antitrafficking endeavors, had the unintended effect of further publicizing the Jewish connection to sex traffic, raising Argentina's visibility on the world stage and provoking the tmeim to build an increasingly elaborate parallel world. Prostitution thus became an integral part of the Argentine Jewish settlement narrative, contributing to the centralization of local institutions.

Jewish community organizations' ongoing involvement in issues like marriage fit into a matrix of broader community concerns about motherhood, procreation, immigration, and family structure and defending those institutions against any connection with prostitution. Ezres Noshim's morality certification system and particular concern with prostitute mothers as a degenerative influence on future generations revealed deep anxiety about the legacy of the substantial local connection between Jews and organized prostitution. Through pressure on immoral and potentially immoral Jewish families, Ashkenazi Jewish social reformers in Argentina attempted to delineate the boundaries of membership in their own community. The self-defensive struggles of the "respectable" Jews against antisemitic exaggerations of Jewish control over financial, cultural, and immoral institutions underline both the vulnerability of migrants and the techniques used by enclave communities and host societies to distinguish between desirable and undesirable new citizens.

Argentine prostitution captured the attention of international reformers organizing against the transnational flow of prostitutes. The League of Nations' efforts to unify divergent national approaches to the global sex traffic were also about the broader question of migration itself, as evidenced by the focus on ports and borders. Within Argentina, even as they blamed police for accepting bribes and otherwise benefiting from the lucrative sex industry, reformers relied on police muscle to enforce evolving regulatory regimes. Despite the inherent anti-semitism of Alsogaray's work, shared with other authorities in this period of rising nationalism, he articulated and helped to realize the moral gatekeeping of local and international Jewish reformers, who publicly expressed their gratitude for his collaboration. Alsogaray's short-lived promotion to a high-level post in the military government reflected both the national quest for order and nativist interest in blaming outsiders for problems—the public trial of the Varsovia Society at that time allowed stereotypical greedy Jewish Others to serve as scapegoat for the nation's prostitution problem.

This story should be seen as more than just a colorful and tragic chapter in the struggling early days of an immigrant community. White slave tales did not reflect the usual experiences of men and women who made transnational journeys to sell sex. Women's choices were limited and often unappealing, but most made at least some decisions along the way, gaining some freedoms even as they lost others. Women asserted their agency as they moved in and out of prostitution, traded lovers, and occasionally amassed wealth or purchased property. Sexual practices themselves and their global variations can also provide insight into women's agential decision making. Migrant sex workers responded to international differentials in sexual economies—particularly how different acts were valued or stigmatized across cultures. Argentina drew experienced sex workers from Europe because higher prices could be commanded thanks to demographic imbalance and economic growth. Examples of women's refusal or agreement to engage in certain sexual behaviors support the broader argument that many women were not hapless victims but able to make life and work decisions, albeit within considerable constraints.

Nor was the pimps' mutual aid organization so exotic: members of the Varsovia Society shared demographics and aspirations with other immigrants, which they expressed in common collective and religious idioms. Like other immigrant voluntary associations, the Society provided important social services before the growth of the welfare state and bridged identity formation tied to old and new homelands. The members of the Society saw themselves as regular businessmen, as landlords rather than as pimps, or as working women rather than prostitutes. While this may have been a disingenuous justification or legal fiction, the unclear line between illicit and licit work winds through many occupational endeavors. Like Esther the Millionaire, some sex workers managed to parlay their wealth into a move out of the shadows, and the Society also provided opportunities for peer recognition and a form of respectability. Morality became a battleground between tmeim and their opponents, as pimps claimed respectability through their voluntary society, prostitutes claimed victimhood when it served their interests, and local and international institutions from Ezres Noshim to the League of Nations used moral claims to shape marriage and migration. Migrant sex workers deployed marriage on the ground as migration strategy, business structure, and romantic endeavor. Even decades after Jews no longer played a significant role in the Argentine underworld, "respectable" Jews continued to scapegoat the tmeim, hoping to protect the Jewish future. The imprint of this history has remained on the centralized structure of local Jewish institutions, the defensiveness of collective historical memory, and the contours of Argentine expressions of antisemitism.

# Acknowledgments

The writing and rewriting of this book have depended on the support of people, communities, and institutions in multiple locales. Wake Forest University has supported this project through the history department, the Griffin Fund, the Office of the Dean of the College, the Provost's Office, the University Publications Fund, and the Humanities Institute. This project could not have been completed without the archival visits, conferences and public conversations, and writing time thus afforded. Will Runyan's assistance with the Argentine Yiddish press aided this project immeasurably. At the Z. Smith Reynolds Library, James Harper worked ILL and technological magic at the last minute, in cahoots with Kathy Shields.

At Rutgers University Press, the generosity of Jeffrey Shandler in particular, along with Marcy Brink-Danan and Matti Bunzel, in commenting on multiple drafts of this work was beyond what I could have hoped for. Their attention to both framing and detail, paired with Elisabeth Maselli's patience and enthusiasm, have been truly invaluable. The expertise of the anonymous readers and Marilyn Campbell propelled me through several plateaus. Mike Siegel's translations of my maps for public consumption could not have been more transparent and efficient.

The history department at Wake Forest University has been a stimulating incubator. Many of my colleagues have read drafts of this work, providing perspectives from various fields as well as advice on the larger process. Sue Rupp's mentorship has included several kind and thorough readings, as has Simone Caron's, and both have been models of principled commitment to teaching and community involvement. Jake Ruddiman and Barry Tractenberg commented on multiple drafts and demystified the stages of the publication process while soothing my anxieties. Monique O'Connell's guidance has been fortifying and patient. Lisa Blee's dedication to community engagement is always an inspiration. An earlier version of the introduction benefited from workshopping in our Faculty Seminar. Laura Gammons has patiently fixed and averted many logistical challenges.

The stalwarts of our Twin City Hive writing group have provided solidarity and strategy through the years. Stephanie Koscak has been a constant trudging buddy, trading chapters, applications, and frustrations. I always appreciate Kristina Gupta's political compass and sharing musical experiences with Elizabeth Clendinning. The participants in our Humanities Institute Beyond Gay Day Seminar helped me connect my research and teaching to larger conversations. The faculty of women, gender, and sexuality studies, Latin American and Latino studies, and Jewish studies have fostered welcome intellectual communities. My students give me daily inspiration and distraction, push me to stay connected to ever-evolving language, and remind me of the excitement of the big questions.

Sharing walks and meals and the things of daily life have fortified me to continue when rewriting seemed endless. Tanisha Ramachandran and Annalise Glauz-Todrank keep me laughing and make sure the work stays in balance with the things that matter more. Sharing the struggles with you keeps everything in perspective. Thanks to Deb and Taiyo and Surjya for sharing. Rian Bowie and Erica and Iris Still have aided these efforts to balance work and play, despite puppy sabotage. Eranda Jayawickreme and Lisa Blee make the best dinners in town, with kitty acrobatics, power tool juggling, and always a good political argument. My fellow Latin Americanists Karin Fredrick and Brian Burke have been stalwart fellow travelers. Joanna Ruocco is my role model for writerly dedication and has livened up the narrative framing of this work—she also reminds me that no matter how much you do it or how smart you are, writing is just hard, which is what makes it worthwhile.

I am grateful to all who have made Winston-Salem my home, most regularly Jessica Lyles, Marlena Del Hierro, Noel Brooke Miles, Lia Scholl, Kevin Edwards and Guy, Tanya Jachimiak and Andrea Dauser, Colin Miller and Sarah Howell-Miller, Mike Pont, Mike Johnson, Ben Harrison, Cheryl Ventura, Henry Lafferty, Allie Garrett, Fran Gordon, and Donna Hampton. I miss Marc Bryson's eye, humor, and music. Cristina Trutanich shared in putting out my first roots here. Alden Caron's responsibility beyond her years made it comfortable for me to travel. I can feel Maria Canal's warmth across continents. Anna Goodman's curiosity lights up every room, and she, along with the other members of my string quartet, Susie Pollack and Jennifer Lane, have provided a regular delightful outlet. Anna and Lionel even braved the Argentine National Library's bureaucracy in an intensive effort to secure printable photographs.

My archival research was aided along the way by many experts: Silvia Hansman, Débora Kacowicz, Lara Milier, and Jana Powazek at Fundación IWO; Monica Testa at CEMLA (Centro de Estudios Migratorios Latinoamericanos);

Adolfo Willy Covi and Adriana Graciela Muñoz at the Centro de Estudios Históricos de la Policía Federal; Eugenio Zappietro at the Museo Policial de la Policía Federal Argentina; Jesse Aaron Cohen at the YIVO Archives; and Eleanor Yadin and Miryem-Khaye Seigel at the New York Public Library's Dorot Jewish Division. Jacques Oberson keeps access to the League of Nations' archive tremendously efficient, and worked technological magic to make this cover image possible. Thanks to Liat Kozma for her advice related to the League of Nations archives and Mollie Lewis Nouwen for her suggestions related to the Argentine Police archives. I am also grateful to the UCLA Latin American Institute, Center for Jewish Studies, and History Department for their support of these archival explorations, as well as the Mellon Foundation for assistance with my research in the League of Nations archives. My time in Buenos Aires was made comfortable by Alejandro Dujovne, Laura Fernandez Cordero and Pablo, Laura Schenquer, Grabiela Rojas Molina, and the Núcleo de Estudios Judios.

Sections of this work have benefited from the expertise shared by Adriana Brodsky, Lila Caimairi, Daniel Llvovich, Raanan Rein, and Eduardo Zimmerman. The core of the project was shaped by my interactions with Adriana Bergero, Robin Derby, José Moya, David Myers, and Kevin Terraciano. I continue to be grateful for my brilliant graduate school cohort, particularly my ongoing relationships with Ben Cowan, Xochitl Flores, Zeb Tortorici, and Dana Velasco-Murillo. Special thanks for contributing to this work go to Jennifer Ansley, Pablo Ben, Liora Halperin, and Sasha Sendlerovich.

Ellen Dubois first showed me that history could be an activist endeavor. She has talked through this work with me from its earliest stages and continues to model an ever-evolving scholarly life. Her home in LA, embellished with Arnie Schwartz, continues to be a grounding spot. Janet Afary offered me a second nurturing home during my LA years, and I am still inspired by the intellectual and activist commitments that she and Kevin Anderson, along with Lena and Leila, embody daily. Thanks to all my creative and quirky Los Angeles crew: Carmen Reginato, Meredith Lee and Judy Rodriguez, Sean Fulkerson, Eli Bartle and Rick, Rebecca Trotsky-Sirr, Alesha Hughes and Alan Weisbart, Kalil Cohen, Christina Webb, Joe Wagner, Paul Schulte, Tara Donley and Leighanna and Angel. Shy Oakes may be my longest-standing intellectual sounding board. From another realm of yiddishkeit, Simcha Frankel has been an inspiration of open-minded dedication.

I am profoundly grateful for a family with whom I share politics and humor. Joan, Denise, Marc, Evan, Jenna, Christoff, Wendy, Bruce, and Mitchell laughed through countless meals and milestones. Joan keeps the spirit of tango alive in the Hollywood Hills. Leo and Evelyn shaped my love of a good story and sense of roots and continue to be sorely missed. Jenny and Mary Block were gracious hosts at several stages of this project. I have always been inspired by the creative examples of Michael, Catherine, and Pepper; and Michael's passing echoes. My broader sense of home and family extends with gratitude to the Kovnat-Lichtenberg clan, Susie, Steve, Jesse, Sylvie, Lucas, Sharon, Samson, Elijah, Silas, Carol, and Ella; the Shaman crew, Donna, Ellen, and Matiah; the Reder-Carlson family; Carla, Jim, and Lydia; Bill, Laura, Casey, and Artie; Cathy Connolly and Lucas; and Puget Ridge Co-housing. The too-early losses of Chris Beahler and Jake Turoff-Martin are still painful. Reed Forrester has been my constant companion in managing the emotional side of this and all my processes; a model of growth, applied intelligence, and patience (thank you, Hazel!). Trudi, Stu, and Dan: your values, wit, evolving curiosity, and profound integrity have been my foundation; thank you.

# Notes

### INTRODUCTION

1. The Society was originally called Varsovia, meaning Warsaw, and changed its name in 1927 to Zwi Migdal. In an effort to reduce confusion, I generally refer to it as the Society or the Varsovia Society, though sometimes as Zwi Migdal if after the name change and thus discussed in primary sources. The term *israelita* has been in common usage to refer to Jews across Latin America and the Caribbean since the colonial era, when antisemitism indelibly stained many related terms. Israelita thus became the polite term, although it has become confusing since the establishment of the State of Israel. See Judith Laikin Elkin, *The Jews of Latin America*, 3rd ed. (Boulder, CO: Lynne Rienner, 2014), 18–19.

2. For more on this language, see Haim Avni, *"Ṭeme'im": Saḥar be-nashim be-Argenṭinah uve-Yiśra'el* (Tel-Aviv: Yedi'ot Aharonot, 2009).

3. This book uses the terms "white slave" and "white slavery" to discuss this narrative trope, without intending to share in the implication (generally picked up by its replacement term "trafficking") that the experiences referenced were always entirely coercive. For narrative flow, "prostitute" and "prostitution," as well as "sex worker" and "sex work," will be often be used interchangeably. While the agency implied in "sex work" fits better with this text's overall argument, it is also an anachronistic term.

4. See, for example, Gretchen Soderlund, *Sex Trafficking, Scandal, and the Transformation of Journalism, 1885–1917* (Chicago: University of Chicago Press, 2013); Brian Donovan, *White Slave Crusades: Race, Gender, and Anti-Vice Activism, 1887–1917* (Champaign: University of Illinois Press, 2006); Marie Sandell, *The Rise of Women's Transnational Activism: Identity and Sisterhood between the World Wars* (New York: I. B. Tauris, 2015).

5. Nazi claim made in Fritz Hippler, dir., *Der ewige Jude* (Deutsche Filmherstellungs und Verwertungs, 1940), 62 min.

6. Federico Rivanera Carles, *Los judíos y la trata de blancas en Argentina* (Buenos Aires: Instituto de Investigaciones sobre la Cuestión Judía, 1986). Although clearly an unreliable source, Carles analyzes the volume of Buenos Aires police mug shots of suspects from 1893 to 1894, in addition to a subsequent volume now missing from the police archive. The extensive documentation of the antisemitism of the Proceso military regime

(1976–1983) includes David Sheinin, "Deconstructing Antisemitism in Argentina," in *The Jewish Diaspora in Latin America and the Caribbean: Fragments of Memory*, ed. Kristin Ruggiero (Brighton: Sussex Academic Press, 2010), 72–85; Daniel Lvovich, *Nacionalismo y antisemitismo en la Argentina* (Buenos Aires: Javier Vergara, 2003); and Leonardo Senkman, ed., *El antisemitismo en la Argentina*, 2nd ed. (Buenos Aires: Centro Editor de America Latina, 1989).

7. E.g., the title claim in Nora Glickman, *The Jewish White Slave Trade and the Untold Story of Raquel Liberman* (New York: Garland, 2000). Haim Avni, an Israeli senior scholar of Argentine Jewry, published a book in Hebrew comparing the Argentine and Israeli experiences of Jewish prostitution. Avni, *"Teme'im."* Israeli poet and journalist Ilan Shainfeld published a book, also only available in Hebrew, framing this as a "silenced story," "Argentine Jewry's dark secret." Ilan Shainfeld, *Ma'aśeh be-ṭaba'at* (Jerusalem: Keter, 2007). The subject has not been silenced in Spanish-language publications in the Southern Cone: Ricardo Feierstein devoted a chapter to the subject in his multiple-edition textbook on Argentine Jews, Victor Mirelman's *Jewish Buenos Aires* includes a chapter on the subject, and Uruguayan Yvette Trochon's hefty tome compares international prostitution across all ethnic groups in Argentina, Brazil, and Uruguay. Ricardo Feierstein, *Historia de los judíos argentinos*, 3rd ed. (Buenos Aires: Galerna, 2006), 266–303; Victor A. Mirelman, *Jewish Buenos Aires, 1890–1930: In Search of an Identity* (Detroit: Wayne State University Press, 1990), 197–220; and Yvette Trochon, *Las rutas de eros: La trata de blancas en el Atlántico Sur: Argentina, Brasil y Uruguay* (Montevideo: Ediciones Santillana/Taurus, 2006), esp. 265–358. Scholars have often used Gerardo Bra's 1982 Argentine work as a source, although it lacks source references and fictionalizes elaborate scenes and Spanish-language dialogue between Yiddish-speaking new immigrants. Gerardo Bra, *La organización negra: La increíble historia de la Zwi Migdal* (Buenos Aires: Corregidor, 1982). Although also lacking a scholarly apparatus and rigorous source citation, Larry Levy's *La mancha de la Migdal: Historia de la prostitución judía en la Argentina* (Buenos Aires: Grupo Editorial Norma, 2007) must be mentioned. A fictionalized version of the Society plays a shadowy role in a 1979 Jonathan Demme murder mystery starring Roy Scheider, based on a Murray Teigh Bloom novel. Jonathan Demme, dir., *Last Embrace* (United Artists, 1979), 102 min.

8. E.g., Robert Weisbrot, *The Jews of Argentina: From the Inquisition to Peron* (Philadelphia: Jewish Publication Society of America, 1979), 62–65.

9. Sandra McGee Deutsch's book on the history of Jewish women in Argentina, the first historical monograph to focus on Jewish women anywhere in Latin America, begins its chapter on prostitution with her concern about the excessive visibility of Argentine Jewish women as prostitutes as opposed to other roles. Sandra McGee Deutsch, *Crossing Borders, Claiming a Nation: A History of Argentine Jewish Women, 1880–1955* (Durham, NC: Duke University Press, 2010), 104–122.

10. Ashkenazi Jews or Ashkenazim, descended from cultural groups that had moved back and forth between Western and Eastern Europe since the eleventh century, made up the majority of world Jewry and this period's migrants to the Americas. Sephardi Jews, descended from those expelled from the Iberian Peninsula in 1492 and largely settled in the Ottoman world, also made up a significant minority of Argentine Jews. For narrative ease, I frequently refer to the Jewish community as a whole, although I focus on the Ashkenazi tmeim and their also Ashkenazi opponents, but I do not intend to flatten the diversity of Jewish experience in Argentina, particularly the differences between

Sephardi and Ashkenazi Jewish life in this period. On the contours of Sephardi vs. Ashkenazi Argentine-Jewish identity, see the work of Adriana M. Brodsky, most notably her comprehensive recent book *Sephardi, Jewish, Argentine: Community and National Identity, 1880–1960* (Bloomington: Indiana University Press, 2016). Numbers for all sectors of the Jewish population are difficult to estimate, but Sephardi Jews probably made up less than 10 percent of the entire Argentine Jewish population between the late nineteenth and mid-twentieth centuries. Brodsky discusses various population estimates (see pp. 14–17). She also examines both Sephardi diversity and the strategic management of collective identity.

11. On antisemitism and nativism, see Lvovich, *Nacionalismo y antisemitismo*.

12. Rebecca Kobrin discusses this skill mismatch across the Ashkenazi diaspora in *Jewish Bialystok and Its Diaspora* (Bloomington: Indiana University Press, 2010). Jose Moya draws the causal connection to sex work along with other gray-market employment in his introduction to *The New Jewish Argentina: Facets of Jewish Experiences in the Southern Cone*, ed. Adriana Brodsky and Raanan Rein (Leiden: Brill, 2013), 12. Jews predominated in the region's sex industry in this period "for the same reason that they were overrepresented in peddling, urban and semi-urban trades, horse trading, money-lending."

13. Moshe Alpherson, quoted in Deutsch, *Crossing Borders*.

14. Pablo Ben, "Plebeian Masculinity and Sexual Comedy in Buenos Aires, 1880–1930," *Journal of the History of Sexuality* 16, no. 3 (September 2007): 436–458; Sandra Gayol, *Sociabilidad en Buenos Aires: Hombres, honor y cafés, 1862–1910* (Buenos Aires: Ediciones del Siglo, 2000); J. L. Guerena, "The Brothel as Space of Sociability (Prostitution, Spain)," *Hispania-Revista Española de historia*, no. 214 (2003): 551–570; Philip Howell, "Sex and the City of Bachelors: Sporting Guidebooks and Urban Knowledge in Nineteenth-Century Britain and America," *Ecumene* 8, no. 1 (2001): 20–50.

15. Feierstein, *Historia de los judíos argentinos*, 278; Gino Germani, *Política y sociedad en una época de transición: De la sociedad tradicional a la sociedad de masas* (Buenos Aires: Editorial Paidós, 1968), 252.

16. Charles Van Onselen discusses the late nineteenth-century Eastern and Western European decrease in brothel prostitution and probability that the demand shift to the New World would have drawn sex workers across the Atlantic. Charles Van Onselen, "Jewish Marginality in the Atlantic World: Organized Crime in the Era of the Great Migrations, 1880–1914," *South African Historical Journal* 43, no. 1 (2000): 103–105.

17. In addition to these examples, discussed later in the book, the Buenos Aires Yiddish press discussed the Torah scrolls and other religious accoutrements used by the Society in several locations, e.g., "Diarestn af rufianes vern fargezetzt in stat un in provintz," *Di Prese*, May 25, 1930, 1.

18. The summary judgment of the court case is reproduced in "Juzgados de instrucción: Número 3—Asociación ilicita," *Gaceta del Foro* 15, no. 4729 (November 1, 1930): 3–23 (henceforth GdF).

19. Much of the historical scholarship on Buenos Aires has focused on the 1890s through the interwar years. During this golden age, the growing capital became a world-famous city of sin, where the tango emerged from legal bordellos that housed thousands of foreign-born prostitutes. Their clients, mostly Southern European immigrant laborers, mingled in the brothels and homosocial spaces immortalized in tango lyrics. On male sociability in this context, see Jean-Luis Guereña, "El burdel como espacio de sociabilidad," *Hispania: Revista española de historia* 63, no. 214 (2003): 551–570; and Howell, "Sex

and the City of Bachelors." For more on Buenos Aires male sociability, see Ben, "Plebeian Masculinity and Sexual Comedy"; and Gayol, *Sociabilidad en Buenos Aires*.

20. Fernando Devoto, *Historia de la inmigración en la Argentina* (Buenos Aires: Editorial Sudamericana, 2003), 49; Germani, *Política y sociedad*, 198.

21. Lila Caimari, *While the City Sleeps: A History of Pistoleros, Policemen, and the Crime
Beat in Buenos Aires before Perón*, trans. Lisa Ubelaker Andrade and Richard Shindell
(Berkeley: University of California Press, 2016), 3.

22. Caimari, *While the City Sleeps*, 5–7. On the extreme right in the Argentine interwar
period, see Federico Finchelstein, *Transatlantic Fascism: Ideology, Violence, and the Sacred
in Argentina and Italy, 1919–1945* (Durham, NC: Duke University Press, 2009); Alberto
Spektorowski, *The Origins of Argentina's Revolution of the Right* (Notre Dame, IN: University of Notre Dame Press, 2003); Sandra McGee Deutsch, *Las Derechas: The Extreme Right
in Argentina, Brazil, and Chile, 1890–1939* (Stanford, CA: Stanford University Press, 1999);
and Sandra McGee Deutsch and Ronald Dolkart, eds., *The Argentine Right: Its History and
Intellectual Origins, 1910 to the Present* (Wilmington, DE: SR Books, 1993).

23. For a classic periodization in Argentine historiography, see, for example, David
Rock, *Argentina 1516–1987: From Spanish Colonization to Alfonsín* (Berkeley: University
of California Press, 1987), though 1930 as an epochal turning point is used in the majority of histories of Buenos Aires and Argentina. Some historians of Buenos Aires, particularly Argentine scholars of popular culture and everyday life, have countered this
periodization with an emphasis on continuity in the interwar period. Lila Caimari's work
falls into this camp, as do, among others, Diego Armus, ed., *Mundo urbano y cultura
popular: Estudios de historia social argentina* (Buenos Aires: Sudamericana, 1990); Lean-
dro Gutiérrez and Luis Alberto Romero, *Sectores populares, cultura y política: Buenos
Aires en la entreguerra* (Buenos Aires: Sudamericana, 1995); Luciano de Privitellio, *Veci-
nos y ciudadanos: Política y sociedad en la Buenos Aires de entreguerras* (Buenos Aires:
Siglo XXI, 2003); Francis Korn and Luis Alberto Romero, eds., *Buenos Aires/Entreguer-
ras: La callada transformación* (Buenos Aires: Alianza, 2006).

24. Caimari, *While the City Sleeps*, 81–82.

25. Although the central argument of this book emphasizes the integration of the tmeim
into the physical and symbolic spaces of Argentine Jewish life, I sometimes use the term
"underworld" to refer to the distinct business and leisure spaces occupied by those who
worked in and around the sex industry. Scholars in several fields have explored the mala
vida. See, for example, Claire Solomon, *Fictions of the Bad Life: The Naturalist Prostitute
and Her Avatars in Latin American Literature, 1880–2010* (Columbus: Ohio State University Press, 2014); Adriana J. Bergero, *Intersecting Tango: Cultural Geographies of Buenos Aires, 1900–1930* (Pittsburgh: University of Pittsburgh Press, 2008). Contemporary
observations include M. Barres, *El hampa y sus secretos* (Buenos Aires: Imprenta López,
1934); Antonio Ferrán, *La mala vida en el 900: Selección de textos* (Buenos Aires: Bolsili-
bros Arca, 1967); and Vincente A. Salaverri, *La mala vida: Drama en un acto, tres cuad-
ros y en prosa* (Buenos Aires: B. Fueyo, 1912).

26. On the French regulatory system, the systemic standard for that period, see Alain
Corbin, *Women for Hire: Prostitution and Sexuality in France after 1850* (Cambridge, MA:
Harvard University Press, 1990). On the British system of regulation, see Philip Howell,
*Geographies of Regulation: Policing Prostitution in Nineteenth-Century Britain and the
Empire* (New York: Cambridge University Press, 2009); and Philippa Levine, *Prostitu-
tion, Race, and Politics: Policing Venereal Disease in the British Empire* (New York: Rout-

ledge, 2003). See also Stephanie A. Limoncelli, "International Voluntary Associations, Local Social Movements and State Paths to the Abolition of Regulated Prostitution in Europe, 1875–1950," *International Sociology* 21, no. 1 (January 2006): 31–59.

27. In the book that launched the historical study of prostitution in Argentina and in Latin America more generally, and continues to be a critical reference for scholars of prostitution across Latin America, Donna Guy overviews the evolution of the Argentine system regulating sex work in *Sex and Danger in Buenos Aires: Prostitution, Family, and Nation in Argentina* (Lincoln: University of Nebraska Press, 1991). The 1875 municipal regulation is outlined on pp. 48–53.

28. Guy, *Sex and Danger*, 39–40, 50–56.

29. "Buenos Aires: Commercialized Prostitution," May 29–30, 1924, and "Buenos Aires: Traffic in Women and Children, Summary," May 25–June 14, 1924, Buenos Aires 1924 Field Reports on Investigation of International Traffic in Women and Children Made for the Special Body of Experts to Study the International Traffic in Women and Children, S148, League of Nations Archive, Geneva (henceforth Buenos Aires Field Reports).

30. Caimari, *While the City Sleeps*, 140–159.

31. Guy, *Sex and Danger*, 50–51.

32. Guy, *Sex and Danger*, 51, 118–119.

33. Guy, *Sex and Danger*, 53.

34. Donna Guy, "Medical Imperialism Gone Awry: The Campaign against Legalized Prostitution in Latin America," in *White Slavery and Mothers Alive and Dead: The Troubled Meeting of Sex, Gender, Public Health, and Progress in Latin America* (Lincoln: University of Nebraska Press, 2000), 20; Guy, *Sex and Danger*, 48.

35. Guy, *Sex and Danger*, 58–59.

36. Guy, *Sex and Danger*, 59–61.

37. Guy, *Sex and Danger*, 61–62.

38. Guy, *Sex and Danger*, 62–64, 73.

39. Guy, *Sex and Danger*, 28–30.

40. Guy, *Sex and Danger*, 117–118.

41. Guy, *Sex and Danger*, 108–111.

42. Jose Moya's magisterial work on Spanish immigrants to Buenos Aires in this period underscores the importance of the host society in shaping immigrant social structure. Jose C. Moya, *Cousins and Strangers: Spanish Immigrants in Buenos Aires, 1850–1930* (Berkeley: University of California Press, 1998), e.g., 302.

43. For example, the works of Lila Caimari, Diego Galeano, Mercedes García Ferrari, and Martín Albornoz, all of which will be further discussed below.

44. Although earlier work was spearheaded by George Reid Andrews, *The Afro-Argentines of Buenos Aires, 1800–1900* (Madison: University of Wisconsin Press, 1980).

45. See the notable range of scholarship collected in Paulina Alberto and Eduardo Elena, eds., *Rethinking Race in Modern Argentina* (Cambridge, MA: Cambridge University Press, 2016), particularly the pieces most relevant to this project by Sandra McGee Deutsch, Ezequiel Adamovsky, Matthew Karush, and Oscar Chamosa.

46. Sandra McGee Deutsch, "Insecure Whiteness: Jews Between Civilization and Barbarism, 1880s–1940s," in Alberto and Elena, *Rethinking Race*, 25–52.

47. Pablo Piccato and Ricardo D. Salvatore have been publishing in this arena for several decades; see, e.g., Pablo Piccato, *City of Suspects: Crime in Mexico City, 1900–1931* (Durham, NC: Duke University Press, 2001); Ricardo D. Salvatore, Carlos Aguirre, and

Gilbert M. Joseph, eds., *Crime and Punishment in Latin America: Law and Society since Late Colonial Times* (Durham, NC: Duke University Press, 2001); Ricardo D. Salvatore, Carlos Aguirre, and Gilbert M. Joseph, eds., *The Birth of the Penitentiary in Latin America: Essays on Criminology, Prison Reform, and Social Control, 1830–1940* (Austin: University of Texas Press, 1996). On the power dynamics and nation-building projects inherent in definitions of criminality, see Julia Rodríguez, *Civilizing Argentina: Science, Medicine, and the Modern State* (Chapel Hill: University of North Carolina Press, 2006); Kristin Ruggiero, *Modernity in the Flesh: Medicine, Law, and Society in Turn-of-the-Century Argentina* (Stanford, CA: Stanford University Press, 2004); Jorge Salessi, *Médicos, maleantes y maricas: Higiene, criminología y homosexualidad en la construcción de la nación argentina (Buenos Aires: 1871–1914)* (Rosario: Beatriz Viterbo Editora, 2000); and Nancy Leys Stepan, *"The Hour of Eugenics": Race, Gender, and Nation in Latin America* (Ithaca, NY: Cornell University Press, 1996). Eric Hobsbawm's bandit-peasant solidarity model inspired Latin Americanists in this field from the 1980s on, as described in the introduction to Luz E. Huertas, Bonnie A. Lucero, and Gregory J. Swedberg, eds., *Voices of Crime: Constructing and Contesting Social Control in Modern Latin America* (Tucson: University of Arizona Press, 2016), 5.

48. The recent work of Lila Caimari and Diego Galeano has been particularly influential among new studies. See, for example, Caimari, *While the City Sleeps*; her chapter, "Police Use of Force and Social Consensus in Buenos Aires," 80–98, among others, in Gema Santamaría and David Carey Jr., eds., *Violence and Crime in Latin America: Representations and Politics* (Norman: University of Oklahoma Press, 2017); and her *Apenas un delincuente: Crimen, castigo y cultura en la argentina, 1880–1955*, 2nd ed. (Buenos Aires: Siglo Veintiuno, 2012). See also Diego Galeano, *Criminosos viajantes: Circulações transnacionais entre Rio de Janeiro e Buenos Aires (1890–1930)* (Rio de Janeiro: Arquivo Nacional, 2016); his *Escritores, detectives y archivistas: La cultura policial en Buenos Aires, 1821–1910* (Buenos Aires: Teseo, 2009); and his chapter "Traveling Criminals and Transnational Police Cooperation in South America, 1890–1920," 17–50, as well as the others in Huertas, Lucero, and Swedberg, *Voices of Crime*.

49. Galeano, "Traveling Criminals and Transnational Police Cooperation"; Mercedes García Ferrari, *Ladrones conocidos/sospechosos reservados: Identificación policial en Buenos Aires, 1880–1905* (Buenos Aires: Prometeo Libros, 2010); and Mercedes García Ferrari, "Dissemination of the Argentine Dactyloscopy System in the Early Twentieth Century: Local, Regional, and International Dimensions," in *Identification and Registration Practices in Transnational Perspective: People, Papers, and Practices*, ed. Ilsen About, James Brown, and Gayle Lonergan (London: Palgrave, 2013), 40–58; and Julia Rodriguez, "South Atlantic Crossings: Fingerprints, Science, and the State in Turn-of-the-Century Argentina," *American Historical Review* 109, no. 2 (2004): 387–416.

50. Recent work argues for this rethinking of center and periphery, such as Kerry Carrington, Russell Hogg, and Máximo Sozzo, "Southern Criminology," *British Journal of Criminology* 56 (2016): 1–20; Máximo Sozzo, *Historias de la cuestión criminal en la Argentina* (Buenos Aires: Editores del Puerto, 2009). In addition to this and the above-listed work on dactyloscopy and policing, Stepan's classic *"The Hour of Eugenics"* underscores Latin American innovations in this arena.

51. On both the symbolic and institutional sides, see especially chap. 5, "The Places of Disorder," in Caimari's *While the City Sleeps*, as well as the rest of the book, and Rodríguez, *Civilizing Argentina*.

52. Ricardo D. Salvatore, "The Normalization of Economic Life: Representations of the Economy in Golden-Age Buenos Aires, 1890–1913," *Hispanic American Historical Review* 81, no. 1 (February 2001): 10. See also his earlier work, which helped define the field of study, e.g., "Criminology, Prison Reform, and the Buenos Aires Working Class," *Journal of Interdisciplinary History* 23, no. 2 (1992): 279–299.

53. Devoto, *Historia de la inmigración*; *Memoria del Departamento General de Inmigración correspondiente al año 1894* (Buenos Aires: Imprenta de Pablo E. Coni e Hijos, 1895); G. Romagnolli, *Aspectos jurídicos e institucionales de las migraciones en la república argentina* (Geneva: International Organization for Migration, 1991), 27–31.

54. See the theoretical discussion of migratory push and pull factors in Moya, *Cousins and Strangers.*

55. Irving Louis Horowitz, *Israeli Ecstasies/Jewish Agonies* (New York: Oxford University Press, 1974), 38; Brodsky, *Sephardi, Jewish, Argentine,* 13–14.

56. Alberto Gerchunoff, *The Jewish Gauchos of the Pampas,* trans. Prudencio de Pereda (Albuquerque: University of New Mexico Press, 1998); Stephen A. Sadow, "Judíos y Gauchos: The Search for Identity in Argentine Jewish Literature," *American Jewish Archives* 34, no. 2 (1982): 164–177.

57. Analyses of Jewish and porteño residential segregation are included in Moya, *Cousins and Strangers,* 180–187; Eugene F. Sofer, *From Pale to Pampa: A Social History of the Jews of Buenos Aires* (New York: Holmes and Meier, 1982), 80–85; and Deutsch, *Crossing Borders,* 47–48.

58. Brodsky, *Sephardi, Jewish, Argentine.*

59. *Memoria del Departamento General de Inmigración.* Chapters 4 and 5 particularly focus on the Jewish population.

60. *Memoria del Departamento General de Inmigración,* 69: "Tan distinta de la demas, tan separada de los argentinos, por raza, lengua, religión y costumbres, es preciso proceder vigorosamente en su educación, teniendo en cuenta que se establecen agrupados, lejos de los centros nacionales . . . para que . . . no sean tampoco un problema social."

61. *Memoria del Departamento General de Inmigración,* 71.

62. Devoto, *Historia de la inmigración,* 360–361.

63. Devoto, *Historia de la inmigración,* 361.

64. On shifts in Argentine immigration policy in relation to the evolution of eugenic thought, see Stepan, *"The Hour of Eugenics,"* 120.

65. Lvovich, *Nacionalismo y antisemitismo.*

66. Minutes and Papers of the Gentlemen's Sub-Committee for Preventative Work, 172–173, Papers of the Jewish Association for the Protection of Girls, Women and Children, Archives of Jewish Care, University of Southampton.

67. Ezres Noshim had conflict, for example, with the larger and more powerful Jewish Union of Polish Residents, or Poilisher Farband, which also worked against the tmeim. Arguments over control of community gatekeeping and the role of Ezres Noshim in the wake of the 1930 court case leave archival traces in an unnumbered packet of Spanish and Yiddish correspondence in box 3, Ezres Noshim Collection, Yidisher Visnshaftlekher Institut, or Instituto Judío de Investigación, Buenos Aires.

68. For example, at its 1910 international conference, the entire international Jewish Association for the Protection of Girls and Women (JAPGW) reported only twenty-nine cases of prevented trafficking in the previous six years. JAPGW, "Official Report of the Jewish International Conference on the Suppression of the Traffic in Girls and Women

Held on April 5th, 6th, and 7th, 1910, in London" (London: JAPGW Central Bureau, 1910), 30.

69. In her recent work on the Jewish community of Tucumán, Argentina, Elisa B. Cohen de Chervonagura connects the social exclusion of two women, a sex worker and a leader of a popular "mestizo" religious cult, to long-term fear of broader social exclusion. Cohen de Chervonagura, *Eshet Jail: Un contrapunto discursive entre dos mujeres judías* (San Miguel de Tucumán: Universidad Nacional de Tucumán, 2015), 19, and her *La comunidad judía de Tucumán: Hombres y mujeres, historias y discursos, 1910–2010* (San Miguel de Tucumán: Universidad Nacional de Tucumán, 2010).

70. Cohen de Chervonagura, *Eshet Jail*, 69–70, underscores the role of possible moral regeneration in Hacer la América.

71. See Jessica R. Pliley, *Policing Sexuality: The Mann Act and the Making of the FBI* (Cambridge, MA: Harvard University Press, 2014).

72. Nathan Englander, *The Ministry of Special Cases* (New York: Knopf, 2007).

73. Her testimony is recounted in the summary of the court case, GdF, 5.

74. Nora Glickman exhaustively surveys related cultural production in *The Jewish White Slave Trade*, including Carlos Luis Serrano's play *Raquel Liberman, una historia de Pichincha*, Humberto Constantini's poem cycle and unfinished novel *Rapsodia de Raquel Liberman*, a fictional biography inspired by her rebellion, Myrtha Schalom's eight-hour 1993 television miniseries *Te llamarás Raquel*, and Glickman's own 1993 play, *Una tal Raquel*, which is based on her research and incorporates Liberman's grandchildren and scenes from Leib Malach's *Ibergus*. Myrtha Schalom has since published a novel based on Liberman's life, *La Polaca: Inmigración, rufianes y esclavas a comienzos del siglo XX* (Buenos Aires: Grupo Editorial Norma, 2003), which has been a best seller in multiple editions in South America. Patricia Suárez published the play *Las Polacas: Historias tártaras, casamentara, la Varsovia* (Buenos Aires: Ediciones Teatro Vivo, 2002). Gabriela Böhm has also produced and directed a short documentary film based on Glickman's research into Liberman's life: *Raquel: A Marked Woman* (USA/Argentina: Böhm Productions, 2014), 34 min.

75. On the Raquel Liberman prize, see www.buenosaires.gob.ar/premioraquelliberman.

76. Isabel Vincent, *Bodies and Souls: The Tragic Plight of Three Jewish Women Forced into Prostitution in the Americas* (New York: William Morrow, 2005).

77. Translation from Spanish by Glickman, *The Jewish White Slave Trade*, 51–52.

78. "Stinking swamp" translated from Yiddish in "Arestirt noch a komisions-mitglider," *Di Prese*, May 29, 1930, 1; and the same article published as "Arestirt noch a komisions-mitglid fun 'Migdal,'" *Di Yidishe Tsaytung*, May 29, 1930, 1.

79. Examples that use this terminology in Spanish and Yiddish press include "Se ha ordenado el procesamiento y la detención de los componentes de la tenebrosa asociación 'Migdal,'" *La Nación*, May 22, 1930, 12; "Fue detenido otro de los miembros de la Sociedad Varsovia," *Crítica*, May 28, 1930, 6; "Arestirt noch a komisions-mitglider," *Di Prese*, May 29, 1930, 1.

80. Related texts that center gender in migration include Laura Agustin, "Migrants in the Mistress's House: Other Voices in the 'Trafficking' Debate," *Social Politics* 12, no. 1 (Spring 2005): 96–117; Laura Agustin, "The Disappearing of a Migration Category: Migrants Who Sell Sex," *Journal of Ethnic and Migration Studies* 32, no. 1 (January 2006): 29–47; Mike Donaldson, ed., *Migrant Men: Critical Studies of Masculinities and the Migration Experience* (New York: Routledge, 2009); Helen Schwenken, "Beautiful Victims

and Sacrificing Heroines: Exploring the Role of Gender Knowledge in Migration Policies," *Signs* 33, no. 4 (Summer 2008): 770-776; Wendy Webster, "Transnational Journeys and Domestic Histories," *Journal of Social History* 39, no. 3 (Spring 2006): 651-666.

81. In 1924 in Buenos Aires, prostitutes charged 5-10 pesos per sex act, and a one-woman brothel brought in 1,200-1,500 pesos per week, of which the prostitute gave half to the property owner. "Traffic in Women and Children: Summary," Buenos Aires Field Reports, 71; "Commercialized Prostitution," Buenos Aires Field Reports, 6; "Prostitute," Buenos Aires Field Reports, 11-12; "Traffic in Women and Children," Buenos Aires Field Reports, 13-14. In comparison, the capital's average male workers in 1925 made 2.5-5 pesos per day if unskilled, 6-10 if skilled, equating to 160-200 pesos per month. Ronald C. Newton, *German Buenos Aires, 1900-1933: Social Change and Cultural Crisis* (Austin: University of Texas Press, 2014), 135; Matthew B. Karush, *Culture of Class: Radio and Cinema in the Making of a Divided Argentina, 1920-1946* (Durham, NC: Duke University Press, 2012), 59.

82. Scholars have become more responsive in recent decades to Salo Baron's 1924 call to develop Jewish history beyond the poles of victimization and triumphalism. Narratives that balance Jewish accommodation and resistance include Natan M. Meir, *Kiev, Jewish Metropolis: A History, 1859-1914* (Bloomington: Indiana University Press, 2010); Elissa Bemporad, *Becoming Soviet Jews: The Bolshevik Experiment in Minsk* (Bloomington: Indiana University Press, 2013); and Jarrod Tanny, *City of Rogues and Schnorrers: Russia's Jews and the Myth of Old Odessa* (Bloomington: Indiana University Press, 2011). Other scholars have sometimes faced criticism for underscoring the lack of unity between all Jews in any given time and place, e.g., the criticism leveled against David Biale's edited tome *Cultures of the Jews: A New History* (New York: Schocken, 2002) and John Efron's *The Jews: A History* (New York: Routledge, 2008). Thanks to Barry Trachtenberg.

83. For one effort at conceptualizing these issues, see Rainer Bauböck and Thomas Faist, *Diaspora and Transnationalism: Concepts, Theories, and Methods* (Amsterdam: Amsterdam University Press, 2010). Some historians have fruitfully approached these challenges by comparing similar groups in different locations, e.g., Samuel L. Baily, *Immigrants in the Lands of Promise: Italians in Buenos Aires and New York City, 1870-1914* (Ithaca, NY: Cornell University Press, 2004). Others have traced migrants from hometowns to host countries, e.g., Moya, *Cousins and Strangers*, and Kobrin, *Jewish Bialystok*. An intriguing approach to the study of mobility is suggested in Torsten Feys's work on shipping companies: Torsten Feys, *The Battle for the Migrants: Introduction of Steamshipping on the North Atlantic and Its Impact on the European Exodus* (Liverpool: Liverpool University Press, 2012).

84. My neighborhood reconstructions are inspired by the seminal work of James Scobie, along with that of Moya and Sofer. James R. Scobie, *Buenos Aires: Plaza to Suburb, 1870-1910* (New York: Oxford University Press, 1974); Moya, *Cousins and Strangers*; Sofer, *From Pale to Pampa*. More recently, Adriana Brodsky physically mapped Sephardi Buenos Aires in *Sephardi, Jewish, Argentine*. Work in the broader field of space and sexuality has also inspired this exploration, although this approach has yet to broadly penetrate Latin American historiography. See Christina Hanhardt, *Safe Space: Gay Neighborhood History and the Politics of Violence* (Durham, NC: Duke University Press, 2013); Kevin J. Mumford, *Interzones: Black/White Sex Districts in Chicago and New York in the Early Twentieth Century* (New York: Columbia University Press, 1997).

85. Jo Doezema traces the parallels between white slave and contemporary victim narratives in "White Slaves, Poor Slavs: Melodrama of Trafficking in Women," *Osteuropa* 56, no. 6 (June 2006): 269. Helen Schwenken makes a similar analysis in "Beautiful Victims and Sacrificing Heroines."

CHAPTER 1 — WHITE SLAVES AND DARK MASTERS

*Epigraphs*: Josephine Butler, "Josephine Butler's Appeal to the Women of America," *Friend's Review* (Philadelphia), July 5, 1888, 49; W. L. [William Leonard] Courtney, "Realistic Drama," *Living Age* (Boston), September 27, 1913, 775.

1. While this chapter predominantly assesses white slave discourses in the United States and Britain, the leadership role of these two countries in international conversations through transnational organizations such as the League of Nations and the International Bureau for the Suppression of the Traffic in Women translated to an outsized voice in world conversations and policy decisions. Further work comparing and contrasting transnational policies and discussions is ongoing, for example, through the UK Arts and Humanities Research Council–funded multinational project on "Trafficking, Smuggling and Illicit Migration in Historical and Gendered Perspective, 1870–2000." See http://gtr.rcuk.ac.uk/projects?ref=AH%2FP003273%2F1. Plentiful French voices from the time have been extensively assessed in such work as Jean-Michel Chaumont, *Le mythe de la traite des blanches: Enquête sur la fabrication d'un fléau* (Paris: La Découverte, 2009), and Jean-Michel Chaumont and Christine Machiels, eds., *Du sordide au mythe: L'affaire de la traite des blanches (Bruxelles, 1880)* (Louvain-la-Neuve: Presses universitaires de Louvain, 2009).

2. An especially rich and formerly underutilized resource, the League of Nations archive in Geneva, holds a massive lode of confidential reports from several years of undercover investigation into international sex trafficking in the mid-1920s, during which investigators posing as pimps and brothel owners circulated in underworlds from Asia to Latin America. These papers extensively assess the Argentine underworld as well as dozens of other sites, and sketch global networks of sex work management, with rich detail on the individuals involved and their work strategies. These data, in conjunction with archival material from other antitrafficking efforts, support arguments about the utility of anti-trafficking work for other nation-building projects, such as the consolidation of the U.S. FBI and the tightening of worldwide immigration policy in the 1920s. Jessica R. Pliley, *Policing Sexuality: The Mann Act and the Making of the FBI* (Cambridge, MA: Harvard University Press, 2014); Pliley, "Sexual Surveillance and Moral Quarantines: A History of Anti-trafficking," *openDemocracy*, April 27, 2015, https://www.opendemocracy.net/beyondslavery/jessica-r-pliley/sexual-surveillance-and-moral-quarantines-history-of-antitrafficking; Julia Laite, *Common Prostitutes and Ordinary Citizens: Commercial Sex in London, 1885–1960* (New York: Palgrave Macmillan, 2012); Stephanie A. Limoncelli, "International Voluntary Associations, Local Social Movements and State Paths to the Abolition of Regulated Prostitution in Europe, 1875–1950," *International Sociology* 21, no. 1 (January 2006): 31–59. Rachel Attwood encourages this kind of criticism, e.g., her "Stopping the Traffic: The National Vigilance Association and the International Fight against the 'White Slave' Trade (1899–c. 1909)," *Women's History Review* 24 (2015): 325–350. A new surge of academic interest in the League of Nations is epitomized by Susan Pedersen, *The Guardians: The League of Nations and the Crisis of Empire* (New York: Oxford University Press, 2015). Recent work in French also engages deeply with the

archives of the League's Traffic in Women Committee, e.g., Chaumont, *Le mythe de la traite des blanches*. Field reports from New York City's early twentieth-century anti-vice Committee of Fourteen, held in the New York Public Library, were written by many of the same investigators, and establish the techniques and genre of this undercover collection of underworld information. I use these reports for comparison.

3. Keely Stauter-Halsted thoroughly contextualizes the versions of these stories that circulated in Eastern Europe in her chapter on "Narratives of Entrapment," Keely Stauter-Halsted, *The Devil's Chain: Prostitution and Social Control in Partitioned Poland* (Ithaca, NY: Cornell University Press, 2015), 117–136. For some standard journalistic examples, a 1913 *New York Times* front-page headline warned "Over 50,000 Girls Disappear in This Country Yearly," and the article reprinted protective societies' warnings such as "Girls should never accept sweets, food, a glass of water, or smell flowers offered them by a stranger; neither should they buy scents or other articles at their doors, as so many things may contain drugs." "Over 50,000 Girls Disappear in This Country Yearly," *New York Times*, September 21, 1913.

4. Gretchen Soderlund examines how the *New York Times* shifted its approach to this subject matter in the 1910s in "Covering Urban Vice: The *New York Times*, 'White Slavery,' and the Construction of Journalistic Knowledge," *Critical Studies in Media Communication*, no. 4 (2002): 438–460. Donna Guy, in *Sex and Danger in Buenos Aires: Prostitution, Family, and Nation in Argentina* (Lincoln: University of Nebraska Press, 1991), shows how the statistics from Argentine municipal prostitutes' health registries were used as evidence not just for the existence of sex work, but for the idea that regulation promoted coercive international trafficking. Mark Connelly assesses the sensationalistic misrepresentation of evidence presented by the 1911 Chicago Vice Commission in subsequent white slavery narratives in *The Response to Prostitution in the Progressive Era* (Chapel Hill: University of North Carolina Press, 2011).

5. Billington-Greig was known for distinguishing her feminism from that of the social purity reformers, rejecting white slavery as gossip and media sensationalism, according to Philippa Levine, *Prostitution, Race, and Politics: Policing Venereal Disease in the British Empire* (New York: Routledge, 2003), 249. The Boston theater critic boldly concluded, "There is not, and apparently has not been in recent years, a single well-tested case in which a girl has been trapped into the white slave traffic in this country against her will. Obviously, there are, of course, cases of seduction, and insidious advertisements are sometimes published enticing girls abroad; but the lurid accounts of compulsory detention and outrage appear to be entirely baseless." Courtney, "Realistic Drama." The critique concluded with the suggestion that reformers take heed of these facts and moderate their efforts.

6. "Missing Girls and False Alarms," *New York Times*, December 9, 1913. Other examples of contemporary expressions of doubt about the veracity of white slave stories include "Is White Slavery Nothing More Than a Myth?," *New York Current Opinion* 55, no. 5 (November 1913), and "Popular Gullibility as Expressed in the New White Slavery Hysteria," *New York Current Opinion* 56, no. 2 (February 1914).

7. Some historians have interpreted white slavery in sociological terms, as a moral panic. Mary Ann Irwin frames the impact of the British *Pall Mall Gazette*'s 1885 publication of Stead's "Maiden Tribute of Modern Babylon" as a moral panic caused by the powerful metaphor of white slavery. Mary Ann Irwin, "'White Slavery' as Metaphor: Anatomy of a Moral Panic," *Ex Post Facto: The History Journal* 5 (History Department, San Francisco

State University, 1996). This moral panic was incited by economic and social tensions that the white slavery metaphor tapped into, due to its interpretation of women's blurred sexual and economic roles as a result of changing industrial and urban conditions. Ronald Weitzer argues that today's organized opposition to sex trafficking, including in U.S. government policy, shares the characteristics of a moral panic, based on false or unsubstantiated claims. Ronald Weitzer, "The Social Construction of Sex Trafficking: Ideology and Institutionalization of a Moral Crusade," *Politics & Society* 35, no. 3 (September 1, 2007): 447–475. See also M. Woodiwiss and D. Hobbs, "Organized Evil and the Atlantic Alliance: Moral Panics and the Rhetoric of Organized Crime Policing in America and Britain," *British Journal of Criminology* 49, no. 1 (January 2009): 106–128; C. Barron and D. Lacombe, "Moral Panic and the Nasty Girl," *Canadian Review of Sociology and Anthropology/Revue Canadienne De Sociologie Et De Anthropologie* 42, no. 1 (February 2005): 51–69. This goes beyond a moral crusade, which Weitzer defines as a perceived unmitigated evil that rallies participants to push political elites and institutions to respond, and becomes a moral panic as the menace is portrayed on a scale far beyond objective reality. Ronald Weitzer, "Moral Crusade against Prostitution," *Society*, March–April 2006, 33. See also Weitzer, "Flawed Theory and Method in Studies of Prostitution," *Violence against Women* 11 (2005): 934–949, and William McDonald, "Traffic Counts, Symbols, and Agendas: A Critique of the Campaign against Trafficking of Human Beings," *International Review of Victimology* 11 (2004): 143–176.

8. E.g., a drawing of a theater proprietor shining a light on an exposed woman hiding her face in A. B. Walker, "The White Slave," *Life* 62, no. 1626 (December 25, 1913): 1155. A 1928 *New York Times* discussion of a Parisian theatrical production based on Londres's *The Road to Buenos Ayres* articulated this dual attraction: "Though vice is denounced and punished and virtue is proclaimed and rewarded in the most approved melodramatic tradition . . . it is probably rather the picture of vice than that of virtue which is expected to attract the public." "The Parisian Season Starts," *New York Times*, September 16, 1928.

9. Quoted in Josephine Butler, *Personal Reminiscences of a Great Crusade* (London: Horace Marshall, 1896), 25.

10. Anne Summers, "Which Women? What Europe? Josephine Butler and the International Abolitionist Federation," *History Workshop Journal*, no. 62 (Fall 2006): 215–231. See also Josephine Butler, *Josephine Butler and the Prostitution Campaigns: Diseases of the Body Politic*, vol. 4: *Child Prostitution and the Age of Consent*, ed. Jane Jordan and Ingrid Sharp (New York: Routledge, 2003); Antoinette M. Burton, "The White Woman's Burden: British Feminists and the Indian Woman, 1865–1915," *Women's Studies International Forum* 13, no. 4 (1990): 295–330; Glen Petrie, *A Singular Iniquity: The Campaigns of Josephine Butler* (London: Macmillan, 1971); Bruno P. F. Wanrooij, "Josephine Butler and Regulated Prostitution in Italy," *Women's History Review* 17, no. 2 (April 2008): 153–171; Petra De Vries, "Josephine Butler and the Making of Feminism: International Abolitionism in the Netherlands (1870–1914)," *Women's History Review* 17, no. 2 (April 2008): 257–277.

11. E.g., Butler, *Personal Reminiscences*, 18.

12. "White Slaves for the East," *New York Times*, May 30, 1886.

13. Butler, "Josephine Butler's Appeal."

14. David Brion Davis, "Declaring Equality: Sisterhood and Slavery," in *Women's Rights and Transatlantic Antislavery in the Era of Emancipation*, ed. Kathryn Kish Sklar and James Brewer Stewart (New Haven, CT: Yale University Press, 2007), 15.

15. Paul Michel Baepler, *White Slaves, African Masters* (Chicago: University of Chicago Press, 1999). See also Robert C. Davis, *Christian Slaves, Muslim Masters: White Slavery in the Mediterranean, the Barbary Coast and Italy, 1500–1800* (New York: Palgrave Macmillan, 2003).

16. Charles Sumner, *White Slavery in the Barbary States* (Boston: John P. Jewett, 1853), 83–90. See also Davis, "Declaring Equality" and Lawrence A. Peskin, *Captives and Countrymen: Barbary Slavery and the American Public, 1785–1816* (Baltimore: Johns Hopkins University Press, 2009).

17. Laura Malosetti Costa, *Rapto de cautivas blancas: Un aspecto erótico de la barbarie en la plástica rioplatense del siglo XIX* (Buenos Aires: University de Buenos Aires, 1994).

18. Linda Colley, "Perceiving Low Literature: The Captivity Narrative," *Essays in Criticism* 53, no. 3 (July 2003): 201. See also Colley, *Captives: Britain, Empire, and the World, 1600–1850* (New York: Anchor, 2004).

19. One scholar of captivity narratives argues that they promoted the imperial designs of the West by underlining "a binary division between captive and captor . . . based on cultural, national, or racial difference." Michelle Burnham, *Captivity and Sentiment: Cultural Exchange in American Literature, 1682–1861* (Hanover, NH: University Press of New England, 1997), 2. For an example of the use of the term "white slavery" applied to Indian captivity narratives, see John Rodgers Jewitt, *White Slaves of the Nootka: Narrative of the Adventures and Sufferings of John R. Jewitt while a Captive of the Nootka Indians on Vancouver Island, 1803–05* (Victoria, BC: Heritage House, 1987).

20. "The Italian Boys," *New York Times*, August 21, 1873.

21. Curtis Brown, "Horrible Slavery of Boys in Europe," *Los Angeles Times*, October 12, 1902.

22. On the 1833 British Factory Act, see Harry Hendrick, "Constructions and Reconstructions of British Childhood: An Interpretative Survey, 1800 to the Present," in *Constructing and Reconstructing Childhood: Contemporary Issues in the Sociological Study of Childhood*, ed. Allison James, 2nd ed. (New York: Routledge, 1997), 40.

23. E.g., "A White Slave," *Life* 50, no. 1288 (July 4, 1907): 45. Reprinted from the *New York Evening Sun*.

24. "White Slavery in Russia," *Times of London*, June 3, 1842; A Poor Governess, "White Slavery: To the Editor of the Times," *Times of London*, January 20, 1857.

25. Sinclair Tousey, "White Slaves" (New York, 1863), in New York Public Library, Science, Industry and Business Library, American Broadsides and Ephemera Collection, Series 1, no. 11440.

26. Hugh Price Hughes, "Evangelization of Great Cities," *Chicago Christian Advocate* 66, no. 45 (November 5, 1891): 745–746; Myron Reed, "Many Pulpit Voices: Religious Thought and Progress in the United States; an Epitome of the Sermons of the Week," *Los Angeles Times*, August 30, 1896.

27. For example, see "Trade Union Tyranny," *Los Angeles Times*, April 15, 1903. For more on the antitrust metaphor, see Mara L. Keire, "The Vice Trust: A Reinterpretation of the White Slavery Scare in the United States, 1907–1917," *Journal of Social History* 35, no. 1 (2001): 7.

28. "A White Slave," 45.

29. David R. Roediger, *The Wages of Whiteness: Race and the Making of the American Working Class* (London: Verso, 1991), 65–66. See also the critique of Roediger's work in Gunther Peck, "White Slavery and Whiteness: A Transnational View of the Sources of

Working-Class Radicalism and Racism," *Labor* 1, no. 2 (June 1, 2004): 41–64. Other important works on Jews and whiteness in the United States include Karen Brodkin, *How Jews Became White Folks and What That Says about Race in America* (New Brunswick, NJ: Rutgers University Press, 1999), and Matthew Frye Jacobson, *Whiteness of a Different Color: European Immigrants and the Alchemy of Race* (Cambridge, MA: Harvard University Press, 1998).

30. Just as a slave could not be free, a slave could not be white. Orlando Patterson references this dichotomy in *Slavery and Social Death* (Cambridge, MA: Harvard University Press, 1982), 7.

31. Sexuality, both coercive and consensual, has increasingly become a subject of study in the history of slavery. A few examples include Gwyn Campbell and Elizabeth Elbourne, eds., *Sex, Power, and Slavery* (Columbus: Ohio University Press, 2015); Vincent Woodard, Justin A. Joyce, and Dwight A. McBride, eds., *The Delectable Negro: Human Consumption and Homoeroticism within U.S. Slave Culture* (New York: New York University Press, 2014); and Gregory D. Smithers, *Slave Breeding: Sex, Violence, and Memory in African American History* (Gainesville: University Press of Florida, 2012). An early work on the link between sexuality and abolitionism is Ronald G. Walters, "The Erotic South: Civilization and Sexuality in American Abolitionism," *American Quarterly* 25 (May 1973): 180.

32. Thomas Washington Shannon, *Self Knowledge and Guide to Sex Instruction: Vital Facts of Life for All Ages* (Marietta, OH: S. A. Mullikin, 1913), 585.

33. On the link between sexuality and the rise and fall of the discourse of "authentic whiteness" in the United States between 1890 and 1940, see Julian B. Carter, *The Heart of Whiteness: Normal Sexuality and Race in America, 1880–1940* (Durham, NC: Duke University Press, 2007).

34. Shannon, *Self Knowledge and Guide to Sex Instruction*, 576.

35. See, for example, the image of a completely naked aristocratic white woman surrounded by men in Richard Harding Davis's 1897 cartoon "Refined Young Women Stripped and Searched by Brutal Spaniards while Under Our Flag on the Olivette," published in the *New York Journal*, reprinted in Howard Zinn, Mike Konopacki, and Paul Buhle, *A People's History of American Empire* (New York: Macmillan, 2008), 42.

36. For an interesting exposition of Orientalism and its counterparts among different groups of women in Egypt in this period, see Mervat Hatem, "Through Each Other's Eyes: Egyptian, Levantine-Egyptian, and European Women's Images of Themselves and Each Other (1862–1920)," *Women's Studies International Forum* 12, no. 2 (1989): 133–198.

37. Unnamed London newspaper cited in "Foreign News," *Baltimore Niles' Weekly Register* 22, no. 569 (August 3, 1822): 358–359.

38. Lisa Z. Sigel, "Name Your Pleasure: The Transformation of Sexual Language in Nineteenth-Century British Pornography," *Journal of the History of Sexuality* 9, no. 4 (October 1, 2000): 402–403.

39. "The Odalisque," *Aldine* 7, no. 22 (October 1, 1875): 426–429; "The Odalisque," *Art Journal (1875–1887)* 2 (January 1, 1876): 15. See Mohja Kahf, *Western Representations of the Muslim Woman: From Termagant to Odalisque* (Austin: University of Texas Press, 1999).

40. See "Uplift for Girl Slave: Beautiful Victim of Opium Dens in Santa Barbara to Be Saved," *Los Angeles Times*, November 5, 1905; Mary Ting Yi Liu, "Saving Young Girls from Chinatown: White Slavery and Woman Suffrage, 1910–1920," *Journal of the History of*

*Sexuality* 18, no. 3 (September 2009): 393–417. For an excellent social history of Chinese involvement in prostitution in nineteenth-century San Francisco, see Benson Tong, *Unsubmissive Women: Chinese Prostitutes in Nineteenth-Century San Francisco* (Norman: University of Oklahoma Press, 2000).

41. "Stop Slave Trade," *Los Angeles Times*, September 1, 1907. Brian Donovan's work on the use of white slavery narratives in anti-vice activism in the U.S. Progressive Era explores the construction of whiteness among immigrant groups as well as Anglo-Saxon fears of African Americans and Chinese immigrants. Brian Donovan, *White Slave Crusades: Race, Gender, and Anti-vice Activism, 1887–1917* (Champaign: University of Illinois Press, 2006).

42. "Slaves Sold to the Turk," *New York Times*, March 28, 1886.

43. S. Louise Weintraub, "Sterility, Especially in Syrian Women," *Philadelphia Medical and Surgical Reporter* 58, no. 3 (January 21, 1888): 72; "Slave-Girls in Egypt," *New York Eclectic Magazine of Foreign Literature* 47, no. 4 (April 1888): 519; "The East African Slaves," *New York Times*, December 8, 1889; Annie Reihardt, "Mohammedan Women," *New York Eclectic Magazine of Foreign Literature* 54, no. 2 (August 1891): 173–181.

44. Jo Doezema, *Sex Slaves and Discourse Masters: The Construction of Trafficking* (London: Zed Books, 2010), 135.

45. Freeman Tilden, "His Offensive Success," *Puck* 74, no. 1899 (July 23, 1913): 3; "The Meaning of the White Slave Act as Shown by Federal Decision," *St. Louis Central Law Journal* 77, no. 15 (October 10, 1913): 261; "'White Slave' Act Upheld: Supreme Court Sustains Law to Stop Traffic," *Los Angeles Times*, February 25, 1913; D. J. Leab, "Women and the Mann Act," *Amerikastudien-American Studies* 21, no. 1 (1976): 55–65. On the Mann Act and the FBI, see Pliley, *Policing Sexuality*. The Mann Act was less likely to be used against black men accused of being involved with white women in this era, however, than was lynching.

46. *Congressional Record*, 62nd Congress, 3rd Session (December 11, 1912): 502–503.

47. Roberta S. Gold, "The Black Jews of Harlem: Representation, Identity, and Race, 1920–1939," *American Quarterly* 55, no. 2 (June 1, 2003): 183.

48. George Kibbe Turner's series in *McClure's* (1907–1909), discussed in the section below on Jewish racialization, argued for the protection of the racial purity of Anglo-Saxon women as the basis of civilization and the preservation of the Anglo-Saxon race. Not all anti-vice activists shared these sentiments: In Brian Donovan's analysis of Jane Addams's work, her pluralistic racial ideology provides a contrast to the nativist ideas about Anglo-Saxon superiority promulgated by many journalists and activists. Donovan, *White Slave Crusades*, 64–71. See also Yoosun Park and Susan P. Kemp, "'Little Alien Colonies': Representations of Immigrants and Their Neighborhoods in Social Work Discourse, 1875–1924," *Social Service Review* 80, no. 4 (December 2006): 705–734; J. Beer and K. Joslin, "Diseases of the Body Politic: White Slavery in Jane Addams' 'A New Conscience and an Ancient Evil' and Selected Short Stories by Charlotte Perkins Gilman," *Journal of American Studies* 33 (1999): 1–18.

49. Buenos Aires socialist politician, doctor, and antiprostitution crusader Angel Giménez donated to the National Library in 1935 a copy of Jose Santalo's *La trata de blancas ante los principios fundamentals del derecho* (Madrid, 1913).

50. Santalo, *La trata de blancas,* 17.

51. Anxiety, however, should be qualified as a causal mechanism. Alan Hunt convincingly warns of the limitations of using the concept of social anxiety to uncover "what is

really going on" underneath social and political controversies, including in campaigns against prostitution. Hunt critiques anxiety theories of social concerns from Stuart Hall's work onward, primarily noting that social anxiety over various changes should not be credited as a causal mechanism, although it can be helpful in linking targets and a range of sources. Alan Hunt, "Anxiety and Social Explanation: Some Anxieties about Anxiety," *Journal of Social History* 32, no. 3 (Spring 1999): 509–528.

52. On the redeemers' side, see Judith R. Walkowitz, *City of Dreadful Delight: Narratives of Sexual Danger in Late-Victorian London* (Chicago: University of Chicago Press, 1992).

53. Women abolitionists were called upon to engage with white slavery as wage slavery, just as they were later appealed to with parallels drawn between chattel slavery and sexual slavery. In an 1892 review of a book of poetry, a Boston minister praised a blank-verse poem entitled "The Slave Girl," written "from the standpoint of a daughter of penury and want, a veritable white slave of the despotism of trade." Although this poem refers to industrial, not sexual, white slaves, the reviewer's emphasis on the nobility, purity, and unselfishness of the "young waifs . . . amid the baneful influences of poverty, and the woeful hardships of child labor," echoes sensationalist seduction stories. His call to the conscience emphasizes the poet's sex and appears to target female readers in particular, as he praises women's leadership role in the abolition of chattel slavery and argues for the importance of women's unique moral position from which to "rouse us to a deep sense of our social wrongs." Rev. Thomas O. Marvin, "In the City by the Lake," *Boston Arena*, no. 34 (September 1892).

54. British feminists' self-positioning as mothers of the race is illuminated by Burton, "The White Woman's Burden," 296.

55. Egal Feldman, "Prostitution, the Alien Woman and the Progressive Imagination, 1910–1915," *American Quarterly* 19, no. 2 (1967): 202–206.

56. Nineteenth-century defenders of industrial white slaves were concerned with working men, women, and children, but as the century drew to a close, female workers moved into the spotlight. Sympathetic depictions portrayed exhausted women in factories and tenement houses, supporting sick husbands and children while suffering from near starvation and painful physical conditions brought on by their working conditions. Hypocritical employers dissimulated, such as the Boston clothing house "which repeatedly assert[ed] that its clothing is not made in tenement houses" yet sold tenement-made bespoke clothing for 500 times the pennies paid its women workers. B. O. Flower, "Society's Exiles," *Arena*, no. 19 (June 1891): 3–27. Into the first decade of the twentieth century, although the general understanding of the term "white slavery" emphasized seduction and prostitution, the industrial meaning could still be applied in order to, for example, bemoan the fate of female white slaves in the garment factories of New York's Lower East Side. "A White Slave," 45. This growing interest in women workers as industrial white slaves may have reflected both the broadening association between white slavery and prostitution and the threat that women's work outside the home posed to some.

57. Captivity narratives, particularly those with female subjects, were generally told by two voices: that of the captive and that of a minister harnessing the story in order to encourage repentance and urge readers to stay close to the congregation in order to avoid a similar fate. The archetypical captivity narrative of Mary Rowlandson emphasized the subject's ultimate redemption and Puritan conversion on the other side of her God-given suffering. See Tara Fitzpatrick, "The Figure of Captivity: The Cultural Work of the Puri-

tan Captivity Narrative," *American Literary History* 3, no. 1 (1991): 1–2, 4. One commentator claimed that the religious beliefs of both American Puritans and British Nonconformists (as opposed to Anglicans) encouraged them to perceive captivity as "a God-given affliction designed to chastise the victim into moral and spiritual reformation." Colley, "Perceiving Low Literature," 202. This perspective resonates with the work of fin-de-siècle moral reformers on both sides of the Atlantic, from Josephine Butler to the Hull House social workers.

58. Argentine authors who expressed progressive sympathy for prostitutes through portraying them as victims included Manuel Gálvez, Samuel Eichelbaum, David Viñas, Alicia Muñoz, and César Tiempo. Discussed in Nora Glickman, *The Jewish White Slave Trade and the Untold Story of Raquel Liberman* (New York: Garland, 2000), 30–37. A fascinating alternative to historical religious responses can be found in the Christian harm reduction model promoted by Lia Claire Scholl in *I Heart Sex Workers: A Christian Response to People in the Sex Trade* (Danvers, MA: Chalice Press, 2013).

59. Discussed in Guy, *Sex and Danger*, 30–31.

60. "Harvester Girls Get Increase: Big Trust to Raise Wages to Eight Dollar Minimum, International Company Announces All Women in Their Employ Will Receive Better Pay as Result of Inquiry in Illinois by Senate White Slave Commission," *Los Angeles Times*, March 20, 1913.

61. "Low Wages Do Not Drive Girls Astray: Social Workers Say Too Much Publicity Has Been Given to This as a Cause," *New York Times*, June 22, 1913.

62. "Low Wages Do Not Drive Girls Astray."

63. "Women Mock Investigation: Reformers Hear They Are on Wrong Track," *Los Angeles Times*, March 13, 1913.

64. By the 1890s, the figure of the shopgirl, or department store saleswoman, became popularly associated with white slavery in its aspects of both labor exploitation and prostitution. These young women were endangered not only by their public exposure and ruthless employers, but by their constant exposure to luxury goods far beyond their reach. On respectability and consumption, see also Eileen J. Suárez Findlay, *Imposing Decency: The Politics of Sexuality and Race in Puerto Rico, 1870–1920* (Durham, NC: Duke University Press, 1999), and Leora Auslander, *Taste and Power: Furnishing Modern France* (Berkeley: University of California Press, 1998). A Boston minister in 1891 warned that "in some of the largest stores in Boston the young women employed are paid disgraceful wages, with an intimation that they must get what more is necessary to maintain themselves in health and food through nameless vice." Hughes, "Evangelization of Great Cities." An 1894 critic of industrial capitalism lamented the predicament of department store saleswomen, exploited by "white slave dealer" employers, and passé after only five years of employment, leaving them no recourse but to find other employment (the sexual nature of such implied). John J. O'Shea, "The White-Slave Trade," *New York Catholic World* 59, no. 351 (June 1894): 418–425. The Committee of Fifteen in New York created a subcommittee to investigate the role of department store employment as a stepping stone to prostitution, and published a report on the subject in 1915, which confirmed the link between the exposure of these young women to a higher standard of living and their downfall, as the most highly paid saleswomen were found to be the most likely to become prostitutes. Citation of the Committee of Fifteen Report from Ruth Rosen's introduction to Maimie Pinzer and Fanny Quincy Howe, *The Maimie Papers: Letters from an Ex-prostitute*, edited by Ruth Rosen, Sue Davidson, and Florence Howe

(New York: Feminist Press, 1997), xxi. See also Pamela Cox's BBC series *Shopgirls: The True Story of Life behind the Counter* (2014).

65. Albert Londres, *Le Chemin de Buenos Aires* (1927); *The Road to Buenos Ayres* (New York: Boni & Liveright, 1928), first published in French as a newspaper series in 1927, and circulating in South America in Spanish in the same year. For press coverage of the book's reception, see, for example, "New Books in Brief Review: The Road to Buenos Ayres," *Independent* 120, no. 4071 (June 9, 1928): 557; "The Parisian Season Starts," *New York Times*, September 16, 1928. Its rise to best-selling status in the United States is described in "'Boss' v. 'Slaves,'" *Time*, May 21, 1928.

66. Butler, "Josephine Butler's Appeal," 2.

67. "German Slaves in the East: Public Sales of European Girls in Constantinople," *New York Times*, October 14, 1888.

68. "Sanitary Matters in Buenos Ayres," *Lancet* 69, no. 1 (January 17, 1891): 156–157.

69. Donna Guy, "'White Slavery,' Citizenship, and Nationality in Argentina," in *White Slavery and Mothers Alive and Dead: The Troubled Meeting of Sex, Gender, Public Health, and Progress in Latin America* (Lincoln: University of Nebraska Press, 2000).

70. "Vice Trust Exposed and Heads Indicted," *New York Times*, June 13, 1913; "Police Want Gangster Who Abducted a Girl: Organized Traffic to South America Charged," *New York Times*, June 23, 1917.

71. "Man's Commerce in Women," *McClure's Magazine* 41, no. 4 (August 1913): 185.

72. "Police Want Gangster Who Abducted a Girl."

73. Paul Knepper, "The 'White Slave Trade' and the Music Hall Affair in 1930s Malta," *Journal of Contemporary History* 44, no. 2 (2009): 205–206.

74. Antoni Marczyński and Anthony Kirkor (pseud.), *The Ravishers: A Novel of White Slavery in Its Heyday* (New York: Ignis, 1955). Translated from the 1930 Polish *Szlakiem hańby*.

75. Dr. Kay Drake, "Philip Guedalla Tangoes through the Argentine," *New York Times*, March 5, 1933.

76. "'Little Bandit' Given: Melodrama Opens at the Public Theatre after Brooklyn Run," *New York Times*, April 19, 1935.

77. Hilary Evans, *Harlots, Whores & Hookers: A History of Prostitution* (New York: Taplinger, 1979), 205. See also Sean O'Callaghan, *Damaged Baggage: The White Slave Trade and Narcotics Trafficking in the Americas* (London: Hale, 1969).

78. Julio L. Alsogaray, *Trilogia de la trata de blancas: Rufianes, policía, municipalidad* (Buenos Aires: L. J. Rosso, 1933), 102.

79. The book's popularity and Irigoyen's reaction noted in "'Boss' v. 'Slaves'"; see also David Rock, *Argentina 1516–1987: From Spanish Colonization to Alfonsín* (Berkeley: University of California Press, 1987), 208.

80. Andrew Thompson, "Informal Empire? An Exploration in the History of Anglo-Argentine Relations, 1810–1914," *Journal of Latin American Studies* 24, no. 2 (1992): 419–436. For further discussion of Argentina's relationship in this era to Britain and the United States, see Ricardo D. Salvatore, "The Unsettling Location of a Settler Nation: Argentina, from Settler Economy to Failed Developing Nation," *South Atlantic Quarterly* 107, no. 4 (Fall 2008): 755–789.

81. H. S. Ferns, *Britain and Argentina in the Nineteenth Century* (Oxford: Clarendon Press, 1960), 492–493; Rock, *Argentina 1516–1987*, 154, 168.

82. The distance between the United States and Argentina was decreased at this time by the establishment in February 1930 of a passenger airline from New York to Buenos Aires, reducing the length of the transcontinental trip to less than one week. "Shrinking the Americas," *Los Angeles Times*, February 15, 1930. At the same time, Argentine exports of beef, flax, alfalfa, and fruit to Europe increased in comparison with the United States, provoking rivalry between the two countries. The U.S. meat industry was in stiff competition with Argentina for the British market, as Argentina surpassed the United States as the major supplier to Britain after 1900. Rock, *Argentina 1516–1987*, 171–172; Simon G. Hanson, *Argentine Meat and the British Market: Chapters in the History of the Argentine Meat Industry* (Stanford, CA: Stanford University Press, 1938), 119–208; Peter H. Smith, *Politics and Beef in Argentina: Patterns of Conflict and Change* (New York: Columbia University Press, 1969). See also David M. K. Sheinin, *Argentina and the United States: An Alliance Contained* (Athens: University of Georgia Press, 2006). While the international image of goods passing in and out of the Rio de la Plata continued to be overshadowed by *The Road to Buenos Ayres*, the international press of early 1930 linked a new fear to Argentina: psittacosis, or parrot fever. As a handful of deaths and widespread parrot fever panic swept the United States, an embargo was placed on parrot imports from South America. "Consider Embargo on Parrot Imports," *New York Times*, January 16, 1930. For broader analysis, see Jill Lepore, "It's Spreading: Outbreaks, Media Scares, and the Parrot Panic of 1930," *New Yorker*, June 1, 2009. Argentina responded defensively to the U.S. embargo and the associated brouhaha. A strongly worded editorial reaction in the Argentine daily *La Prensa* connected the international fears of parrot fever to other allegations against Argentine animal and agricultural exports. Cited in "Buenos Aires Paper Lays Trouble to Us," *New York Times*, March 13, 1930. The *La Prensa* editorial claimed that the United States had launched anti-Argentine propaganda campaigns in Germany, France, and Great Britain, which associated Argentine beef with hoof and mouth disease and Argentine fruit with the Mediterranean fruit fly. The parrot fever panic, asserted the editors of *La Prensa*, was also instigated by U.S. propagandists, and was equally unfair: not only did official investigations reveal the safety of these Argentine exports, it was a well-known fact that no parrots were exported from Argentina. The Argentine press thus blamed recent European criticisms of Argentine imported food products on the inaccurate parrot fever allegations, promulgated by the United States and its worries about Argentine trade competition in the European marketplace. *La Prensa* thus attempted to vindicate Argentina in European eyes from the jealous rumor mongering of the United States, and free the nation from accusations of contagion, an analogy easily drawn to prostitution. Fundamentally, international concerns with both parrot fever and the white slave traffic to Argentina were rooted in fears about cross-border flows, the consequences of travel and trade, and the dangers of cross-cultural contact.

83. E.g., "Inem land fun frien handl" (In the Land of Free Trade), *Di Prese*, June 2, 1930, 6.

84. At the time of the Special Body of Experts' investigation into the traffic, in the mid-1920s, Argentina was not a member of the League (it was a founding member, left in 1921 and returned in 1933). Argentina did have a League of Nations Association, which Bascom Johnson, the Experts' director of investigations, spoke of with high praise. The Argentine Association's leader Lodi told him that the nation's rejoining of the League

was only blocked by those in Congress aligned with the Irigoyen faction. National politics thus shaped Argentina's position on the League's world map. Letter from Bascom Johnson in Montevideo to William F. Snow (June 19, 1924), 5, S171, League of Nations Archive, Geneva.

85. "Commission Revises White Slave Report: Latin Nations at Geneva Charge It Criticizes Them and Whitewashes Anglo-Saxons," *New York Times*, November 27, 1927.

86. "Commission Revises White Slave Report"; League of Nations, *Report of the Special Body of Experts on Traffic in Women and Children*, part 2 (Geneva: League of Nations, 1927) (henceforth League of Nations, *Experts' Report*, pt. 2).

87. Luisi surprised Snow and Johnson with her pushback, as she had led the successful effort to convince the Uruguayan government to accept the League's 1921 convention. But after the second volume of the *Experts' Report* was published, she became its most vocal critic, boycotted the fourth, fifth, and sixth sessions of the committee, and criticized the report intensely at the seventh session. She refused to sign the final product, and proposed that it be published along with her statement that it was not satisfactory from the South American perspective. She complained in a letter to the League's secretary general Eric Drummond that the South American research had been "very insufficient and somewhat superficial" and that the researchers had chosen their sites based on where the most comfortable and convenient hotels were located. See Paul Knepper, "The International Traffic in Women: Scandinavia and the League of Nations Inquiry of 1927," *Journal of Scandinavian Studies in Criminology and Crime Prevention* 14, no. 1 (May 1, 2013): 73, on Snow's 1927 letter to Drummond of December 5, 1927, S181, League of Nations Archive, Geneva.

88. League of Nations, *Report of the Special Body of Experts on Traffic in Women and Children*, part 1 (Geneva: League of Nations, 1927), 12.

89. Feldman, "Prostitution."

90. Rutvica Andrijasevic makes a similar claim for contemporary activists against Eastern European trafficking in women, throughout "Beautiful Dead Bodies: Gender, Migration, and Representation in Anti-trafficking Campaigns," *Feminist Review* 86, no. 1 (2007): 24-44.

91. "Respectable Persons" section in "Codebook [to code used in Field Reports]," Field Reports on Investigation of International Traffic in Women and Children Made for the Special Body of Experts to Study the International Traffic in Women and Children, S171, League of Nations Archive, Geneva. On Johnson's career, see Allan M. Brandt, *No Magic Bullet: A Social History of Venereal Disease in the United States since 1880*, 2nd ed. (New York: Oxford University Press, 1987), 59, 73-75, 94; Thomas C. Mackey, *Pursuing Johns: Criminal Law Reform, Defending Character, and New York City's Committee of Fourteen, 1920-1930* (Columbus: Ohio State University Press, 2005), 251n1; Kevin J. Mumford, *Interzones: Black/White Sex Districts in Chicago and New York in the Early Twentieth Century* (New York: Columbia University Press, 1997), 19n20; "Bascom Johnson, Lawyer, 76, Dead," *New York Times*, October 21, 1954, 27; and Knepper, "International Traffic in Women."

92. Kinzie's ruse exemplified, e.g., "Traffic in Women and Children: Summary," May 25-June 14, 1924, Buenos Aires Field Reports, Field Reports on Investigation of International Traffic in Women and Children Made for the Special Body of Experts to Study the International Traffic in Women and Children, S148, League of Nations Archive, Geneva, 14 (henceforth Buenos Aires Field Reports); "Traffic in Women and Children:

General Summary," July 24, 1924, Rio de Janeiro Field Reports, Field Reports on Investigation of International Traffic in Women and Children Made for the Special Body of Experts to Study the International Traffic in Women and Children, S148, League of Nations Archive, Geneva, 33 (henceforth Rio Field Reports).

93. "Tunis, Tunisia: Traffic in Women and Children," February 23-24, 1925, Field Reports on Investigation of International Traffic in Women and Children Made for the Special Body of Experts to Study the International Traffic in Women and Children, S148, League of Nations Archive, Geneva, 2-3.

94. "Houses of Prostitution," Buenos Aires Field Reports, 3-4; "Vice Trust Exposed and Heads Indicted," New York Times, June 13, 1913, 4; "Accuses the Police in Vice Trust Plot," New York Times, August 31, 1915, 6; "Slavery Evidence Stolen," New York Times, October 4, 1916, 7; "Head of Vice Trust Faces Court Today: 'Mortche' Goldberg, Indicted in 1913, Caught after Flight to Argentina," New York Times, March 25, 1915, 5.

95. Notecards in Boxes 43 and 50, Committee of Fourteen Collection, Rare Books and Manuscripts Division, New York Public Library.

96. Dame Rachel Crowdy, the head of the League's Social Questions Section, pushed back against the support that the head of the League's Latin American bureau had offered Luisi's protest. Luisi had expressed concern that Jack London's recent popular publication unfairly centered South America in the international traffic in women, and must have been based on supposedly confidential police evidence. Crowdy points out that Luisi must have confused London, deceased for several years, with Albert Londres's The Road to Buenos Ayres, but does not address the implied data leak. Letter from Rachel Crowdy to Cristobal Rodriguez, December 12, 1927, S166, League of Nations Archive, Geneva, 2-3.

97. "Traffic in Women and Children: Summary."

98. "Traffic in Women and Children: General Summary."

99. My analysis of pages 11-186 of League of Nations, Experts' Report, pt. 2.

100. The n-word was used without censorship in field reports and notes, while sexual terms were replaced with dashes. E.g., "Marseilles, France: Traffic in Women and Children," January 1-5, 1925, Field Reports on Investigation of International Traffic in Women and Children Made for the Special Body of Experts to Study the International Traffic in Women and Children, S148, League of Nations Archive, Geneva, 1 (henceforth Marseilles Field Reports), and Rio Field Reports, 11.

101. "Head of the White Slavers?," Buenos Aires Herald, June 24, 1930.

102. On similarities and differences between European and Latin American experts in this era, see Nancy Leys Stepan, "The Hour of Eugenics": Race, Gender, and Nation in Latin America (Ithaca, NY: Cornell University Press, 1996), e.g., 137-139.

103. Annexes II and III, 196-197, in League of Nations, Experts' Report, pt. 2.

104. Buenos Aires Field Reports, 16.

105. League of Nations, Experts' Report, pt. 2, 6.

106. E.g., Luisi's protest, discussed above. Her concern was in part to distinguish Uruguayan antitrafficking efforts from Argentine failures. "Commission Revises White Slave Report."

107. "Hablan de la trata de blancas en la liga de naciones," La Calle, September 19, 1928, 15.

108. Analysis of page counts from League of Nations, Experts' Report, pt. 2, 11-192.

109. See Texas railroad map at http://www.lib.utexas.edu/maps/atlas_texas/rail_road_texas_1860.jpg.

110. League of Nations, *Experts' Report*, pt. 2, 15, 131, 138.

111. Traffic in Women and Children, Salto, Uruguay, and Concordia, Argentina, Report from Montevideo, June 28, 1924, in Montevideo Field Reports, June 22–July 3, 1924, Field Reports on Investigation of International Traffic in Women and Children Made for the Special Body of Experts to Study the International Traffic in Women and Children, S179, League of Nations Archive, Geneva, 7–8 (henceforth Salto and Concordia Field Report).

112. Salto and Concordia Field Report, 14.

113. December 31, 1923, law 817 restricting immigration discussed in G. Romagnolli, *Aspectos jurídicos e institucionales de las migraciones en la república argentina* (Geneva: International Organization for Migration, 1991), 15–17; Fernando Devoto, *Historia de la inmigración en la Argentina* (Buenos Aires: Editorial Sudamericana, 2003), 360–361.

114. Jessica R. Pliley analyzes the relationship between border control and antitrafficking efforts in the U.S. context in *Policing Sexuality* and "Sexual Surveillance and Moral Quarantines."

115. Devoto, *Historia de la inmigración*, 361.

### CHAPTER 2 — JEWISH TRAFFIC IN WOMEN

*Epigraph*: Sholem Aleichem, "The Man from Buenos Aires," in *Tevye the Dairyman and The Railroad Stories*, trans. Hillel Halkin (New York: Schocken Books, 1987), 176 (originally published in 1909 as "Der mentsch fun Buenos Aires"). Although Hillel Halkin substitutes the term "Hanukkah candles," Sholem Aleichem's term "etrogim" comes from the Hebrew word for the ritual fruit, a citron, used in the celebration of the harvest holiday of Sukkot as a symbol of purity and perfection. This symbol provides an ironic juxtaposition between purity and the violation of purity at the core of the man's actual business.

1. Aleichem, "The Man from Buenos Aires," 167, 176.

2. Sholem Asch, *Motke Ganef* (New York: Forverts, 1916), initially published serially in the New York Yiddish newspaper *Forverts* and the Warsaw-based *Haynt*. See Nora Glickman's analysis of his work in *The Jewish White Slave Trade and the Untold Story of Raquel Liberman* (New York: Garland, 2000), 18–19.

3. Oral history quoted in Val Marie Johnson, "Protection, Virtue, and the 'Power to Detain': The Moral Citizenship of Jewish Women in New York City, 1890–1920," *Journal of Urban History* 31, no. 5 (2005): 655.

4. *Di Prese*, September 8, 1930.

5. Isaac Bashevis Singer, *Scum*, trans. Rosaline Dukalskv Schwartz (New York: Farrar, Straus & Giroux, 1991). Glickman further analyzes his work on the subject in *The Jewish White Slave Trade*, 26–28. See also Maxine A. Hartley, *Guide to the Works of Isaac Bashevis Singer* (New York: Vantage, 2009).

6. White supremacist internet message boards recycle versions of the Jew as white slaver, both as pimp and reversing the natural order of things by enslaving the white man for the benefit of the black man. David Duke has spoken and published on white supremacist sites about Jewish sexual enslavement of non-Jewish white women for profit, e.g., www.stormfront.org/forum/t1095380/ and www.stormfront.org/forum/t1112725/. The famous (and fictitious) formulation of this trope in *The Protocols of the Elders of Zion* has continued to circulate since its initial publication in 1903.

7. Frank Felsenstein, *Anti-Semitic Stereotypes: A Paradigm of Otherness in English Popular Culture, 1660–1830* (Baltimore, MD: Johns Hopkins University Press, 1995), 54–55.

8. Matthew Biberman, *Masculinity, Anti-Semitism and Early Modern English Literature: From the Satanic to the Effeminate Jew* (Burlington, VT: Ashgate, 2004), 153.

9. Sander L. Gilman, "Sibling Incest, Madness, and the 'Jews,'" *Social Research* 65, no. 2 (1998): 401-433.

10. Matthew Frye Jacobson, "Looking Jewish, Seeing Jews," in *Whiteness of a Different Color: European Immigrants and the Alchemy of Race* (Cambridge, MA: Harvard University Press, 1998), 170-199. See also Eric Goldstein, *The Price of Whiteness: Jews, Race, and American Identity* (Princeton, NJ: Princeton University Press, 2006); Karen Brodkin, *How Jews Became White Folks and What That Says about Race in America* (New Brunswick, NJ: Rutgers University Press, 1999); K. Hodl, "The Black Body and the Jewish Body: A Comparison of Medical Images," *Patterns of Prejudice* 36, no. 1 (January 2002): 17-34; and Sander L. Gilman, *The Jew's Body* (New York: Routledge, 1991).

11. Jeffrey Lesser, *Welcoming the Undesirables: Brazil and the Jewish Question* (Berkeley: University of California Press, 1995), 4-6.

12. Marion A. Kaplan, *Dominican Haven: The Jewish Refugee Settlement in Sosua, 1940-1945* (New York: Museum of Jewish Heritage, 2008), 23, 26.

13. "Camara criminal y correccional de la capital de la República: Asociación ilicita—prision preventiva," *Jurisprudencia Argentina*, vol. 35, year 1931 (Buenos Aires: Revista de Jurisprudencia Argentina, 1932), 9-19.

14. On nationalism and antisemitism, see Daniel Lvovich, *Nacionalismo y antisemitismo en la Argentina* (Buenos Aires: Javier Vergara, 2003). During this nationalist peak, antisemitic publications included the anonymous *Historia de una infamia judia* (Buenos Aires: Cuadernos Antijudios, 1938), which elaborated on the Protocols of the Elders of Zion and advertised to the "anti-Jewish Argentine" wishing to collaborate in the "anti-Jewish struggle" materials for purchase at six different price levels that included monthly delivery of multiple copies of anti-Jewish flyers, leaflets, broadsheets, postcards, stickers for their own use, and distribution as well as daily issues of the newspaper *Crisol*.

15. G. Joseph, "Taking Race Seriously: Whiteness in Argentina's National and Transnational Imaginary," *Identities* 7, no. 3 (2000): 333-371.

16. "Philip Bernstein now in uniform. . . . Being of the [Jewish] race of which the majority of that district are composed, it would seem that he was fitted for the place." Letter from Committee of Fourteen Secretary Thomas H. Reed to Theodore A. Bingham, November 20, 1908. "The younger of the two women was of the unusual type of Italian, very tall for that race." Letter from Thomas H. Reed to John H. Russell, July 9, 1908. Both in box 13, Committee of Fourteen, New York Public Library Manuscripts and Archives Division.

17. "Commercialized Prostitution," Rio de Janeiro Field Reports, Field Reports on Investigation of International Traffic in Women and Children Made for the Special Body of Experts to Study the International Traffic in Women and Children, S148, League of Nations Archive, Geneva, 1 (henceforth Rio Field Reports).

18. Reginald Wright Kauffman, *The House of Bondage* (New York: Grosset & Dunlap, 1910), 19, 31.

19. E.g., "Pursued by Police: Midnight Hunt for White Slavers," *Buenos Aires Herald*, May 22, 1930.

20. "Wiles of the White Slave Trader: Charitable Institution as 'Exchange,'" *Buenos Aires Herald*, May 11, 1930.

21. Rio Field Reports, 11.

22. My survey of index cards in box 50, Committee of Fourteen, New York Public Library Manuscripts and Archives Division.

23. "Head of the White Slavers?," *Buenos Aires Herald*, June 24, 1930.

24. Albert Londres, *The Road to Buenos Ayres* (New York: Boni & Liveright, 1928). First published in French as a newspaper series the previous year.

25. For press coverage of the book's reception, see, for example, "New Books in Brief Review: *The Road to Buenos Ayres*," *Independent* 120, no. 4071 (June 9, 1928): 557; "The Parisian Season Starts," *New York Times*, September 16, 1928. Its rise to best-selling status in the United States is described in "'Boss' v. 'Slaves,'" *Time*, May 21, 1928.

26. William T. Stead, *The Maiden Tribute of Modern Babylon: The Complete Exposé by the Pall Mall Gazette of the Illicit Traffic in Children, Illustrating the Prevalence of the Criminal Practices through Which They Are Decoyed from Their Homes into a Life of Shame* (London: International, 1885).

27. Londres, *The Road to Buenos Ayres*, 166–167.

28. Londres, *The Road to Buenos Ayres*, 176.

29. E.g., "Hoy," *Crítica*, May 22, 1930: "Pudicamente, con una hipocresia un tanto digna de la mentalidad puritana, se puso el grito en el cielo cuando un escritor como Albert Londres, en un libro célèbre que ha tenido el destino de darle a nuestra ciudad una mala fama mundial, puso el dedo en la enorme llaga" (Basically, with a hypocrisy somewhat worthy of the Puritan mentality, the cry went up to the heavens when a writer like Albert Londres, in a famous book that has had the fate of giving our city a bad reputation world-wide, put his finger in the gaping wound). One article in the Yiddish press took the opposite tack, deliberately misreading his book and offering statistics that minimized the Jewish role: "The focus remains now as before all around the 'Migdal' issue, as if there could be found the only, or at least the greatest source of procuring. Statistics show best that this is not so: each year Argentina 'consumes' around 10,000 'new' prostitutes who are brought by woman traffickers, at most 1,500 of them by Jews. The 'rest' are supplied by the French, Italians and others, and thus the Jewish pimps take such a small place in the well known book *The Road to Buenos Ayres*." "Der kamf mitn rufianizm," *Der shpigl: Vokhnzhurnal far visn, literatur un untervalt* 2, no. 65 (October 6, 1930): 3–4.

30. See Beatriz Kushnir, *Baile de máscaras: Mulheres judias y prostituaição; As polacas e suas associações de ajuda mútua* (Rio de Janeiro: Imago Ed., 1996), 83, on French and Jewish women as exotic in Rio de Janeiro in the late nineteenth century.

31. *Ruso* and *rusa* predominated as the usual term in the earlier period of Jewish migration to Argentina, as in the series of memoirs from the national immigration department from the early to mid-1890s archived at the Centro de Estudios Migratorios Latinoamericanos in Buenos Aires, e.g., *Memoria del Departamento General de Inmigracion Corespondiente al año 1894*, presented by the Comisario General Juan A. Alsina (BA: Imprenta de Pablo E. Coni e Hijos, 1895); chap. 6 of the 1892 volume.

32. Patricia Suárez, *Las polacas: Historias tártaras, casamentara, la Varsovia* (Buenos Aires: Ediciones Teatro Vivo, 2002); Myrtha Schalom, *La polaca: Inmigracion, rufianes y esclavas a comienzos del siglo XX* (Buenos Aires: Grupo Editorial Norma, 2003). The label of "polaca" as a generic name for Jewish prostitutes historically is discussed in Ernesto Goldar, *La "mala vida"* (Buenos Aires: Centro Editor de América Latina, 1971), 48, and Glickman, *The Jewish White Slave Trade*, 7.

33. Antoni Marczyński and Anthony Kirkor (pseud.), *The Ravishers: A Novel of White Slavery in Its Heyday* (New York: Ignis, 1955), uses the term "polaca" to refer to all prostitutes in Argentina, regardless of whether or not they were Jewish or from Poland. Note that this is a Polish publication. See also Ana María Shua, *El libro de los recuerdos* (Buenos Aires: Sudamericana, 1994), 1, 9, and related discussion in Silvia G. Dapía, "Polish and Jewish Identities in the Narratives of Ana María Shua," *Polish American Studies* 65, no. 2 (October 1, 2008): 65.

34. Ruth Walkinshaw, "Special Report to Miss Grace Abbot: Some Facts about Prostitution and Traffic in Women in Rio de Janeiro, Sao Paulo, and Santos, Brazil," January 1925, 1 in Buenos Aires Correspondence, S171, League of Nations Archive, Geneva.

35. Walkinshaw, "Special Report to Miss Grace Abbot," 3.

36. Donna Guy articulates this policy trend in "Medical Imperialism Gone Awry: The Campaign against Legalized Prostitution in Latin America," in *White Slavery and Mothers Alive and Dead: The Troubled Meeting of Sex, Gender, Public Health, and Progress in Latin America* (Lincoln: University of Nebraska Press, 2000), 17–32.

37. *Las camareras y el diablo verde: Historia complete para hombres solos* (Francisco Matera: Buenos Aires, 1909), 7. Thanks to Pablo Ben.

38. *Las camareras y el diablo verde*, 6.

39. *Las camareras y el diablo verde*, 7.

40. E.g., "El pan dulce del cesante," from Roberto Arlt's *Nuevas aguafuertes portenas* (Buenos Aires: Hachette, 1960), 103–107. On Roberto Arlt, see his *Los siete locos: Novela* (Buenos Aires: Editorial Claridad, 1929), and *Los lanzallamas* (Buenos Aires: Editorial Claridad, 1931); and for interesting interpretations of his work, see M. Sierra, "Gender Constructions in Avantgarde Argentine Literature: Productivity and the Human Body in the Works of Raul Scalabrini Ortiz, Roberto Arlt and Enrique Gonzalez Tunon," *Revista de estudios hispanicos* 35, no. 1 (2001): 21–47; and Abelardo Hernando, "Clase social y genero sexual en la formacion del sujeto pequeno burgues: Buenos Aires 1920–1940" (PhD diss., University of California, San Diego, 1998). Borges's short story "Emma Zunz" features a Jewish character in the Argentine underworld; Ilan Stavans, "Emma Zunz: The Jewish Theodicy of Jorge Luis Borges," *Modern Fiction Studies* 32, no. 3 (1986): 469–475.

41. J. Eugenio Sallot, *La trata de blancas o sea los negociantes de carne humana y variadas décimas modernas para cantar con guitarra* (Buenos Aires: Biblioteca Criolla Lehmann-Nitsche, 1912).

42. Victorio Luis Bessero, *Los tratantes de blancas en Buenos Aires: El escandalo de la pseuda sociedad "Varsovia" o "Migdal"* (Buenos Aires: Aspasia, 1930), 3.

43. Julio L. Alsogaray, *Trilogia de la trata de blancas: Rufianes, policía, municipalidad* (Buenos Aires: L. J. Rosso, 1933), 72, 92.

44. Alsogaray, *Trilogia de la trata de blancas*, 87.

45. Analysis of Martel's work based on Sandra McGee Deutsch, *Las Derechas: The Extreme Right in Argentina, Brazil, and Chile, 1890–1939* (Stanford, CA: Stanford University Press, 1999), 27–28.

46. Tiberio Lolo, *El peligro semita en la República Argentina: Algunas reflexiones y observaciones hechas a la ligera y sin mayores pretensiones* (Buenos Aires: America Latina, 1919).

47. D. S. Castro, "The Sainete Porteño, 1890–1935: The Image of Jews in the Argentine Popular Theater," *Studies in Latin American Popular Culture* 21 (2002): 29–57.

48. For example, Jewish stinginess and the large nose are exaggerated in a cartoon published in *Crítica* in the midst of the 1930 arrests of Varsovia Society members, in which a Jew complaining of a stomachache awakens a coreligionist pharmacist friend in the middle of the night, who tells him he doesn't need a prescription when he can just drink a warm glass of water. Sancha, "Una Mala Noche," *Crítica*, May 17, 1930, 10.

49. Examples of this kind of antisemitic expression include *Un judío contesta a tres argentinos* (Buenos Aires: Folleto del Judische Wochenscha, 1946), a thirty-page anonymous letter that purports to be by a Jew and justifies antisemitic characterizations of Jews as "truhanes, gangsters, canallas y traficantes de blancas" (46). The work's publisher also advertises in the back of the work a Spanish translation of *The Protocols of the Elders of Zion*, and other works on Henry Ford, the Rothchilds, and the link between Judaism and masonry. See also the elaboration of the Jewish threat to Argentina in Jacques Zoilo Scyzoryk's *El imperio judeo-sionista y la desintegracion argentina* (Buenos Aires: Continente Indoamericano, 1972). Similar subjects are dealt with by right-wing nationalist Federico Rivanera Carles in *Los judíos y la trata de blancas en Argentina* (Buenos Aires: Instituto de investigaciones sobre la cuestion judia, 1986), which was widely available in the 1980s in urban street corner newspaper kiosks and used reproductions of police records from the 1890s to lay exclusive blame on the Jews for the country's entire history of "white slavery." The same author also published *El judaismo y la semana tragica: La verdadera historia de los sucesos de enero de 1919* (Buenos Aires: Instituto de investigaciones sobre la cuestion judia, 1986) and *¡Los judios son nuestros enemigos! Sus leyes ordenan apartar, odiar, robar, oprimir y asesinar a los no-judios* (Buenos Aires: Instituto de investigaciones sobre la cuestion judia, 1987).

50. Bessero, *Los tratantes de blancas en Buenos Aires*, 3.

51. Alsogaray, *Trilogia de la trata de blancas*, 58–59.

52. Alsogaray, *Trilogia de la trata de blancas*, 60–61.

53. A contemporary international business parallel can be drawn to the concentration of Jews in the international ostrich feather trade. Sarah Abrevaya Stein, *Plumes: Ostrich Feathers, Jews, and a Lost World of Global Commerce* (New Haven, CT: Yale University Press, 2008).

54. Ira Rosenswaike, "The Jewish Population of Argentina: Census and Estimate, 1887–1947," *Jewish Social Studies* 22, no. 4 (October 1960): 196; Ricardo Feierstein, *Historia de los judíos argentinos*, 3rd ed. (Buenos Aires: Galerna, 2006), 136–137.

55. Rosenswaike, "The Jewish Population of Argentina," 196.

56. Boleslao Lewin, *Cómo fue la inmigración judía a la Argentina* (Buenos Aires: Plus Ultra, 1983), 206–207.

57. Lewin, *Cómo fue la inmigración judía a la Argentina*, 208–209. My calculations based on the same numbers yield a higher proportion of Jewish involvement than Lewin's calculations, 29.9 percent rather than his "somewhat higher than 25%."

58. Lewin, *Cómo fue la inmigración judía a la Argentina*, 207.

59. Out of 164, 157 have Ashkenazi names and parents with Ashkenazi names, and emigrated from Russia, Romania, or Austria, from where at that time the overwhelming majority of migrants to Argentina were Jewish. Policía de la Capital, *Galería de sospechosos*, vol. 1 (Buenos Aires: Imprenta y encuadernación de la policía de la capital, 1894).

60. Rosenswaike, "The Jewish Population of Argentina," 195. Moya connects this census to the SS *Weser* in his introduction to *The New Jewish Argentina: Facets of Jewish*

*Experiences in the Southern Cone*, ed. Adriana Brodsky and Raanan Rein (Leiden: Brill, 2013), 8.

61. Rosenswaike, "The Jewish Population of Argentina," 197.

62. 1909 data in James R. Scobie, *Buenos Aires: Plaza to Suburb, 1870–1910* (New York: Oxford University Press, 1974), 260, from 1909 Buenos Aires Census, 3–17. 1899–1915 raw numbers from Lewin's citation of Carlos Bernaldo de Quiros, 208. My calculations. 1910–1923 numbers in Victor A. Mirelman, *Jewish Buenos Aires, 1890–1930: In Search of an Identity* (Detroit: Wayne State University Press, 1990), 205, from Records of Buenos Aires Municipal Health Department. I correlated these with an identical version of this data from June 16, 1924, in LON archive, S171, which also notes that "up to 1921 the Poles were counted as Russians and in some instances as Austro-Hungarians." For January to May 1924, my calculations from reply to League of Nations questionnaire sent by Jacinto Fernandez, Buenos Aires Police, July 30, 1924, p. 6, 12/39498/28338, League of Nations Archive, Geneva.

63. Arthur R. Moro, "Letter to JCA from JAPGW," April 9, 1901, Series 1, Roll MKM 15.169 no. 4, folders 32–35, HIAS-HICEM Archives, Yidisher Visnshaftlekher Institut, or Institute for Jewish Research, New York, NY, 4–6.

64. Egal Feldman, "Prostitution, the Alien Woman and the Progressive Imagination, 1910–1915," *American Quarterly* 19, no. 2 (1967): 204, here citing the Misch article.

65. Feldman, "Prostitution," 203.

66. Fictionalized in the 1908 Yiddish work by E. N. Frenk, *Der alfonsen pogrom in varshe* (Warsaw: Druk y Edelshteyn, 1908). While generally represented as a self-defensive act by "respectable" Jews that quieted local brothel activity for a time, it has also been suggested that this was a turf battle between rival underworld factions. See Keely Stauter-Halsted, *The Devil's Chain: Prostitution and Social Control in Partitioned Poland* (Ithaca, NY: Cornell University Press, 2015), 97, 214–216, 220.

67. Jewish Association for the Protection of Girls and Women, "Official Report of the Jewish International Conference on the Suppression of the Traffic in Girls and Women Held on April 5th, 6th, and 7th, 1910, in London, Convened by the Jewish Association for the Protection of Girls and Women" (London: JAPGW Central Bureau, 1910), 93 (henceforth 1910 JAPGW Conference Report).

68. 1910 JAPGW Conference Report, 65.

69. Paula E. Hyman, "Gender and the Shaping of Modern Jewish Identities," *Jewish Social Studies* 8, nos. 2/3 (January 1, 2002): 153–161; 158; Paula E. Hyman, "The Jewish Body Politic: Gendered Politics in the Early Twentieth Century," *Nashim: A Journal of Jewish Women's Studies & Gender Issues*, no. 2 (April 1, 1999): 37–51.

70. Many local Jewish institutions testified against the Varsovia Society in court, "Juzgados de instrucción: Número 3—Asociación ilicita," *Gaceta del Foro* 15, no. 4729 (November 1, 1930): 7.

71. On the JAPGW in Argentina, see also Susana Bianchi, *Historia de las religiones en la Argentina: Las minorias religiosas* (Buenos Aires: Sudamericana, 2004), 115–118. In comparison, the JAPGW did not found a branch in Rio de Janeiro until 1925.

72. "Tzu vos shitn zamd in di oigen," *Di Prese*, September 1, 1933; "Tzu der idisher efentlichkeit," *Di Prese*, September 9, 1933; "An antfer af der derklerung Ezras Noschim," *Di Prese*, September 13, 1933; "A derklerng fun dem 'Ezras Noschim,'" *Di Prese*, October 19, 1933.

73. "'Ezras Noschim' un 'imigrantn-shutz farain' rufn a delegatn farzamlung," *Di Prese*, June 16, 1930.

74. Correspondence between Samuel Cohen and Rachel Crowdy, September 13, 1928—October 15, 1928, 12/39498/28338, League of Nations Archive, Geneva.

75. Rachel Crowdy's notes on the 1927 London JAPGW conference, submitted to the League Committee on Traffic July 24, 1927, 12/60144/647, League of Nations Archive, Geneva, 1–3.

76. Crowdy's 1927 notes.

77. Crowdy's 1927 notes.

78. Buenos Aires Field Reports, Field Reports on Investigation of International Traffic in Women and Children Made for the Special Body of Experts to Study the International Traffic in Women and Children, S148, League of Nations Archive, Geneva, 71.

### CHAPTER 3 — MARRIAGE AS RUSE, OR MIGRATION STRATEGY

1. Naomi Seidman, *The Marriage Plot: Or, How Jews Fell in Love with Love, and with Literature* (Stanford, CA: Stanford University Press, 2016).

2. Shaul Stampfer, *Families, Rabbis and Education: Traditional Jewish Society in Nineteenth-Century Eastern Europe* (Portland, OR: Littman Library of Jewish Civilization, 2010), 27–30.

3. Stampfer, *Families, Rabbis and Education*, 27–28.

4. Seidman, *The Marriage Plot*, 105.

5. Stampfer, *Families, Rabbis and Education*, 32–34.

6. ChaeRan Y. Freeze, *Jewish Marriage and Divorce in Imperial Russia* (Hanover, NH: University Press of New England for Brandeis University Press, 2002), 97–98.

7. Edward J. Bristow, *Prostitution and Prejudice: The Jewish Fight against White Slavery, 1870–1939*, 2nd ed. (New York: Schocken Books, 1983), 102–108.

8. See, for example, Nathan Englander, *The Ministry of Special Cases* (New York: Knopf, 2007), 93; David Pivar, *Purity and Hygiene: Women, Prostitution, and the "American Plan," 1900–1930* (Westport, CT: Greenwood Press, 2002), 90n75.

9. Bristow, *Prostitution and Prejudice*, 102–108.

10. "Wiles of the White Slaver: Charitable Institution as 'Exchange,'" *Buenos Aires Herald*, May 11, 1930, 1.

11. "A Vendung . . . Rodriguez Ocampo," *Di Prese*, May 23, 1930, 5.

12. For an example of the modified choice argument, see Wendy Chapkis, *Live Sex Acts: Women Performing Erotic Labor* (New York: Routledge, 1997). Jo Doezema pushes this further, calling for a move beyond this "modified choice" model. She promotes the conceptualization of sex workers as "desiring" rather than vulnerable subjects, seeking to practice freedom rather than waiting to be granted rights. Jo Doezema, *Sex Slaves and Discourse Masters: The Construction of Trafficking* (London: Zed Books, 2010), 24–25, 175.

13. "Prostitutes Alleged to be Under 21 Years of Age," July 22, 1924, Rio de Janeiro Field Reports, Field Reports on Investigation of International Traffic in Women and Children Made for the Special Body of Experts to Study the International Traffic in Women and Children, S148, League of Nations Archive, Geneva, 36 (henceforth Rio Field Reports).

14. Rio Field Reports, 36.

15. Rio Field Reports, 21. On the postage stamp as primary immigration agent for Spanish migrants to Argentina, see Jose C. Moya, *Cousins and Strangers: Spanish Immigrants in Buenos Aires, 1850–1930* (Berkeley: University of California Press, 1998).

16. Rio Field Reports, 36.

17. "Traffic in Women and Children: Summary," May 25–June 14, 1924, Buenos Aires Field Reports, Field Reports on Investigation of International Traffic in Women and Children Made for the Special Body of Experts to Study the International Traffic in Women and Children, S148, League of Nations Archive, Geneva, 10 (henceforth Buenos Aires Field Reports).

18. In addition to Raquel Liberman, other examples appear in these sources of women moving in and out of prostitution over their lives; e.g., Ike Rosen brought Dolly or Dottie from Warsaw, where she engaged in some sex work but not extensively, as well as while passing through Paris and London: "She did a little, but not much." Rio Field Reports, 22.

19. "Juzgados de instrucción: Número 3—Asociación ilicita," *Gaceta del Foro* 15, no. 4729 (November 1, 1930), 8 (henceforth GdF).

20. "Police Raids a 'Wash-Out': Only Ten White Slavers Caught," *Buenos Aires Herald*, May 23, 1930, 1, 8.

21. "La Sociedad Varsovia vista por dentro según el relato de uno de sus socios," *El Orden*, May 30, 1930, 3.

22. "La Sociedad Varsovia vista," 3.

23. Naomi Seidman builds on the work of Iris Parush to connect Jewish women's reading habits to shifts in marriage ideals. Seidman, *The Marriage Plot*, 63–65; Iris Parush, *Reading Jewish Women: Marginality and Modernization in Nineteenth-Century Eastern European Jewish Society*, trans. Saadya Sternberg (Waltham, MA: Brandeis University Press, 2004), 166, 245.

24. "La Sociedad Varsovia vista," 3.

25. Jewish Association for the Protection of Girls and Women (henceforth JAPGW), "Official Report of the Jewish International Conference on the Suppression of the Traffic in Girls and Women Held on April 5th, 6th, and 7th, 1910, in London, Convened by the Jewish Association for the Protection of Girls and Women" (London: JAPGW Central Bureau, 1910), 109–110.

26. "'Ezras Noschim' un 'Imigrantn-shutz Farain' Rufn a Delegatn Farzamlung," *Di Prese*, June 16, 1930, 1.

27. Albert Londres, *The Road to Buenos Ayres* (New York: Boni & Liveright, 1928), 171.

28. Quoted in Egal Feldman, "Prostitution, the Alien Woman and the Progressive Imagination, 1910–1915," *American Quarterly* 19, no. 2 (1967): 197; George Kibbe Turner, "The City of Chicago: A Study of the Great Immoralities," *McClure's* 28, no. 6 (April 1907): 575; George Kibbe Turner, "Tammany's Control of New York by Professional Criminals," *McClure's* 33, no. 2 (June 1909): 117; George Kibbe Turner, "The Daughters of the Poor: A Plain Story of the Development of New York City as a Leading Center of the White Slave Trade of the World, under Tammany Hall," *McClure's* 34, no. 1 (November 1909): 45.

29. "Jewish Girls Are Sacrificed: Sensational Disclosures in Chicago Ghetto," *Los Angeles Times*, October 21, 1907, I1.

30. Cited in Feldman, "Prostitution," 196.

31. Comite Argentino de Moralidad Publica to William Alexander Coote, "En nombre del Comite tengo el agrado de dirigirme a Ud.," January 8, 1915, Women's Library's Collection, International Bureau for the Suppression of Traffic in Persons, 4IBS/6 FL112.

32. JAPGW, *Annual Report* (London: JAPGW, 1928), 32.

33. Anna R. Igra, "Marriage as Welfare," *Women's History Review* 15, no. 4 (September 2006): 601–610.

34. Jack Nusan Porter, ed., *Women in Chains: A Sourcebook on the Agunah* (Lanham, MD: Jason Aronson, 1995).

35. For more on prostitution in Poland in this era, see Keeley Stauter-Halsted's excellent *The Devil's Chain: Prostitution and Social Control in Partitioned Poland* (Ithaca, NY: Cornell University Press, 2015).

36. "Jewish Ritual Weddings" section of "Memorandum and Proposals of the Polish National Committee for the Suppression of Traffic in Woman [*sic*] and Children submitted to the VII International Congress on the Subject of the Suppression of Traffic in Women," June 1927, 12/58389/647, League of Nations Archive, Geneva, 7-9.

37. Jews continued to be blamed for the origination of prostitution in Poland and its international aspect in the 1939 Polish policewoman's memoir Stanislawa Paleolog, *The Women Police of Poland (1925 to 1939)*, trans. Eileen Garlinska (Westminster: Association for Moral and Social Hygiene, 1939), e.g., 4.

38. "Jewish Ritual Weddings," 7-9.

39. "Big Percentage of Jewish Prostitution in Poland: The Effect of the Immigration Quota Restrictions," in Jewish Telegraphic Association section of conference notes for VII International Congress on the Subject of the Suppression of Traffic in Women, June 24, 1927, 12/60144/647, League of Nations Archive, Geneva, 3.

40. League of Nations, *Traffic in Women and Children: Summary of Annual Reports for 1929 Prepared by the Secretariat* (Geneva: League of Nations, 1931), 139-140.

41. "Big Percentage of Jewish Prostitution in Poland," 2.

42. "Big Percentage of Jewish Prostitution in Poland," 2.

43. "Big Percentage of Jewish Prostitution in Poland," 2.

44. Handwritten notes from Argentine investigation, June 1-15, 1924, Field Reports on Investigation of International Traffic in Women and Children Made for the Special Body of Experts to Study the International Traffic in Women and Children, S171, League of Nations Archive, Geneva, 1.

45. JAPGW, *Annual Report*, 31.

46. Mir Yarfitz, "Uprooting the Seeds of Evil: Ezras Noschim and Jewish Marriage Regulation, Morality Certificates, and Degenerate Prostitute Mothers in 1930s Buenos Aires," in *The New Jewish Argentina: Facets of Jewish Experiences in the Southern Cone*, ed. Adriana Brodsky and Raanan Rein (Leiden: Brill, 2012), 55-80.

47. Victor A. Mirelman, *Jewish Buenos Aires, 1890-1930: In Search of an Identity* (Detroit: Wayne State University Press, 1990), 87, esp. section on rabbis, 86-99.

48. Mirelman, *Jewish Buenos Aires*, 88-90; Adriana M. Brodsky, *Sephardi, Jewish, Argentine: Community and National Identity, 1880-1960* (Bloomington: Indiana University Press, 2016), chap. 3.

49. On restriction of divorces, see Mirelman, *Jewish Buenos Aires*, 91; on restriction of marriages, see this book's final chapter and Yarfitz, "Uprooting the Seeds of Evil."

50. The average marriage age among Eastern European Jews rose in the last third of the nineteenth century from 24.95 in 1867 to 28.14 in 1902 for males and from 22.24 to 24.38 for females. While many marriages continued to be arranged by parents, this rise in age afforded youth greater possibilities of exerting their own influence on their choice of mates. David Biale, *Eros and the Jews: From Biblical Israel to Contemporary America* (New York: Basic Books, 1992), 163-165. Also see Jacques Silber, "Some Demographic Characteristics of the Jewish Population in Russia at the End of the Nineteenth Century," *Jewish Social Studies* 42, nos. 3-4 (1980): 277-278.

51. Rio Field Reports, 25.

52. Rio Field Reports, 25.

53. Stephanie Coontz, *Marriage, a History: How Love Conquered Marriage* (New York: Penguin, 2006), provides an excellent overview of the transition to the historically unique love match.

54. "Big Percentage of Jewish Prostitution," 4.

55. Freeze, *Jewish Marriage and Divorce*, 17.

56. "Uncover Huge Slave Band: Latvian Police Report Sale of Hundreds of Girls from Russia to South American Buyers," *Los Angeles Times*, December 10, 1925.

57. David Englander, *"Stille Huppah* (Quiet Marriage) among Jewish Immigrants in Britain," *Jewish Journal of Sociology* 34, no. 2 (December 1992): 93–94.

58. Englander, *"Stille Huppah,"* 102–103.

59. Fernando Devoto, *Historia de la inmigración en la Argentina* (Buenos Aires: Editorial Sudamericana, 2003), 361.

60. "Algiers, Algeria: Traffic in Women and Children," February 14–16, 1925, Field Reports on Investigation of International Traffic in Women and Children Made for the Special Body of Experts to Study the International Traffic in Women and Children, S148, League of Nations Archive, Geneva, 9 (henceforth Algiers Field Reports).

61. E.g., Algiers Field Reports, 9.

62. "Marseilles, France: Traffic in Women and Children," January 1–5, 1925, Field Reports on Investigation of International Traffic in Women and Children Made for the Special Body of Experts to Study the International Traffic in Women and Children, S148, League of Nations Archive, Geneva, 7 (henceforth Marseilles Field Reports).

63. "Prostitutes Alleged to be under 21 Years of Age," 22 July 1924, Rio Field Reports, 37; GdF, 21. The creation and control of the passport system in this period, particularly after World War I, was a new articulation of nationality that both facilitated and restricted movement. Many migrants challenged government efforts to limit their national identification and mobility by altering and falsifying passports and other documentation both during and after migratory processes. See Devi Mays, "Transplanting Cosmopolitans: The Migrations of Sephardic Jews to Mexico, 1900–1934" (PhD diss., Indiana University, 2013), 38–41.

64. Marseilles Field Reports, 12–14.

65. Marseilles Field Reports, 9.

66. December 31, 1923, law 817 restricting immigration discussed in G. Romagnolli, *Aspectos jurídicos e institucionales de las migraciones en la república argentina* (Geneva: International Organization for Migration, 1991): 15–17; Devoto, *Historia de la inmigración*, 360–361.

67. Romagnolli, *Aspectos jurídicos*, 15–17.

68. For example, "Iz der froien-handl nar fun oisland?," *Di Prese*, October 7, 1930.

69. "The Paper Barrier," *Buenos Aires Herald*, June 25, 1930, 6. On the language of desirability in relation to Jewish immigrants to Latin America, see Jeffrey Lesser, *Welcoming the Undesirables: Brazil and the Jewish Question* (Berkeley: University of California Press, 1995).

70. For example, in Genoa a prostitute describes the process of quitting a registered house, thus getting out of the system, and then getting a passport with no record that the individual had ever been registered. "Genoa, Italy: Traffic in Women and Children," March 5–10, 1925, Field Reports on Investigation of International Traffic in Women and

Children Made for the Special Body of Experts to Study the International Traffic in Women and Children, S148, League of Nations Archive, Geneva, 5.

71. "Exhibit M: Uruguay," Questionnaire C.L. 61, 1924, Commission of Experts, Traffic in Women and Children, S180, League of Nations Archive, Geneva, 1.

72. "Romagnolli, *Aspectos jurídicos,* 15-17; Marseilles Field Reports, 7-9.

73. Ezres Noshim (henceforth EN) Letter Report No. 96, EN box 2, November 14, 1923, 391-441.

74. GdF, 18.

75. Buenos Aires Field Reports, 12.

76. Buenos Aires Field Reports, 12.

77. Buenos Aires Field Reports, 12; see "Classification of Houses," Rio Field Reports, 1, for an example of a previously practicing prostitute who said she came from Warsaw to Rio to make more money, though the investigator is suspicious of her age and story.

78. Marseilles Field Reports, 13-14.

79. "Police Raids a 'Wash-Out': Only Ten White Slavers Caught," *Buenos Aires Herald,* May 23, 1930.

80. Sholem Asch, *God of Vengeance,* in *The Great Jewish Plays,* trans. Joseph C. Landis (New York: Horizon Press, 1972), 73-113.

81. GdF, e.g., 18.

82. GdF, 18.

83. GdF, 5.

84. Buenos Aires Field Reports, 38.

85. E.g., Buenos Aires Field Reports, 16-17.

86. Buenos Aires Field Reports, 46.

87. Policía de la Capital, *Galería de sospechosos,* vol. 1 (Buenos Aires: Imprenta y encuadernación de la policía de la capital, 1894).

88. Marseilles Field Reports, 7-9.

89. Marseilles Field Reports, 8-9.

90. Marseilles Field Reports, 7, 12-14.

91. Buenos Aires Field Reports, 44-45.

92. Buenos Aires Field Reports, 45.

93. Rio Field Reports, 37.

94. "La Sociedad Varsovia vista," 3.

95. "Naples, Italy: Traffic in Women and Children," March 15-16, 1925, Field Reports on Investigation of International Traffic in Women and Children Made for the Special Body of Experts to Study the International Traffic in Women and Children, S148, League of Nations Archive, Geneva, 2 (henceforth Naples Field Reports).

96. Rio Field Reports, 29-30, 39.

97. Multiple uses of the term "sweetheart" for pimp, e.g., Rio Field Reports, 21, 30.

98. Naples Field Reports, 4.

99. Rio Field Reports, 27.

100. E.g., Goldberg's property on Sarmiento.

101. As Goldberg told Kinzie: "If a fellow wants a wife, a respectable woman who don't hustle (solicit), yes. That's how I got mine. It cost me 4,000 pesos, but she had 80,000 pesos! She was a widow. My wife (in the U.S.A.) is supposed to be dead." Buenos Aires Field Reports, 26.

102. GdF, 8-9.

103. GdF, 9, 13.

104. "Exhibit M: Uruguay," Questionnaire C.L. 61, 1924, Commission of Experts, Traffic in Women and Children, S180, League of Nations Archive, Geneva, 1.

105. GdF, 18–19.

106. Buenos Aires Field Reports, 39.

107. Buenos Aires Field Reports, 49.

108. "Constantinople, Turkey: Traffic in Women and Children," May 18–23, 1925, Field Reports on Investigation of International Traffic in Women and Children Made for the Special Body of Experts to Study the International Traffic in Women and Children, S148, League of Nations Archive, Geneva, 7.

109. Buenos Aires Field Reports, 40.

110. E.g., discussion of green girl from Warsaw, Buenos Aires Field Reports, 44–45.

111. Buenos Aires Field Reports, 32.

112. Buenos Aires Field Reports, 16.

113. Buenos Aires Field Reports, 16.

114. Buenos Aires Field Reports, 32.

115. Buenos Aires Field Reports, 32.

116. Buenos Aires Field Reports, 40.

117. Marseilles Field Reports, 13–14.

118. Buenos Aires Field Reports, 17. Absela is probably a corruption of *bsule*, virgin, from *a bsile*, a virgin, in the Polish dialect of Yiddish.

119. Buenos Aires Field Reports, 17.

### CHAPTER 4 — IMMIGRANT MUTUAL AID AMONG PIMPS

1. Jewish Association for the Protection of Girls and Women (henceforth JAPGW), *Official Report of the Jewish International Conference on the Suppression of the Traffic in Girls and Women Held on April 5th, 6th, and 7th, 1910, in London* (London: JAPGW Central Bureau, 1910), 67.

2. JAPGW, *Official Report of the Jewish International Conference*, 69.

3. Scholars have primarily viewed the group's purported structure as a sham. Robert Weisbrot characterizes the association as a "grim parody of Jewish concern for social welfare and communal responsibility." Robert Weisbrot, *The Jews of Argentina: From the Inquisition to Peron* (Philadelphia: Jewish Publication Society of America, 1979), 62. He expresses shock that the tmeim desired the larger Jewish community's recognition of their identity as Jews. While Donna Guy acknowledges that the organization's members may have sought to maintain a religious life alongside their nontraditional profession, she also notes that the group only "ostensibly functioned as a mutual aid society." Donna Guy, *Sex and Danger in Buenos Aires: Prostitution, Family, and Nation in Argentina* (Lincoln: University of Nebraska Press, 1991), 22.

4. "Supervision of Juridical Societies," *Buenos Aires Herald*, May 23, 1930.

5. Julio L. Alsogaray, *Trilogia de la trata de blancas: Rufianes, policía, municipalidad* (Buenos Aires: L. J. Rosso, 1933), 80, 121–122. Victorio Luis Bessero echoes this opinion in his tract *Los tratantes de blancas en Buenos Aires: El escándalo de la pseuda sociedad "Varsovia" o "Migdal"* (Buenos Aires: Editorial Aspasia, 1930).

6. Produced by the Varsovia Society for its own members, this thirty-six-page annual financial report in Yiddish and Spanish lays out nearly three hundred active members' names and their itemized payments to the organization in 1925 and 1926. Cited as

Varsovia Society 1925–26 Financial Report, Ezres Noshim Collection, Yidisher Visn-shaftlekher Institut, or Instituto Judío de Investigación, Buenos Aires (henceforth IWO). This invaluable document, in combination with legal, immigration, and police records, provides the basis for my portrait of the Society's members. This is supplemented by ship manifests from transatlantic vessels arriving in Buenos Aires, handwritten immigration lists catalogued by the Centro de Estudios Migratorios Latinoamericanos, which provide another untapped source of these migrants' demographic information (although multiple spellings of names and uses of aliases make confirming matches difficult). In *Gaceta del Foro*, a detailed legal summary of the Society's 1930 prosecution supplies further demographic information, which can also be correlated with the Buenos Aires police department's *Órdenes del Día*, or arrest orders, from late May and early June 1930.

7. "Juzgados de instrucción: Número 3—Asociación ilicita," *Gaceta del Foro* 15, no. 4729 (November 1, 1930): 10–11, 19 (henceforth GdF). Their denials of knowing one another or their work presumably relate to the central legal charge, that of corruption and collusion ("asociación ilicita"). The legal summary points out that nearly all the members had previous police records related to prostitution management, and the fact that they all responded in strikingly similar terms to questioning on the witness stand can be seen as both conscious refutation of the collusion charge and proof of collusion's existence. The legal record states that "nearly all the members of the Z. Migdal were known to the Police as immoral, which shows that their dealings, in one way or another, had become known to the Police, and that all the persons who applied for admission to the Z. Migdal knew perfectly well who the other members were and for what purpose they were united."

8. "La Sociedad Varsovia vista por dentro según el relato de uno de sus socios," *El Orden*, May 30, 1930, 3.

9. "La Sociedad Varsovia vista por dentro según el relato de uno de sus socios," *El Orden*, May 30, 1930, 3.

10. "La Sociedad Varsovia vista por dentro según el relato de uno de sus socios," *El Orden*, June 1, 1930, 3.

11. "La Sociedad Varsovia vista por dentro según el relato de uno de sus socios," *El Orden*, May 29, 1930, 3.

12. "La Sociedad Varsovia vista por dentro según el relato de uno de sus socios," *El Orden*, June 1, 1930, 3.

13. Ronaldo Munck, "Mutual Benefit Societies in Argentina: Workers, Nationality, Social Security, and Trade Unionism," *Journal of Latin American Studies* 30, no. 3 (1998): 573–590, at 578. See also Samuel L. Baily, "Mutual Assistance Societies and the Development of the Italian Community in Buenos Aires, 1858–1918," *Desarrollo Economico* 21, no. 84 (1982): 485–514.

14. In a 2005 special issue of the *Journal of Ethnic and Migration Studies* devoted to the subject, Jose C. Moya defines the immigrant voluntary association and surveys the historiography of this institution in North and South America. He delineates the category as an intermediary institution between basic kinship ties and such nonvoluntary structures as the state. Jose C. Moya, "Immigrants and Associations: A Global and Historical Perspective," *Journal of Ethnic and Migration Studies* 31, no. 5 (September 2005): 833–864, at 834–835. While many scholars have emphasized either the continuation of premigratory practices or the influence of the host society in their analyses of the formation and operation of such groups, Moya argues that the process of migration disrupted both tra-

ditional and modern social welfare institutions, from local kinship and religious structures to state welfare and insurance providers, creating the need for health care and other social services to be filled by voluntary associations. Migration also produced stronger ethnic or national identification against host society natives and other newly arriving groups. In their introductory article to the same journal issue, Marlou Schrover and Floris Vermeulen underscore the significance of voluntary associations in defining immigrant identity, as new arrivals come together either to protect their interests in the face of exclusion or to distinguish themselves from the host society, emphasizing their differences. Marlou Schrover and Floris Vermeulen, "Immigrant Organisations," *Journal of Ethnic and Migration Studies* 31, no. 5 (2005): 823–832, at 824–826. Moya argues against Daniel Soyer's observation that the host environment was the central shaping factor in the structure of immigrant associations, though Soyer does not ignore Old World institutions; Moya, "Immigrants and Associations," 837–840. See Daniel Soyer, *Jewish Immigrant Associations and American Identity in New York, 1880–1939* (Detroit: Wayne State University Press, 2002).

15. For examples of analyses of Jewish criminal associations, see Rose Keefe, *The Starker: Big Jack Zelig, the Becker-Rosenthal Case, and the Advent of the Jewish Gangster* (Nashville: Cumberland House, 2008); Charles Van Onselen, *The Fox and the Flies: The Secret Life of a Grotesque Master Criminal* (New York: Walker, 2007) and "Jewish Marginality in the Atlantic World: Organized Crime in the Era of the Great Migrations, 1880–1914," *South African Historical Journal* 43 (November 2000): 96–137; Daniel Vyleta, "Jewish Crimes and Misdemeanours: In Search of Jewish Criminality (Germany and Austria 1890–1914)," *European History Quarterly* 35, no. 2 (April 2005): 299–325; Robert Rockaway, *But He Was Good to His Mother: The Lives and Crimes of Jewish Gangsters* (New York: Gefen, 2000); and Jenna Weissman Joselit, *Our Gang: Jewish Crime and the New York Jewish Community, 1900–1940* (Bloomington: Indiana University Press, 1983).

16. Ronaldo Munck has published the historical work most focused on these institutions in Argentina, tied to class and labor history. Membership in such groups peaked in Argentina just before the First World War, with, according to one estimate, over 60 percent of the skilled porteño working class in 1913 affiliated with a mutual aid society, with the highest concentration of full members among first-generation immigrants. He claims that the percentage of mutual aid society members plummeted in the 1920s and thereafter (particularly under Peronism) as labor unions and government social security programs took over their most important functions. Munck, "Mutual Benefit Societies in Argentina," 579. See also Michael R. Weisser, *A Brotherhood of Memory: Jewish Landsmanshaftn in the New World* (New York: Basic Books, 1985).

17. My compilation from Policía de la Capital, *Galería de sospechosos*, vol. 1 (Buenos Aires: Imprenta y encuadernación de la policía de la capital, 1894).

18. Data on founders from Policía de la Capital, *Galería de sospechosos*.

19. Names, as elsewhere in League field reports, decoded in "Codebook [to code used in Field Reports]," Field Reports on Investigation of International Traffic in Women and Children Made for the Special Body of Experts to Study the International Traffic in Women and Children, S171, League of Nations Archive, Geneva, 57, 60.

20. Buenos Aires Field Reports, 50.

21. Standard Yiddish transliteration would render this *khevre*, but the spelling *Hevra* was used in League reports. E.g., "Buenos Aires: Commercialized Prostitution," June 10,

1924; "Tunis: Traffic in Women and Children," February 27–28, 1925; "Tunis: Official Interviews," February 25–27, 1925; "Constantinople: Traffic in Women and Children," May 18–19 and 20–21, 1925; "New York City: Law Enforcement, Police," September 11, 1925; all in Field Reports, S148, League of Nations Archive, Geneva.

22. This route discussed in, e.g., "Constantinople, Turkey: Traffic in Women and Children," May 18–23, 1925, Field Reports on Investigation of International Traffic in Women and Children Made for the Special Body of Experts to Study the International Traffic in Women and Children, S148, League of Nations Archive, Geneva, 6–7 (henceforth Constantinople Field Reports).

23. These routes are generally articulated throughout the League's second Expert Report. Paul Knepper describes these as two distinct routes in "The International Traffic in Women: Scandinavia and the League of Nations Inquiry of 1927," *Journal of Scandinavian Studies in Criminology and Crime Prevention* 14 (May 1, 2013): 73.

24. This presumably refers to the Polish Yiddish dialect *gris*, for the standard Yiddish *grus*, meaning greeting.

25. Constantinople Field Reports, 2.

26. Goldberg advised: "Always have a poor mouth. Make it appear that you are traveling on borrowed gelt (money). . . . Don't be a yold (fool)! His price is $100 American gold. After you get the girl and you are about to board the steamer, show him a check, and address it to me here. He will understand. I will send it back to him. . . . Whenever you invest a dollar in anything, see what you are going to get for your money!'" Buenos Aires Field Reports, 50, 54.

27. League of Nations, *Report of the Special Body of Experts on Traffic in Women and Children*, part 2 (Geneva: League of Nations, 1927), 138.

28. Traffic in Women and Children, Montevideo Field Reports, June 22–July 3, 1924, Field Reports on Investigation of International Traffic in Women and Children Made for the Special Body of Experts to Study the International Traffic in Women and Children, S148, League of Nations Archive, Geneva, 2; Ezres Noshim (henceforth EN) Letter Report No. 96 (from Ganapol and Halphon to Cohen), EN box 2, November 14, 1923, 391–441.

29. Policía de la Capital, *Galería de sospechosos*.

30. The 1906 Jewish Encyclopedia, with information from this period, lists community newspapers only in Judeo-Spanish (Ladino). http://www.jewishencyclopedia.com /articles/4623-constantinople#anchor12. Names from Policía de la Capital, *Galería de sospechosos*.

31. Constantinople Field Reports, 2–7.

32. Constantinople Field Reports, 8.

33. Description in Algiers Field Report of a "boy" who went to "Constantine" from where he brought a seventeen-year-old Jewish girl back to Algiers, then to Paris. "Algiers, Algeria: Traffic in Women and Children," February 14–16, 1925, Field Reports on Investigation of International Traffic in Women and Children Made for the Special Body of Experts to Study the International Traffic in Women and Children, S148, League of Nations Archive, Geneva, 10.

34. E.g., Rifat N. Bali, *The Jews and Prostitution in Constantinople, 1854–1922* (Istanbul: Isis Press, 2008).

35. Bali, *The Jews and Prostitution in Constantinople*; Nancy Wingfield, "Destination: Alexandria, Buenos Aires, Constantinople; 'White Slavers' in Late Imperial Austria," *Journal of the History of Sexuality* 20, no. 2 (May 2011): 300–301. See also Minna Rozen,

*The Last Ottoman Century and Beyond: The Jews in Turkey and the Balkans 1808–1945* (Tel Aviv: Tel Aviv University, 2005).

36. Bertha Pappenheim, *Sisyphus-Arbeit: Reise-briefe aus dem Jharen 1911 und 1912* (Leipzig, 1924), referenced in Lloyd P. Gartner, "Anglo-Jewry and the Jewish International Traffic in Prostitution, 1885–1914," *AJS Review* 7 (1982): 135.

37. Constantinople Field Reports, 8. Another example: "I introduced myself to Rosita Steinman as a friend of one of the boys from the American Legion, and then accompanied her into the dining room of the house where we conversed in Yiddish." Rio de Janeiro Field Reports, Field Reports on Investigation of International Traffic in Women and Children Made for the Special Body of Experts to Study the International Traffic in Women and Children, S148, League of Nations Archive, Geneva, 36 (henceforth Rio Field Reports).

38. These transliterations often vary from YIVO standard Yiddish but are intelligible, as are the translations. Constantinople Field Reports, 3, 7–8, 11; Rio Field Reports 19, 22, 31–32.

39. Rio Field Reports, 34.

40. Buenos Aires Field Reports, 32; emphasis in original.

41. "Los socios de la Zwi Migdal," *El Ideal* (Buenos Aires), May 27, 1931.

42. Buenos Aires Field Reports, 37.

43. According to Kinzie's reports, brothel owner Goldberg contradicts himself on this, saying, "We have a little club and . . . the French pimps do the same thing. They help one another," in direct opposition to his quote in the prior sentence. Buenos Aires Field Reports, 19. The League's summary report denies French organization. "Investigation on the Spot for the Commission of Experts Appointed by the Council of the League of Nations to Study, in Collaboration with Governments, the Conditions under Which the Traffic in Women and Children Is Carried On," Field Reports on Investigation of International Traffic in Women and Children Made for the Special Body of Experts to Study the International Traffic in Women and Children, S148, League of Nations Archive, Geneva, 12. The Yiddish press reported several times on French-organized prostitution, particularly in the midst of the Varsovia court case, perhaps to deflect attention away from Jewish domination. E.g., "La Sociedad Varsovia vista por dentro según el relato de uno de sus socios," *El Orden*, June 1, 1930, 3.

44. "Investigation on the Spot," Buenos Aires Field Reports, 12.

45. Varsovia Society 1925–26 Financial Report, president's introduction on page 1.

46. Varsovia Society 1925–26 Financial Report, 1.

47. Varsovia Society 1925–26 Financial Report, inside cover and 1.

48. Varsovia Society 1925–26 Financial Report, 3.

49. Titles of officers and burial society functions mirror those of two New York Jewish family circles whose bylaws are reproduced in William E. Mitchell, *Kinship, Et'nicity and Voluntary Associations: Jewish Family Life in New York City* (New Brunswick, NJ: Aldine Transaction, 2009), 217–226.

50. Varsovia Society 1925–26 Financial Report, 33.

51. GdF, 16.

52. GdF, 11.

53. Varsovia Society 1925–26 Financial Report, 1.

54. On the demographics of Argentine immigration in this period, see Fernando Devoto, *História de la inmigración en la Argentina* (Buenos Aires: Editorial Sudamericana, 2003);

Jose C. Moya, *Cousins and Strangers: Spanish Immigrants in Buenos Aires, 1850–1930* (Berkeley: University of California Press, 1998); and Haim Avni, *Argentina and the Jews: A History of Jewish Immigration* (Tuscaloosa: University of Alabama Press, 1991). See also Samuel L. Baily and Eduardo José Míguez, eds., *Mass Migration to Modern Latin America* (Lanham, MD: Rowman & Littlefield, 2003).

55. Ship manifests from transatlantic vessels arriving in Buenos Aires, archived at the Centro de Estudios Migratorios Latinoamericanos, allow for analysis of the arrivals of some of the Varsovia Society's members. Spelling variations complicate the use of these data, but when correlated with birthdates and other arrest data, they allow around ninety of the members of the Varsovia Society to be cross-referenced. These data include dates and ports of arrival and departure, age upon arrival, nationality, civil status, stated profession, and occasionally birthplace. This information also suggests whether group members traveled together, made multiple trips, or traveled together with others sharing their last name. This includes multiple trips by the same individual, but eliminates possible redundancies across different source data sets. Overall Jewish immigration data from Ricardo Feierstein, *Historia de los judíos argentinos*, 3rd ed. (Buenos Aires: Galerna, 2006), 399. He draws these data from Simón Weill, *Población Israelita en la República Argentina* (Buenos Aires: Bené Berith, 1936), which, although problematic, is the most complete body of data on Jewish immigration available for this period. Ira Rosenswaike discusses the problems with charting Argentine Jewish demographics through census and other data, including Weill's data. Ira Rosenswaike, "The Jewish Population of Argentina: Census and Estimate, 1887–1947," *Jewish Social Studies* 22, no. 4 (October 1960): 195–214, esp. 195–196. Haim Avni compares several other sources for the period from 1901 to 1914 in *Argentina y las migraciones judías: De la Inquisición al Holocausto y despues* (Buenos Aires: Editorial Milá, 2005), 458.

56. Rosenswaike, "The Jewish Population of Argentina," 197, 201–204, 210–211.

57. For overall European immigration in this period, see Devoto, *Historia de la inmigración*, esp. the graph on 248.

58. The content and implications of this law are discussed by Guy, *Sex and Danger*, 61–62.

59. William P. Dillingham, *Importing Women for Immoral Purposes: A Partial Report from the Immigration Commission on the Importation and Harboring of Women for Immoral Purposes* (Washington, DC: GPO, 1909), 23–24; "Five 'White Slave' Trade Investigations," *McClure's* 35 (July 1910): 347; "Jerome Its Counsel: On Condition Association Tells All It Knows of White Slavery," *New York Times*, March 2, 1910; Egal Feldman, "Prostitution, the Alien Woman and the Progressive Imagination, 1910–1915," *American Quarterly* 19, no. 2 (1967): 194–195.

60. On Jewish family clubs and occupational assistance, see Mitchell, *Kinship, Ethnicity and Voluntary Associations*, 86.

61. Out of a total of 168 individuals for whom these data are available, in the most commonly listed categories, 35 percent state their profession as merchant or trader (*comerciante*), 9 percent as tailor or dressmaker, 5 percent as hairdresser or barber, 5 percent as day laborer, 4 percent as farmworker, and 3 percent as traveling salesman or peddler. This reflects the patterns of other Jewish immigrants, as articulated, for example, in Benjamin Nathans, *Beyond the Pale: The Jewish Encounter with Late Imperial Russia* (Berkeley: University of California Press, 2002), 100–103. According to the 1931 Polish census, only 4 percent of Jews worked in agriculture, as opposed to 60 percent of non-Jews. Also,

37 percent of Jews were in commerce, versus only 6 percent of non-Jews, and 42 percent of Jews were artisans, versus 19 percent of non-Jews. Commerce is defined broadly in these data to include banking and insurance, and artisanship is lumped together with mining and industry, where presumably more of the non-Jews were concentrated. Joseph Marcus, *Social and Political History of the Jews in Poland, 1919–1939* (Berlin: Mouton, 1983), 437. While a small number of highly successful Jewish merchants were granted special privileges and mobility, thus tending to remain in Eastern Europe rather than emigrate, most were in less privileged fields such as petty trading, brokerage, or pawnshop ownership. Nathans, *Beyond the Pale*, 40, 59, 86. One estimate for 1935 associates 57 percent of Argentine Jews with commercial activity, with only 9 percent in agricultural labor. Feierstein, *Historia de los judíos argentinos*, 132. In Argentina as in Eastern Europe, the category of comerciante reflected a broad range of earnings and prestige. Mark D. Szuchman and Eugene F. Sofer, "State of Occupational Stratification Studies in Argentina: Classificatory Scheme," *Latin American Research Review* 11, no. 1 (1976): 159–171, at 164.

A breakdown of overall Argentine immigrants' trades in the period 1894 to 1903 provides a picture quite distinct from that of Jews, with the largest categories and most relevant smaller categories as follows: 41.6 percent farmworkers, 15.7 percent day laborers or workmen, 4 percent merchants, 3.8 percent dressmakers, 3.8 percent servants, 0.8 percent shoemakers, 0.6 percent tailors, 0.2 percent barbers. Immigration Department, Ministry of Agriculture, Argentine Republic, "The Immigration Offices and Statistics from 1857 to 1903: Information for the Universal Exhibition of St. Louis (U.S.A.)" (Buenos Aires: Argentine Weather Bureau, 1904), 26. Another comparison can be drawn from the Argentine census data processed by James Scobie. He notes the numbers of those employed in various professions in 1869, 1895, and 1914 and the percentage of each of those in the latter two dates who are foreign-born. While he does not include the merchant category or the underworld, his statistics show that in general, the foreign-born are overrepresented as agricultural or day laborers as well as tailors and shoemakers. James R. Scobie, *Buenos Aires: Plaza to Suburb, 1870–1910* (New York: Oxford University Press, 1974), 265.

62. GdF, 6.

63. Alsogaray, *Trilogia de la trata de blancas*, 123; GdF, 6; Victor A. Mirelman, *Jewish Buenos Aires, 1890–1930: In Search of an Identity* (Detroit: Wayne State University Press, 1990), 81. For more on Jewish cemeteries in Latin America, see Aviva Ben-Ur and Rachel Frankel, *Remnant Stones: The Jewish Cemeteries of Suriname: Epitaphs* (Cincinnati: Hebrew Union College Press, 2009).

64. GdF, 18–19. Although if not tainted by "impurity," they could presumably have joined the larger Jewish community's burial society.

65. This is the Spanish spelling of the burial society's name, as was typically used— standard Yiddish would have been *khevre kedishe*. On membership numbers, see Eugene F. Sofer, *From Pale to Pampa: A Social History of the Jews of Buenos Aires* (New York: Holmes and Meier, 1982), 7–8. His social history of the broader Jewish community is based on an analysis of the records of 1,514 Eastern European Jews born in or immigrated to Argentina between 1890 and 1930, which he argues is a representative cross-section because 85 to 95 percent of Jews belonged to this organization in the years prior to 1945.

66. These sixteen photographs of the cemetery are kept in box 3 of the Ezres Noshim Collection, IWO. Birth information for Lewek Migdal from the Mormon Church's online

Jewish Records Indexing for Poland, Warszawa Gubernia, Lowicz Births 1837–1865, film 811071, http://data.jewishgen.org/wconnect/wc.dll?jg~jgsys~jripllat2. These data correspond to those in Policía de la Capital, *Galería de sospechosos*.

67. Avni goes so far as to suggest that these Hebrew inscriptions marked them as "traditional Jews." Haim Avni, *"Ţeme'im": Saḥar be-nashim be-Argenţinah uve-Yiśra'el* (Tel-Aviv: Yedi'ot Aḥaronot, 2009), 88.

68. GdF, 16.

69. Varsovia Society 1925–26 Financial Report, 33–34.

70. Varsovia Society 1925–26 Financial Report, 3. This new land is here described as measuring 3071.22 v.c., which stands for *varas cuadradas*. The *vara* is a unit of measurement of roughly 34.1 inches, and *cuadrada* means squared; thus this is around 3,000 square yards. This information confirms that the Ashquenasum Society existed as an independent entity before the 1927 name change from Varsovia to Zwi Migdal, the point at which some contemporary and later observers have asserted that the Ashquenasum was founded as a splinter group.

71. This theory that the Ashquenasum split off from the Varsovia Society in 1927 is put forth in Alsogaray, *Trilogia de la trata de blancas*, 139; and GdF, 11.

72. Alsogaray deplores these events, which he describes as made even more shameful by being held on national holidays. Alsogaray, *Trilogia de la trata de blancas*, 62–63.

73. See, for example, photo spread in "Los tenebrosos de la 'Migdal' gustan del confort: Hace tres meses el fiscal Barberis solicitó que se allanara la Migdal," *Crítica*, May 27, 1930, 8.

74. Varsovia Society 1925–26 Financial Report, 33–34.

75. Varsovia Society 1925–26 Financial Report, 3.

76. A *La Nación* article confirms that the mansion was legally registered in the names of five individual members rather than that of the Society. "El Consejo Nacional de Educación reclama los bienes de la Migdal," *La Nación*, June 6, 1930, 30.

77. Varsovia Society 1925–26 Financial Report, 1.

78. "El sensacional proceso a la sociedad Migdal," *Caras y Caretas* 33, no. 1653 (June 7, 1930): 81.

79. "Se hace difícil la búsqueda," *La Última Hora*, 3.

80. Varsovia Society 1925–26 Financial Report, 23, 32–34.

81. Varsovia Society 1925–26 Financial Report, 3, 6.

82. She was also known as Esther Kohn or Cohen and as Masha or Maria Fischer, along with variant spellings of these names. For simplicity, I refer to her here as Esther. The *New York Times* reported that after the 1930 arrest sweeps "several women over 60 years of age have been held, one of whom is alleged to have amassed more than 1,000,000 pesos ($424,000 at par)." "South America Pushes White Slave Inquiry," *New York Times*, May 26, 1930.

83. GdF, 17; Varsovia Society 1925–26 Financial Report, 9.

84. "A froienhendlerke a milionerke," *Di Prese*, May 25, 1930, 1; "El juez confia limpiar al pais de tenebrosos: La policia no consigue dar con los tratantes de blancas acusados," *Crítica*, May 24, 1930, 6.

85. "El juez confia limpiar"; "La policia ha detenido algunos otros individuos pertenecientes a la tenebrosa asociación Migdal," *La Nacion*, May 24, 1930, 26.

86. "Zwi Migdal Case: Millionairess Arrested," *Buenos Aires Herald*, May 25, 1930, 8.

87. "El juez confia limpiar"; "A froienhendlerke a milionerke"; "Arum kampf gegn di froien-handel," *Di Yidishe Tsaytung,* May 25, 1930, 1.

88. E.g., Goldberg's property on Sarmiento, Buenos Aires Field Reports, 16.

89. Guy, *Sex and Danger,* 108.

90. Guy, *Sex and Danger,* 108–110, underscores the expansion of managerial control and ineffective efforts to control police. League sources suggest how this law increased property-owning opportunities, and how the hevra network supported one another through loans. E.g., Buenos Aires Field Reports, 22–23, 25–26, 47, 55–56.

91. GdF, 19.

92. GdF, 13.

93. E.g., GdF, 6, says thirty-seven women members; the Varsovia Society 1925–26 Financial Report lists closer to twenty. On women's collective property, see GdF, 11; and "El gobierno debe limpiar al pais de la verguenza de la trata de blancas," *Crítica,* September 17, 1930.

94. As explained by Goldberg to Kinzie, Buenos Aires Field Reports, 22.

95. A madam in Rio who owns a house that she would like to sell to Goldberg suggests to Kinzie that Goldberg might do this with his own wife, bringing her to Rio and leaving her in charge of the house for a period to get a sense of its profitability. Rio Field Reports, 7.

96. Buenos Aires Field Reports, 27.

97. GdF 6.

98. Buenos Aires Field Reports, 7.

99. GdF, 9.

100. GdF, 9.

101. GdF, 9.

102. Lara Putnam's work on West Indian migrants to Costa Rica and Eileen Findlay's on Puerto Rican sex workers provide particularly apt parallels. Lara Putnam, *The Company They Kept: Migrants and the Politics of Gender in Caribbean Costa Rica, 1870–1960* (Chapel Hill: University of North Carolina Press, 2002), esp. 139–172; Eileen J. Suárez Findlay, *Imposing Decency: The Politics of Sexuality and Race in Puerto Rico, 1870–1920* (Durham, NC: Duke University Press, 1999).

103. Soyer, *Jewish Immigrant Associations,* 42; Guy, *Sex and Danger,* 22.

### CHAPTER 5 — THE IMPURE SHAPE JEWISH BUENOS AIRES

1. Robert Weisbrot, *The Jews of Argentina: From the Inquisition to Peron* (Philadelphia: Jewish Publication Society of America, 1979), 62, 59–66.

2. Brodsky, in *Sephardi, Jewish, Argentine,* discusses throughout the broader differences between Sephardim and Ashkenazim and begins her first chapter with a discussion of the Moroccan Jewish community's willingness to share cemetery space with the tmeim. Adriana M. Brodsky, *Sephardi, Jewish, Argentine: Community and National Identity, 1880–1960* (Bloomington: Indiana University Press, 2016).

3. Weisbrot himself underscores the "unprecedented centralization" of Buenos Aires Jewry, "united to a degree unmatched by any other substantial Jewish community in the Diaspora." He attributes this to "the threat of anti-Semitism in forms more virulent than any encountered by American Jews" and Jewish concentration in the Argentine capital. *The Jews of Argentina,* 57.

4. This narrative is indebted to Victor Mirelman's chapter in his 1990 history of Jewish Buenos Aires, in which he traces many contours of the developments in this battle against the tmeim, including the self-defensive impulse of a marginal community smaller and of a more stigmatized religion and ethnicity than those of other European immigrants. Victor A. Mirelman, *Jewish Buenos Aires, 1890–1930: In Search of an Identity* (Detroit: Wayne State University Press, 1990), chap. 9.

5. This alienation characterized, e.g., by Daniel J. Elazar, *Jewish Communities in Frontier Societies: Argentina, Australia, and South Africa* (New York: Holmes and Meier, 1983), 9. On this period's political upheaval, see Alberto Spektorowski, *The Origins of Argentina's Revolution of the Right* (Notre Dame, IN: University of Notre Dame Press, 2003).

6. Jewish Association for the Protection of Girls and Women, *Official Report of the Jewish International Conference on the Suppression of the Traffic in Girls and Women* (London, 1910), 18.

7. "Preserve your honor! Appeal to Jews in Argentina: We should live like people and not like filthy animals!" (n/d), Ezres Noshim (henceforth EN) box 3.

8. This map can be viewed in an interactive format, with details on each address, numbers of Jewish and non-Jewish prostitutes in each brothel, and source citations, at https://maps.google.com/maps/ms?msid=205801690951610780493.0004c576 e16f6e5e3e529&msa=0.

9. Marisa Donadío, "La ciudad de las esclavas blancas," *Documentos e investigaciones sobre la historia del tango* 3, no. 3 (1996): 173–176.

10. Eugene F. Sofer, *From Pale to Pampa: A Social History of the Jews of Buenos Aires* (New York: Holmes and Meier, 1982); Ricardo Feierstein, *Historia de los judíos argentinos*, 3rd ed. (Buenos Aires: Galerna, 2006), 146–152.

11. Donadío, "La ciudad de las esclavas blancas," 140–143. Although this source reproduces the census data, my project is the first to notice and map out this one-block concentration. The 1895 census manuscripts are now available online, and, in addition to name, profession, sex, civil status, nation or Argentine province of origin, religion, and occupation, also include literacy, education, property ownership, children and years married, illness or disability, and if orphaned by father or mother. See https://familysearch .org.

12. The symbolic significance of this location was immortalized in a poem by César Tiempo, in which the streets Lavalle and Junin are repeated as a refrain in each verse. Poem quoted in Feierstein, *Historia de los judíos argentinos*, 160.

13. Donadío, "La ciudad de las esclavas blancas."

14. Donadío, "La ciudad de las esclavas blancas," 157–163. The brothels in this zone cannot be mapped, as they are listed by census block rather than address.

15. Donadío, "La ciudad de las esclavas blancas," 145–147.

16. Out of 164, 157 have Ashkenazi names and parents with Ashkenazi names and immigrated from Russia, Romania, or Austria, from where at that time the overwhelming majority of migrants to Argentina were Jewish. Policía de la Capital, *Galería de sospechosos*, vol. 1 (Buenos Aires: Imprenta y encuadernación de la policía de la capital, 1894).

17. Further analysis of Argentine criminology can be found in Julia Rodríguez, *Civilizing Argentina: Science, Medicine, and the Modern State* (Chapel Hill: University of North Carolina Press, 2006) and "South Atlantic Crossings: Fingerprints, Science, and the State in Turn-of-the-Century Argentina," *American Historical Review* 109, no. 2 (2004): 387–416.

18. Jose Moya makes a suggestion in this direction in "The Positive Side of Stereotypes: Jewish Anarchists in Early-Twentieth-Century Buenos Aires," *Jewish History* 18 (2004): 21-22.

19. Donna Guy, *Sex and Danger in Buenos Aires: Prostitution, Family, and Nation in Argentina* (Lincoln: University of Nebraska Press, 1991), 108.

20. Houses with multiple women did continue to operate in a clandestine fashion, maintained through bribery of the police. Guy, *Sex and Danger*, 108-109.

21. Guy, *Sex and Danger*, 110.

22. Buenos Aires 1924 Field Reports on Investigation of International Traffic in Women and Children Made for the Special Body of Experts to Study the International Traffic in Women and Children, S148, League of Nations Archive, Geneva, 70 (henceforth Buenos Aires Field Reports).

23. Goldberg told Kinzie "more money can be made in Buenos Aires under this system than was made when the large houses of prostitution with 10 and 15 inmates flourished here." Buenos Aires Field Reports, 71.

24. Buenos Aires Field Reports, 68.

25. Buenos Aires Field Reports, 5.

26. Goldberg describes his use of the corner lot strategy with a duplex he owns with doors on two separate streets, at 295 Ayacucho and 1996 Sarmiento. Buenos Aires Field Reports, 4-5.

27. Buenos Aires Field Reports, 68.

28. Sofer, *From Pale to Pampa*, 73.

29. For interactive map with details on each address and sources, see https://maps .google.com/maps/ms?msid=205801690951610780493.0004c522c16bb0b2b4324 &msa=0.

30. Sofer describes this plaza as central in 1895 in *From Pale to Pampa*, 66.

31. These addresses come primarily from the legal testimony in "Juzgados de instrucción: Número 3—Asociación ilicita," *Gaceta del Foro* 15, no. 4729 (November 1, 1930): 3-23 (henceforth GdF), with others mentioned in Julio L. Alsogaray, *Trilogia de la trata de blancas: Rufianes, policía, municipalidad* (Buenos Aires: L. J. Rosso, 1933), 46, 50; "Un Tenebroso indagado hoy compro una casa al contado en novecientos mil pesos," *Crítica*, June 3, 1930, 8; "El gobierno debe limpiar al pais de la verguenza de la trata de blancas," *Crítica*, September 17, 1930, 1; EN Letter Report 99, May 19, 1924, 454-472, EN box 2, Ezres Noshim Collection, Yidisher Visnshaftlekher Institut, or Instituto Judío de Investigación, Buenos Aires (henceforth IWO); EN Letter Report 140, p. 2, December 10, 1928, EN box 1, IWO; Letter Report 144, p. 45, February 5, 1929, EN box 1, IWO; Letter Report 144, p. 45, February 5, 1929, EN box 1, IWO; Letter Report 148, pp. 84, 87, 97, 99, July 10, 1929, EN box 1, IWO; Letter Report 149, pp. 127, 131-132, 137-138, September 4, 1929, EN box 1, IWO; EN "Memoria" 1936, pp. 17-21, EN box 3, IWO; "Codebook [to code used in Field Reports]," Field Reports on Investigation of International Traffic in Women and Children Made for the Special Body of Experts to Study the International Traffic in Women and Children, S171, League of Nations Archive, Geneva, 2-5; "Casas de confianza y buen trato," in *Nueva guia nocturna* (August 1920), S171, League of Nations Archive, Geneva.

32. Reprinted in Feierstein, *Historia de los judíos argentinos*, 267-268.

33. GdF, 14.

34. GdF, 12.

35. EN "Memoria" 1936, 17–21, EN box 3, IWO.

36. Addresses from Sofer, *From Pale to Pampa*, 67; Feierstein, *Historia de los judíos argentinos*, 157, 163, 171, 188–191, 199, 231; masthead of *Di Prese* and *Di Yidishe Tsaytung*; letterhead of Federacion Sionista Argentina from letter of February 12, 1932, EN box 2, IWO.

37. EN Letter Report 146, p. 59, May 3, 1929, EN box 1, IWO.

38. Feierstein, *Historia de los judíos argentinos*, 155.

39. Feierstein, *Historia de los judíos argentinos*, 163.

40. This cemetery address, marked with a black square in the center of Avellaneda, was given to the Inspeccion de Sociedades Juridicas by the Registro Civil de Avellaneda as the headquarters of the organization, in response and refusal of the attempt to repeal the organization's juridical status April 19, 1921, denied May 19, 1921. GdF, 11.

41. Sofer, *From Pale to Pampa*, 73; Feierstein, *Historia de los judíos argentinos*, 150. Address for the National Association from a report related to a League of Nations investigation by "the Committee on Trata de Mujeres y Ninas, July 1934 to Dec 1934," 7, 9, EN box 2, IWO.

42. "El gobierno debe limpiar al pais de la verguenza de la trata de blancas," *Crítica*, September 17, 1930, 1.

43. Jewish Association for the Protection of Girls and Women (henceforth JAPGW), *Official Report of the Jewish International Conference on the Suppression of the Traffic in Girls and Women Held on April 5th, 6th, and 7th, 1910, in London* (London: JAPGW Central Bureau, 1910), 69.

44. A. L. Schusheim, "Letoldot haishuv hayehudi be-Argentina," in *Sefer Argentina* (Buenos Aires, 1954), 32, cited in Mirelman, *Jewish Buenos Aires*, 77.

45. From the 1905 doctoral dissertation about Argentine white slavery by Manuel Galvez, "Recuerdos de la vida literaria," out of print, excerpt published in Marisa Donadío, "La ciudad de las esclavas blancas," 215–218.

46. Mirelman, *Jewish Buenos Aires*, 80.

47. Mirelman, *Jewish Buenos Aires*, 207–209.

48. Mirelman, *Jewish Buenos Aires*, 81.

49. Feierstein, *Historia de los judíos argentinos*, 233–235.

50. Elisa Cohen de Chervonagura, *Eshet Jail: Un contrapunto discursive entre dos mujeres judías* (San Miguel de Tucumán: Universidad Nacional de Tucumán, 2015), throughout and 78–81.

51. Yankev Sh. Liakhovetsky, "The Dead in Avellaneda: A Shameful Blemish for the Living," *Avezshaneder shtime*, date unspecified (from content, it appears to be from around the time of the cemetery's establishment), 3, EN box 3, IWO. This author is a famous founder of Jewish journalism in BA, involved in various newspapers and Zionist organizations.

52. Mirelman, *Jewish Buenos Aires*, 352, and Nora Glickman, *The Jewish White Slave Trade and the Untold Story of Raquel Liberman* (New York: Garland, 2000), 6, note these fears.

53. Liakhovetsky, "The Dead in Avellaneda," 3.

54. "Iz der froien-handl nar fun oisland?," *Di Prese*, October 7, 1930.

55. A day-by-day search through twenty-two Argentine newspapers for the period of the court case and select moments earlier in the 1920s yielded over five hundred articles about white slavery, the Varsovia Society, and the role of Jews in and against local pros-

titution. Most of these newspapers were dailies, published out of Buenos Aires and nearby provinces, with seventeen in Spanish, four in Yiddish, and one in English. Nine of these papers each published at least twenty to sixty stories on the subject in this period: *Buenos Aires Herald, Crítica, El Diario, Di Prese, Mundo Israelita, La Nación, El Orden* (Santa Fe), *La Última Hora,* and *Di Yidishe Tsaytung.* I did most of this research in Buenos Aires archives and libraries and the New York Public Library. I was aided in additional Yiddish press discoveries beyond the two principal dailies by Will Runyan, whose attention to detail and translation skill aided this project immeasurably. I added additional stories from international publications (primarily available in English, mostly from New York and London) through digital searching. Although the tedium of daily searching (and following newspaper runs between multiple sites and archives) was required by technological and archival limitations, it had the benefit of highlighting the larger conversations in which both the Jewish and non-Jewish presses were simultaneously engaged, particularly around national identity and the turbulent political moment of the court case.

56. *Israel Illustrada* notably did not mention the subject during the months of police raids and court proceedings, though it did run the JAPGW's ads for missing husbands sought by abandoned wives in Eastern Europe.

57. E.g., in the middle of the court case, *Di Prese* criticized other Jewish publications for printing ads for businesses that belonged to traffickers in women: "They justified this by saying that from their perspective no merchants are better than others, and they did not see why they should publish one merchant's ads and not another's. They are still printing such ads today." "Inem land fun froien handl," *Di Prese,* June 2, 1930, 6. *Di Prese* had pushed back against the tmeim for years, as in a 1925 series of editorials and letters bemoaning the active presence of the tmeim in Yiddish theater audiences and their influence over the content of productions, e.g., "Di rufianes un dem teater," *Di Prese,* November 20, 1925, 4; and "Vegn intzident in 'idishen teater,'" *Di Prese,* November 22, 1925, 5.

58. GdF, 7.

59. GdF, 7.

60. GdF, 7.

61. Alsogaray, *Trilogia de la trata de blancas,* 140; GdF, 7.

62. GdF, 7, 21.

63. It was sometimes still called Varsovia after the change, as in "Solo dos nuevas detenciones ha realizado hoy la policía," *Crítica,* May 23, 1930.

64. Jewish Association for the Protection of Girls and Women, "League of Nations' Advisory Commission for the Protection and Welfare of Children and Young People, Traffic in Women and Children Committee, Seventh Session: Report of the Jewish Association for the Protection of Girls and Women for the Year Ending December 31st, 1927" (Geneva, 1928), 5.

65. "El problema de la trata de blancas es internacional," *Crítica,* May 24, 1930.

66. "El problema de la trata de blancas es internacional."

67. On the challenges of this centralization process, see Mirelman, *Jewish Buenos Aires,* 221–231.

68. "Ezras Noshim rufn a delegatn farzamlung," *Di Prese,* May 23, 1930.

69. GdF, 7.

70. Ezres Noshim, Letter to Max Glucksmann, April 23, 1930, IWO.

71. Ezres Noshim, Letter Report 146, May 3, 1929; Ezres Noshim, Letter to Leonard G. Montefiore, President du Comite Financier, JAPGW, December 20, 1928.

72. Ezres Noshim, *Reseña de las Actividades desde el 1 de Julio de 1943 Hasta el 30 de Junio de 1944* (1944), 5, IWO.

73. Ezres Noshim, *Reseña de las Actividades desde el 1 de Julio de 1944 Hasta el 30 de Junio de 1945* (1945), 5, IWO.

74. JAPGW—Ezres Noshim, *Informe Primer Semestre de 1934, Presentado por Secretaria al Comité Ejecutivo el día 20 de noviembre de 1934*, IWO, 19.

75. JAPGW, *Annual Report* (London: JAPGW, 1925), 24.

76. Minutes and Papers of the Gentlemen's Sub-Committee for Preventative Work, 154–156, Papers of the Jewish Association for the Protection of Girls, Women and Children, Archives of Jewish Care, University of Southampton.

77. JAPGW, *Annual Report* (1925), 24.

78. JAPGW—Ezres Noshim, *Informe Primer Semestre de 1934*, 111–120.

79. "Woman Who Fought White Slave Traffic," *Buenos Aires Herald*, clipping in Archives of the International Bureau for the Suppression of Traffic in Persons 4IBS/6, FL112, 1J, Women's Library, London.

80. JAPGW, *Annual Report* (1925), 33.

81. Samuel Halphon, "Letter to S. E. el Sr. Ministerio de Hacienda de la Republica Argentina," November 14, 1921; Selig Ganapol and Samuel Halphon, "Letter to Samuel Cohen," February 8, 1922, IWO.

82. See Lila Caimari, *While the City Sleeps: A History of Pistoleros, Policemen, and the Crime Beat in Buenos Aires before Perón*, trans. Lisa Ubelaker Andrade and Richard Shindell (Berkeley: University of California Press, 2016); Rodríguez, *Civilizing Argentina*; and Kristin Ruggiero, *Modernity in the Flesh: Medicine, Law, and Society in Turn-of-the-Century Argentina* (Stanford, CA: Stanford University Press, 2004).

83. Nancy Leys Stepan, *"The Hour of Eugenics": Race, Gender, and Nation in Latin America* (Ithaca, NY: Cornell University Press, 1996), 51.

84. Mary Gibson, "The Female Offender and the Italian School of Criminal Anthropology," *Journal of European Studies* 12, no. 47 (1982): 155–165, at 157.

85. Stepan, *"The Hour of Eugenics"*; Julia Rodríguez, *Civilizing Argentina: Science, Medicine, and the Modern State* (Chapel Hill: University of North Carolina Press, 2006); Ruggiero, *Modernity in the Flesh*.

86. Rodríguez, *Civilizing Argentina*, 117.

87. Cesare Lombroso and William Ferrero, *The Female Offender* (New York, 1895), 153.

88. For more on Argentine state and social agencies' regulatory responses to motherhood in this period, see Marcela Nari, *Políticas de maternidad y maternalismo político: Buenos Aires, 1890–1940* (Buenos Aires: Biblos, 2004); and Donna Guy, "Mothers Alive and Dead: Multiple Concepts of Mothering in Buenos Aires," in *White Slavery and Mothers Alive and Dead: The Troubled Meeting of Sex, Gender, Public Health, and Progress in Latin America* (Lincoln: University of Nebraska Press, 2000), 191–206.

89. Memorias de la "Ezras Noschim" de Buenos Aires (1936), 5, EN box 3, IWO.

90. Memorias de la "Ezras Noschim" de Buenos Aires, 4–6.

91. Ezres Noshim, box 3, item 30, IWO.

92. Memorias de la "Ezras Noschim" de Buenos Aires, 37.

93. Memorias de la "Ezras Noschim" de Buenos Aires, 35.

94. Memorias de la "Ezras Noschim" de Buenos Aires, 35–36.

95. Memorias de la "Ezras Noschim" de Buenos Aires, 36–37.

96. Factory work was also criticized as a source of women's degeneration, as, for example, noted by Nari in *Políticas de maternidad y maternalismo político*, 86–88.

97. Memorias de la "Ezras Noschim" de Buenos Aires, 38.

98. Memorias de la "Ezras Noschim" de Buenos Aires, 40.

99. Memorias de la "Ezras Noschim" de Buenos Aires, 53–54.

100. Memorias de la "Ezras Noschim" de Buenos Aires, 10.

101. Memorias de la "Ezras Noschim" de Buenos Aires, 10.

102. Memorias de la "Ezras Noschim" de Buenos Aires, 68. The 1934 annual report mentioned that the group's secretary and "one of the most active advisors," Efroim Dubrowsky, in the face of certain defects in the organization of "Jupe-Kedischen," "are studying the best way of organizing this religious service, in order to make Ezras Noschim's control more efficient." JAPGW—Ezres Noshim, *Informe Primer Semestre de 1934*, 11.

103. Flyer titled "Ezras Noshim, Regulamen far religyeze khasenes," attached to page 70 of Memorias de la "Ezras Noschim" de Buenos Aires.

104. Memorias de la "Ezras Noschim" de Buenos Aires, 48.

105. E.g., rejected marriage permission application example, October 30, 1935, EN box 2.

106. JAPGW, *Annual Report* (London: JAPGW, 1932), 30.

107. "Planilla estadistica correspondiente al periodo comprendido desde el 1 de enero 1935 hasta la fecha 18 diciembre 1935," JAPGW, *Annual Report* (London: JAPGW, 1935).

108. JAPGW, *Annual Report* (1925), 33.

109. Memorias de la "Ezras Noschim" de Buenos Aires, 42.

110. Memorias de la "Ezras Noschim" de Buenos Aires, 42.

111. Memorias de la "Ezras Noschim" de Buenos Aires, 43.

112. Memorias de la "Ezras Noschim" de Buenos Aires, 44.

113. Memorias de la "Ezras Noschim" de Buenos Aires, 44–45.

114. JAPGW—Ezres Noshim, *Informe Primer Semestre de 1934*, 20.

115. For example, "Personas Buscadas," *Israel Illustrada*, June 11, 1926, 17; "Personas Buscadas," *Israel Illustrada*, August 2 and 9, 1929, 17.

116. Sociedad Israelita de Proteccion a Niñas y Mujeres (Ezras Noschim), *Informe sintetico sobre las actividades desde el 1º de julio de 1943 hasta el 30 de junio de 1944* (Buenos Aires, 1944), 4, IWO.

117. JAPGW—Ezres Noshim, *Informe Primer Semestre de 1934*, 10–11, 16, 55.

118. Memorias de la "Ezras Noschim" de Buenos Aires, 47.

119. Memorias de la "Ezras Noschim" de Buenos Aires, 51.

120. GdF, 7.

121. Polish Minister Plenipotentiary refers to both Poilisher Farband and Ezres Noshim leading the battle against the tmeim in a note to the court, and Poilisher Farband President Felix Herselkovitch testified that this was one of the reasons for the organization's foundation. GdF, 7.

122. Ezres Noshim box 3, 11th item in box, in unnumbered packet of Spanish and Yiddish correspondence, IWO.

123. Nora Glickman and Gloria F. Waldman, eds. and trans., *Argentine Jewish Theatre: A Critical Anthology* (Lewisburg, PA: Bucknell University Press, 1996), 9.

124. Manuel Galvez, *Recuerdos de la vida literaria*, out of print, excerpt published in Marisa Donadío, "La ciudad de las esclavas blancas," 215–218; also discussed in Feierstein, *Historia de los judíos argentinos*.

125. Glickman, *The Jewish White Slave Trade*, 9, citing Gerardo Bra, *La Organización Negra: La increíble historia de la Zwi Migdal* (Buenos Aires: Corregidor, 1982), 90–91.

126. Guy, *Sex and Danger*, 61–62.

127. E.g., "such a movement was once created and it worked. Unfortunately we have seen how they creep yet further into our souls." "Vegn Intzident in 'Idishen teater,'" *Di Prese*, November 22, 1925.

128. "Tsu alle yidishe arbeiter" (n/d), EN box 3.

129. "The Jewish Theater Noah's Ark in Buenos Aires" (n/d), EN box 3.

130. "The Jewish Theater Noah's Ark."

131. "The Jewish Theater Noah's Ark."

132. Timothy Gilfoyle notes the mixed audiences of concert saloons, *City of Eros: New York City, Prostitution, and the Commercialization of Sex, 1790–1920* (New York: W. W. Norton & Company, 1992), 231.

133. Poster example reproduced in Silvia Hansman, Susana Skura, and Gabriela Kogan, *Oysfarkoyft, Localidades Agotadas, Sold Out: Afiches del teatro ídish en la Argentina, Yiddish Theater Posters in Argentina* (Buenos Aires: Editorial Del Nuevo Extremo, 2006).

134. GdF, 7.

135. Glickman and Waldman, *Argentine Jewish Theatre*, 21; Glickman, *The Jewish White Slave Trade*, 20–22. See also Harley Erdman, "Jewish Anxiety in 'Days of Judgement': Community Conflict, Antisemitism, and the *God of Vengeance* Obscenity Case," *Theatre Survey* 40, no. 1 (1999): 51–74; and Boleslao Lewin, *Cómo fue la inmigración iudía a la Argentina* (Buenos Aires: Plus Ultra, 1983), 211.

136. "Those who seek salvation though foreign naive innocent creatures who are still muttering a backwards *lekha dodi* [liturgical Shabbat song]. . . . The tune of false sabbath hymns quietly stirs in your souls. And so you seek to drown out the melody that comes from your false hearts, with the hypocritical prayer of 'pimp ideology.'" "Tsum gantsn yidishn" (n/d), EN box 2.

137. Zachary Baker, "Art Patronage and Philistinism in Argentina: Maurycy Minkowski in Buenos Aires, 1930," *Shofar* 3 (2001): 117–118n13.

138. See Nahma Sandrow, *Vagabond Stars: The World History of Yiddish Theater* (New York: Harper and Row, 1977).

139. Isaac Bashevis Singer, "The Colony," *Commentary* 46 (November 1968): 57–61. Glickman analyzes Singer's work on the subject in *The Jewish White Slave Trade*, 26–28. See also Maxine A. Hartley, *Guide to the Works of Isaac Bashevis Singer* (New York: Vantage, 2009).

140. Sandra Deutsch discusses the tradition of Jewish women as repositories of communal honor in *Crossing Borders, Claiming a Nation: A History of Argentine Jewish Women, 1880–1955* (Durham, NC: Duke University Press, 2010), 124–127.

## CONCLUSION

1. The 120 members imprisoned were released after 8 months. "Not Proven: Zwi Migdal Members Released," *Buenos Aires Herald*, January 28, 1931. Argentine consuls in Europe were notified that all these deportees were deprived of their Argentine citizenship and were not to be given visas to return to Argentina. Letter from R. Lighton Robinson to Sempkins, no. 83, February 12, 1931, London, Women's Library, International Bureau for the Suppression of Traffic in Persons, 4IBS/6, FL112, folder 1J-Argentine—Zwii Mygdal case [*sic*].

2. E.g., Julio L. Alsogaray, *Trilogia de La Trata de Blancas: Rufianes, Policía, Municipalidad* (Buenos Aires: L. J. Rosso, 1933); Isabel Vincent, *Bodies and Souls: The Tragic Plight of Three Jewish Women Forced into Prostitution in the Americas* (New York: William Morrow, 2005); and Edward J. Bristow, *Prostitution and Prejudice: The Jewish Fight against White Slavery, 1870–1939,* 2nd ed. (New York: Schocken Books, 1983). Glickman praises Alsogaray's support of Liberman.

3. Edward J. Bristow, *Prostitution and Prejudice: The Jewish Fight against White Slavery, 1870–1939,* 2nd ed. (New York: Schocken Books, 1983), 316; Vincent, *Bodies and Souls,* 172.

4. In general, Guy is neither laudatory nor critical of Alsogaray, but does make this connection. Donna Guy, *Sex and Danger in Buenos Aires: Prostitution, Family, and Nation in Argentina* (Lincoln: University of Nebraska Press, 1991), 129.

5. Memorias de la "Ezras Noschim" de Buenos Aires (1936), 5, Ezres Noshim box 3, Yidisher Visnshaftlekher Institut, or Instituto Judío de Investigación, Buenos Aires (henceforth IWO), 89–90. The Jewish organization may have been particularly angered by Alsogaray putting these words in its mouth: in his memoir, he wrote that according to a 1932 report by the Jewish Association for the Protection of Girls and Women, the roughly four hundred traffickers and brothel owners of the Varsovia Society were solely responsible for the anti-Jewish sentiments of the larger population against the three hundred thousand Jews in Argentina. Alsogaray, *Trilogía de la trata de blancas,* 259.

6. In the first pages of his memoir, he distinguishes the "good sons of Israel" from the bad and lists names of several exemplary (though non-Argentine) Jews from Lombroso to Einstein. Alsogaray, *Trilogía de la trata de blancas,* 13–15.

7. "In the report of Commissioner Alsogaray, he stated that in many cases, dealing with the offence of corruption, the Migdal Society and its members were always more or less involved." "Juzgados de instrucción: Número 3—Asociación ilicita," *Gaceta del Foro* 15, no. 4729 (November 1, 1930): 4 (henceforth GdF).

8. Alsogaray, *Trilogía de la trata de blancas,* 78.

9. Alsogaray, *Trilogía de la trata de blancas,* 15.

10. Alsogaray, *Trilogía de la trata de blancas,* 20–21.

11. Alsogaray, *Trilogía de la trata de blancas,* 25.

12. "Irigozshenistisher rezshis geshtirtzt," *Di Prese,* September 7, 1930. Alsogaray's appointment was highlighted alongside the dissolution of the government, various arrests and resignations, and the casual mention of a bloody slaughter in the plaza in front of the houses of government. The police journal also describes his promotion: "Nuevo jefe de policia," *Revista de Policia* (Buenos Aires), September 16, 1930, 1117–1118.

13. "Der komisar alsogarai tetik in zain nayen amt," *Di Prese,* September 9, 1930; "Der komisar alsogaray hot tzugeshtelt a barict vegn di froien-hendler," *Di Prese,* September 18, 1930.

14. "Der komisar alsogaray hot tzugeshtelt a barict vegn di froien-hendler," *Di Prese,* September 18, 1930.

15. *Homenaje al Senor Comisario de Órdenes Don Julio L. Alsogaray, Octubre 11 de 1930* (Buenos Aires: Tip. Luis Veggia, [1930/1931?]), 6.

16. Martin Edwin Andersen, *La policía: Pasado, presente y propuestas para el futuro* (Buenos Aires: Editorial Sudamericana, 2002), 98; September 9, 1930, and December 4, 1930, police arrest orders, Policia de la Capital Federal, *Orden del Dia,* vol. 49, year 1930 (Buenos Aires: Servicio de Aprovisionamiento, 1936), 526–528, 752.

17. Lila Caimari, *While the City Sleeps: A History of Pistoleros, Policemen, and the Crime Beat in Buenos Aires before Perón*, trans. Lisa Ubelaker Andrade and Richard Shindell (Berkeley: University of California Press, 2016), 76.

18. Caimari, *While the City Sleeps*, especially "Detecting Disorder."

19. "Argentine Rabbi Praised: Dr. Halphon, Sailing for Europe, Lauded for His Work," *New York Times*, December 9, 1930.

20. Court finding quoted in "Not Proven," *Buenos Aires Herald*, January 28, 1931.

21. Rosalie Lighton Robinson, Letter to Frederick Sempkins, January 1931, Archives of the International Bureau for the Suppression of Traffic in Persons 4IBS/6, FL112, 1J, Women's Library, London.

22. Robinson's obituary confirms that she continued the job beyond March 1931. "Woman Who Fought White Slave Traffic," *Buenos Aires Herald*, n/d.

23. "La colectividad israelita de Buenos Aires, ofrecio hoy un homenaje al Comisario Julio L. Alsogaray," *Crítica* 14, no. 4854 (February 5, 1927), 2.

24. Policing and crime have been expanding fields in both Argentine and transnational contexts, and scholars in those fields might appreciate the alliances of Jewish institutions with Commissioner Alsogaray as well as the discussions of bribery, respectability, and criminology. Lila Caimari emphasizes the central mission of Buenos Aires police to abolish social disorder. Caimari, *While the City Sleeps*, 9–10. See also Lila Caimari, ed., *La Ley de Los Profanos: Delito, Justicia y Cultura en Buenos Aires (1870–1940)* (Buenos Aires: Fondo de Cultura Económica, 2007); Charles Van Onselen, "Jewish Police Informers in the Atlantic World, 1880–1914," *Historical Journal* 50, no. 1 (March 2007): 119–144; Julia Rodríguez, *Civilizing Argentina: Science, Medicine, and the Modern State* (Chapel Hill: University of North Carolina Press, 2006); Kristin Ruggiero, *Modernity in the Flesh: Medicine, Law, and Society in Turn-of-the-Century Argentina* (Stanford, CA: Stanford University Press, 2004); Mathieu Deflem, *Policing World Society: Historical Foundations of International Police Cooperation* (New York: Oxford University Press, 2004); Lila M. Caimari, "Whose Criminals Are These? Church, State, and Patronatos and the Rehabilitation of Female Convicts (Buenos Aires, 1890–1940)," *Americas* 54, no. 2 (1997): 185–208; Beatriz C. Ruibal, "El Control Social y la Policia de Buenos Aires: Buenos Aires 1880–1920," *Boletin del Instituto de Historia Argentina y Americana "Dr. E. Raviginani"* 3, no. 2 (1990): 75–90; Lyman L. Johnson, ed., *The Problem of Order in Changing Societies: Essays on Crime and Policing in Argentina and Uruguay* (Albuquerque: University of New Mexico Press, 1990).

25. Nora Glickman, *The Jewish White Slave Trade and the Untold Story of Raquel Liberman* (New York: Garland, 2000).

26. Glickman, *The Jewish White Slave Trade*, 53–54.

27. Although this is a part of her larger endeavor to reveal new aspects of Liberman's life, Glickman, in *The Jewish White Slave Trade*, 55–56, reiterates the version in Alsogaray's memoir that Liberman did not know of Korn's membership nor that Simon Bruskevich was the Society's president when she went to him for assistance.

28. GdF, 9.

29. GdF, 9.

30. Ezres Noshim box 2, item 16, Ezres Noshim Collection, IWO.

31. Ezres Noshim box 2, item 3, Ezres Noshim Collection, IWO. Glickman also translates this document into English in *Jewish White Slave Trade*, 77–78.

32. Philippa Levine, *Prostitution, Race, and Politics: Policing Venereal Disease in the British Empire* (New York: Routledge, 2003); Judith R. Walkowitz, *Prostitution and Victorian Society: Women, Class, and the State* (Cambridge: Cambridge University Press, 1982). In 1900, the Jewish reformers in Britain working to found the Jewish Association for the Protection of Girls and Women used the Contagious Diseases Acts as shorthand for the concept of the regulatory system, noting that the "Contagious Diseases Acts [were] in force in the Argentine Republic." Minutes and Papers of the Gentlemen's Sub-Committee for Preventative Work, 188–189, Papers of the Jewish Association for the Protection of Girls, Women and Children, Archives of Jewish Care, University of Southampton.

33. Most of those involved with the League of Nations' Traffic in Women and Children Committee held this perspective, as did the leaders of international reform organizations such as the International Bureau for the Suppression of Traffic in Women and the Jewish Association for the Protection of Girls and Women.

34. Kathleen Barry's most influential work on this subject is *Female Sexual Slavery* (New York: New York University Press, 1979). For a critique of Barry's position and the Coalition Against Trafficking in Women, see, e.g., Jo Doezema, "Ouch! Western Feminists' 'Wounded Attachment' to the 'Third World Prostitute,'" *Feminist Review*, no. 67 (Winter 2001): 16–38. Other key works articulating this position include Catharine MacKinnon, *Toward a Feminist Theory of the State* (Cambridge, MA: Harvard University Press, 1989), and Sheila Jeffreys, *The Idea of Prostitution* (Melbourne: Spinifex Press, 1997), rearticulated as a global phenomenon in Jeffreys's *The Industrial Vagina: The Political Economy of the Global Sex Trade* (New York: Taylor & Francis, 2009). On the feminist "sex wars," see the epilogue to Alice Echols, *Daring to Be Bad: Radical Feminism in America 1967–1975* (Minneapolis: University of Minnesota Press, 1989), 287–298, and Jane Gerhard, *Desiring Revolution: Second-Wave Feminism and the Rewriting of American Sexual Thought, 1920 to 1982* (New York: Columbia University Press, 2001).

35. Jo Doezema's scholarship highlights the parallels between today's anti-human and sex trafficking activism and the images invoked in the historical "myth of white slavery." Jo Doezema, *Sex Slaves and Discourse Masters: The Construction of Trafficking* (London: Zed Books, 2010). *Women's Studies International Forum* hosted a debate between the radical feminist and sex work responses to trafficking in volume 32 (2009).

36. Gerhard, *Desiring Revolution*, 149–196.

37. See Emma Goldman, *The White Slave Traffic* (New York: Mother Earth, 1909), revised into "The Traffic in Women." In a draft of this article, she argued with George Kibbe Turner against the accusations of Jewish dominance of the Chicago traffic as Jewish women could not have been attractive or acculturated enough. Emma Goldman, "The White Slave Traffic," 6–7, Emma Goldman Papers, International Institute of Social History, Amsterdam.

38. Much has been written on the language of sex work and this feminist position; see, for example, Elizabeth Bernstein, "What's Wrong with Prostitution? What's Right with Sex Work? Comparing Markets in Female Sexual Labor," *Hastings Women's Law Journal* 10 (1999): 91; Kamala Kempadoo and Jo Doezema, eds., *Global Sex Workers* (New York: Routledge, 1998); L. McLaughlin, "Discourses of Prostitution, Discourses of Sexuality," *Critical Studies in Mass Communication* 8, no. 3 (September 1991): 249–272; Shonali Choudhury, "'As Prostitutes, We Control Our Bodies': Perceptions of Health and

Body in the Lives of Establishment-Based Female Sex Workers in Tijuana, Mexico," *Culture, Health & Sexuality* 12, no. 6 (August 2010): 677–689; Laura Oso Casas, "Money, Sex, Love, and the Family: Economic and Affective Strategies of Latin American Sex Workers in Spain," *Journal of Ethnic and Migration Studies* 36, no. 1 (January 2010): 47–65.

39. Jo Doezema pushes further in granting agency to historical and present-day sex workers, suggesting that women's desires for various forms of freedom might make sex work less oppressive than other employment options. Prostitutes might thus have more room to shape their working conditions than waitresses, into whose work sexuality enters implicitly but cannot be directly negotiated. Doezema, *Sex Slaves and Discourse Masters*, 12.

40. Nearly all of the forty panelists at the Conference on Trafficking, Smuggling, and Illicit Migration in Historical Perspective at University of London, Birkbeck, June 18–20, 2015, shared this position. Laura María Agustín has been one of the most influential scholars to interpret trafficking in a migratory framework; see her *Sex at the Margins: Migration, Labour Markets, and the Rescue Industry* (London: Zed Books, 2007); "The Conundrum of Women's Agency: Migrations and the Sex Industry," in *Sex Work Now*, ed. M. O'Neill and R. Campbell (Cullompton, UK: Willan, 2006), 116–140; "The Disappearing of a Migration Category: Migrants Who Sell Sex," *Journal of Ethnic and Migration Studies* 32, no. 1 (January 2006): 29–47; "The Cultural Study of Commercial Sex," *Sexualities* 8, no. 5 (2005): 618–631; and "Migrants in the Mistress's House: Other Voices in the 'Trafficking' Debate," *Social Politics* 12, no. 1 (Spring 2005): 96–117. On the migration connection, see also Sallie Yea, "'Shades of Grey': Spaces in and beyond Trafficking for Thai Women Involved in Commercial Sexual Labour in Sydney and Singapore," *Gender, Place & Culture* 19, no. 1 (2012): 42–60; Veronica Magar, "Rescue and Rehabilitation: A Critical Analysis of Sex Workers' Antitrafficking Response in India," *Signs* 37, no. 3 (March 1, 2012): 619–644; Rutvica Andrijasevic, "Beautiful Dead Bodies: Gender, Migration, and Representation in Anti-trafficking Campaigns," *Feminist Review* 86, no. 1 (2007): 24–44; M. F. Manalansan, "Queer Intersections: Sexuality and Gender in Migration Studies," *International Migration Review* 40, no. 1 (Spring 2006): 224–249; Tanja Bastia, "Stolen Lives or Lack of Rights? Gender, Migration, and Trafficking," *Labour, Capital, and Society* 39, no. 2 (2006): 21–47; Kamala Kempadoo, Jyoti Sanghera, and Bandana Pattanaik, eds., *Trafficking and Prostitution Reconsidered: New Perspectives on Migration, Sex Work, and Human Rights* (Boulder, CO: Paradigm, 2005); Laura Oso Casas, "Money, Sex, Love, and the Family: Economic and Affective Strategies of Latin American Sex Workers in Spain," *Journal of Ethnic and Migration Studies* 36, no. 1 (January 2010): 47–65. Julietta Hua provides a thought-provoking critique of human rights discourse around trafficking in *Trafficking Women's Human Rights* (Minneapolis: University of Minnesota Press, 2011).

41. For an example of the modified choice argument, see Wendy Chapkis, *Live Sex Acts: Women Performing Erotic Labor* (New York: Routledge, 1997). On consent, see also Ilse van Liempt, "Trafficking in Human Beings: Conceptual Dilemmas," 27–42, and Donna Dickenson, "Philosophical Assumptions and Presumptions about Trafficking for Prostitution," 43–53, both in *Trafficking and Women's Rights*, ed. Christien van den Anker and Jeroen Doomernik (New York: Palgrave Macmillan, 2006). Doezema critiques this model in *Sex Slaves and Discourse Masters*, 24–25.

42. Quoted in Glickman, *The Jewish White Slave Trade*, 38, from his novel *A las 20:25 la señora entró en la inmortalidad* (1981).

43. This suggestion follows conversations with individuals involved in current antitrafficking efforts that do focus on these areas but are in the minority. E.g., Reverend Lia Claire Scholl, author of *I Heart Sex Workers: A Christian Response to People in the Sex Trade* (Danvers, MA: Chalice Press, 2012).

44. Guy argues in *Sex and Danger* that shifts in local prostitution regulations were fundamentally about elite assertion of control over the behavior of all working-class women. E.g., Guy, *Sex and Danger*, 44.

# Index

*Note*: Page numbers in *italics* indicate figures.

Abbott, Grace, 33
abolitionism, 21–22, 24, 160n53. *See also*
    prostitution/prostitutes; white slavery/
    white slaves
Abraham, Malka, 114
Addams, Jane, 33, 159n48
Adler, Hermann, 52, 79, 101, 104
Adler, Stella, 127
African chattel slavery, 21–22, 25–26, 27,
    43, 137, 160n53. *See also* abolitionism
agency, 14–15, 27, 33, 62, 135–136, 139, 145n3,
    196n39
*agunah*, 63
Aleichem, Sholem, 41, 166n
Algiers, Algeria, 23, 25, 180n33
Alphonse (Pimp) Pogrom, 52, 171n66
Alsogaray, Julio: jurisdiction, 106, 110,
    129–130, 139; Liberman's accusations, 1,
    133; memoir, 31, 50, 193n5; Varsovia
    Society as front, 79–80, 92; Varsovia
    Society court trial, 5, 48, 49, 74, 104
American, Sadie, 53
American Social Hygiene Association,
    33, 34
AMIA (Asociación Mutual Israelita
    Argentina), 138: Jewish Community
    Center, 13. *See also* Chevrah Keduscha
    Ashkenazi
anarchism, 5, 68
antisemitism: associations, 46; conflated
    with anticommunism, 44, 167n14;
    coverage of Varsovia Society, 115–116;

Jews linked to white slavery, 51, 104,
    193n5; novels, 48; social exclusion, 12, 53,
    120; stereotypes, 48, 138, 170n48
Argentina: age of minors, 68–69; border,
    39; Committee for Public Morality, 63;
    crime, 8–9; exclusionary policies, 4,
    10–11; flash point for international
    controversies, 2; immigration policy, 10,
    11, 58, 87–88; Jewish link to prostitution,
    41–43, 49–51, 87; Jewish migration, 4,
    87–88, *88*; law 817, 68–69; League of
    Nations' Expert Report, 37; military
    dictatorship, 6, 11, 128; national identity,
    8; nationalism, 44; national reputation,
    31; nation-building efforts, 8–9, 128;
    population, 6, 50; presidential coup, 6;
    prostitution legalization, 31; prostitution
    regulation, 6–7, 76, 88; racial and sexual
    order battleground, 17; racial categories,
    8; state-sponsored brothel system, 6;
    trade relationships, 163n82
Argentine National Association against
    the White Slave Trade, 113
Argentine Zionist Federation, 111
Arlt, Roberto, 47, 110
Arnold K. (former Varsovia Society
    member), 60–61, 72, 80–81
Asch, Sholem, 41, 70
Ashkenazi Jews: Buenos Aires residences,
    110; burial society, 90, 112, 113–114;
    cemetery, 105; cultural disconnect with
    Sephardi Jews, 104; diaspora, 56;

# About the Author

Mir Yarfitz is an assistant professor in the Wake Forest University Department of History. His research and teaching bridge modern Latin American history, Jewish history, and women's, gender, and sexuality studies, with particular interests in migration, masculinity, and cultural responses to trans bodies before the development of contemporary language.